The Renewal of All Things

The Renewal of All Things

An Alternative Missiology

WALDRON BYRON SCOTT

WIPF & STOCK · Eugene, Oregon

THE RENEWAL OF ALL THINGS
An Alternative Missiology

Wipf & Stock
A Division of Wipf and Stock Publishers
199 W. 8th Ave., Suite 3
Eugene, OR 97401
www.wipfandstock.com

ISBN 13: 978-1-60608-562-2

Manufactured in the U.S.A.

To my grandchildren:
Justine (Hawk), Gillian (Canary), and Damian;
Scott, Daniel, Kendra, and Jonathan;
Brianna; Dustin and Travis; Brittney;
and to their generation

Even when I am old and gray, do not forsake me, my God,
Till I declare your power to the next generation,
Your mighty acts to all who are to come

PSALM 71:18

Contents

Preface

No SOONER HAD I finished writing *What about the Cross?* than I realized a sequel was required. For in that book I had sketched an alternative model of the atonement without relating it to certain other major blocs of Christian belief; without elaborating on its missionary relevance, if any, in a world of religious pluralism and secular ideologies; and without developing its practical application to our daily lives in sufficient detail.

Further, I had found it impossible to develop a relevant model of the atonement and the gospel apart from the context of contemporary science and the late modern or postmodern worldviews. The whole world lives in what has been called a "planetary postmodern movement."[1] Although I am not part of the so-called Christian postmodern emergent movement spearheaded in North America by Brian McLaren, I share many of the concerns of its participants.[2] Like them, I read the Bible seriously but differently. As they are, I am intrigued by the disparities between the Old Testament and the New but equally by those between the gospels and the epistles. For me, it is Jesus' life and mission that ultimately define my relationship with God. Jesus is aptly named Emmanuel.[3]

As the reader will see, contemporary science and a theistic perspective on evolution condition my worldview. Postmodern people are comfortable with both of these. The kingdom of God preoccupies me more than the institutional church. I am notably sympathetic to theologies of liberation and social justice. I am distressed by the ambiguous ethics and morals of evangelicals in responsible positions, beginning with myself, and I believe the sensual nature of *Homo sapiens* is more complex than most of us realize.

---

1. Cf. Raschke, *GloboChrist*, 23.

2. For a sample of emergent movement thinking, see McLaren, *Everything Must Change.* Cf. McKnight, "Ironic Faith of Emergents," 62–63.

3. Meaning: "God with us."

For me, contextualization is the defining feature of all missional activity. Thus I share the postmodern concern with the relativity of language and context. It will not surprise the reader that my missionary career has made me thoroughly multicultural. The obvious point at which I diverge from the postmodern perspective is the value of metanarrative. Postmodern folk tend to be suspicious of all metanarrative, including the biblical story. In contrast, I value the biblical metanarrative[4] highly and base this book upon it.

A friend suggested that I should try to write more loosely and supply more detail in order to make my perspective as convincing to others as it is to me. It is true that I tend to write compactly, synthesizing conclusions derived from wide reading but sometimes failing to amplify the explicit reasoning that led to each conclusion. In this book I will try to correct these deficiencies as best I can.

But there's the rub. Thinking about God is an adventure exceeding anything Indiana Jones might imagine. Theology, especially missiology rightly done, is perpetual discovery.[5] Each book completed seems to call for another. This present volume, which is a further exploration of the themes of atonement and salvation in the context of Christian mission, is oriented toward eschatology.[6] Traditionally, eschatology is supposed to be about the last times or the end of history. But as Jürgen Moltmann has correctly insisted, eschatology is not about the end at all. It is about a new beginning, "the new creation of all things."[7] Or, as I have titled this book, the renewal of all things.

The primary audiences for this book are students at both the university and seminary levels, and other intellectually engaged laypersons who appreciate the role of science in contemporary society yet are at the same time responsive to issues of faith and spirituality. I do not write argumentatively in order to be refuted or falsified but to stir imagination and provoke fresh thought. I am less interested in expositing evangelical

4. Metanarrative: a comprehensive story meant to explain historical experience or knowledge.

5. Missiology: the formal study and practice of mission, especially Christian mission.

6. Eschatology: traditionally, theological beliefs related to the final events in the history of the world or humankind. In this book the term is used somewhat differently, encompassing the totality of the new age inaugurated by the Christ event.

7. Cf. Moltmann, *Coming of God*, xi.

dogma than in exploring the Christian tradition from new angles. In this I shadow Jürgen Moltmann and Walter Brueggemann. But I like to think that in some modest degree I am also following Jesus' methodology. As Thomas Talbott puts it:

> [Jesus's] whole manner of expressing himself . . . was intended to awaken the spiritual imagination of his disciples and to leave room for reinterpretation as they matured in the faith; it was not intended to provide final answers to their theological questions (emphasis added).[8]

My background in Christian mission is fairly extensive. I served with The Navigators for twenty-five years, pioneering their outreach to the Middle East and North Africa, leading their mission in Asia and Australasia, and functioning as their international field director for a brief period. For six years (1975–1980) I served the broader ecumenical arena as general secretary of the World Evangelical Fellowship (now World Evangelical Alliance). I think of myself as an ecumenical evangelical or an evangelical ecumenical. For three years I was president of American Leprosy Missions—superb preparation for the founding (with my wife Georgia) of Holistic Ministries International in Paterson, New Jersey. Paterson is a quintessential third world city.

The main text of *The Renewal of All Things* consists of three parts. Part I focuses on the setting or background that necessitates God's program of renewal. The first chapter introduces the scientific worldview. My objective here is simply to affirm the validity of a scientific worldview within the Judeo-Christian horizon. Chapter 2 explores the early chapters of Genesis, showing how theistic evolution illuminates the stories preserved there. Chapter 3 surveys the remainder of the Old Testament. Here my aim is to forcefully demonstrate God's faithful commitment—his unfailing love—to a people he chose as emissaries to reveal his character and salvation to the whole world. This people, Israel, was not notably successful in the enterprise; so chapter 4 describes spiritual developments in the rest of the world, notably those in the so-called Axial Age[9] that began about eight hundred years before the Christ event.

8. Talbott, *Inescapable Love*, 43. Cf. John 16:13.

9. Axial Age: a term invented by the philosopher Karl Jaspers to describe the six-hundred-year period from 800 to 200 B.C.E. [B.C.E.: before the Common Era = B.C.; C.E.: Common Era = A.D. B.C.E. AND C.E. are considered religiously neutral designations of historical eras.] During this time unique religious developments occurred in Greece, the

Part 2 is titled Good News. Chapter 5 portrays the Christ event "from the bottom up." That event was revolutionary, not least to the immediate followers of Jesus. Chapter 6 investigates how they understood and appropriated it, emphasizing the different interpretations evident within the various New Testament writings themselves. Taking the same contextual approach, chapter 7 demonstrates the variety of ways Christian leaders have interpreted the Christ event within their own times and cultures. This approach validates my personal effort to understand the gospel in the context of our late modern or postmodern culture. Chapter 8 includes descriptions of contemporary thinkers such as RenéGirard and notable black, feminist, and womanist scholars. It concludes with a brief presentation of my own model of the atonement, seen in the larger context of God's purpose to renew all things.

Part 3 is titled Universal Redemption. Chapter 9 lays out the biblical and patristic[10] bases for the hope of universal redemption; chapter 10 does the same with respect to the theological and philosophical grounds. In my judgment, understanding and proclaiming the gospel in terms of universal redemption offers a fresh and potentially more effective avenue for Christian world mission. The final two chapters are specifically missional. Chapter 11 explores the missiological and personal implications of the themes of evolution, contextualization, religious pluralism, and universal salvation as they prepare the way for God's renewal of all things—first with respect to the world's religions and then in the broader secular arena. Finally, in chapter 12, I offer "my gospel"—not as dogma but as a forthright discussion of how I have appropriated the good news during a long and tumultuous life.

Because this monograph is a sequel, I have condensed and appropriated brief segments from my earlier books, *Bring Forth Justice* and *What about the Cross?* Most of the biblical citations and references herein are from the gender-neutral Today's New International Version (TNIV) or the New Revised Standard Version (NRSV) of the Bible, also gender-neutral. Occasionally I have made my own translation of a particular text. I will refer to God in gender-neutral terms as often as possible but I find it unnecessarily awkward to do so consistently. I trust no reader will

Middle East, South Asia, and East Asia. The reader is referred to chapter 4 below.

10. Patristic: relating to the fathers of the early church.

take offense.[11] I do not have a computer program that allows me to create a good index and I apologize for this lack. Given the readership I have in mind, however, I have provided an appendix outlining the standard theory of evolution; a glossary of terms that may be unfamiliar to my audience; and a complete bibliography of works and web sites cited in the main text.

I am especially grateful to my wife Georgia for her encouragement through the whole process of writing *Renewal*. My indebtedness to scholars and others will be apparent from the quotations and citations of writings that appear in the footnotes. I am grateful also for friends who took the time and trouble to critique early drafts of *The Renewal of All Things*: Messrs. Colin Watson, Sr., Donald McGilchrist, Jim Petersen, and Dick Fischer; Drs. John Ridgway, Bisharah Libbus, and Nabeel Jabbour, Dr. Sik Ming Chong, and his wife, Mei Mang; Mrs. Laurel Van Der Wende and Mrs. Debra Algera; and the Rev. Dan Groh. I learned much from their observations, positive and negative, and this book is better because of their suggestions.

11. Cf. McDermott, "God and the Masculine Pronoun," in *God's Rivals*, 169.

PART ONE

The Setting

1

The Big Bang

He stretches out the heavens like a tent.

PSALM 104:2

WE WERE WALKING TOWARD Ground Zero in lower Manhattan, my grandson Scott and I. After reflecting on the evil events of September 11, 2001, we fell to discussing whether God had created the universe. I argued that God had. At the time, Scott was a graduate student at Duke University in North Carolina, working on a doctorate in statistics. Between long strides he remonstrated, "Why must the universe be thought to be created? Why should we not think it simply *is*, in the same way Christians believe God simply *is*?"

A good question and one that is raised repeatedly. The Temple University mathematician John Allen Paulos argues that if everything has a cause, then as a matter of infinite regression God does too.[1] And if there is any "something" that *doesn't* have a cause, he continues, that something may just as well be the physical universe as God.[2]

For ten thousand years and likely much longer, human beings have wondered about the origin of all things, or whether the notion of origin itself is an illusion. The question seems important to many people in their search for ultimate truth and reality. The philosopher Gottfried Leibniz famously asked, "Why is there anything at all?" Origins are also important because human beings suspect they may convey existential answers to the meaning and purpose of human life:

---

1. Infinite regression: a form of circular reasoning. Applied linearly, it signifies an extended causal relationship or relationships for which there can be no beginning; e. g., "God created the universe." "But who or what created God?" And so on *ad infinitum*.

2. Paulos, *Irreligion*.

- Who am I?
- Where did I come from?
- Why am I here?
- Do I have value and significance?
- What is my destiny?

Some look to science or to some scientific theory for the answer to these questions. But questions of ultimate value cannot be answered scientifically—only philosophically, theologically, or ideologically as an expression of one's worldview. The theory of evolution, for example, is a valid scientific model. Evolution*ism*, which holds that there is no God, is not science but mere ideology. As the renowned South African cosmologist[3] George F. R. Ellis cogently notes, "People need to be aware that there is a range of models that could explain the [scientific] observations .... We are using philosophical criteria in choosing our models. A lot of cosmology tries to hide that."[4]

Nontheistic and theistic (no-God and God-affirming) worldviews inform *both* scientific and philosophic religious inquiry. Five thousand years ago Eastern civilizations were forming myths about the origin of the universe. Hindu mythology portrayed the universe as coming into being through the dismemberment of a cosmic man, or originating from within a dream of Brahma, the creator god, or arising from the tears of Prajapati, lord of all creatures. The unknown authors of the ancient Hindu scriptures, the *Upanishads,* ultimately decided that the source of creation is profoundly unknowable.

Living during the Axial Age in the fifth century B.C.E., the Buddha also thought it was a waste of time to speculate about the origin of the universe. Our limited minds and limitless cravings make such speculation a useless task, he insisted. Yet even the Buddha intuited or formulated ideas about the nature of reality and whether the universe had a beginning. In the Buddhist canon known as the *Agganna Sutta,* the Buddha described the universe as contracting and then re-evolving into its present form over countless millions of years. Life, he theorized, first formed on the surface of the water and again, over countless millions of years, evolved from

---

3. Cosmologist: an astronomer who studies the evolution and space-time relations of the universe.

4. Cited in Gibbs, "Profile," 55.

simpler into more complex organisms. All these processes are without beginning or end, he asserted, and are set in motion by natural causes.[5]

What these natural causes included, the Buddha did not say. He lived 2550 years ago and was a sage, not a scientist. He insisted that people should be preoccupied with the immediate problem of suffering rather than the origin of the universe. In our time, both the Estonian astrophysicist Ernst Öpik and the late American quantum physicist[6] David Bohm, like the Buddha, believe in an oscillating or pulsating universe that has no alpha or omega. Bohm is remembered as saying,

> I propose something like this: Imagine an infinite sea of energy filling empty space, with waves moving around in there, occasionally coming together and producing an intense pulse. Let's say one particular pulse comes together and expands, creating our universe of space-time and matter.[7]

For others who believe the universe simply *is*, some version of the steady-state model adequately describes its existence. The British astronomer Sir Fred Hoyle promoted this model throughout his career. Such plasma[8] cosmologists as the late Swedish Hannes C. Alfvén also assume a universe with no beginning and no end. Alfvén wrote,

> There is no rational reason to doubt that the universe has existed indefinitely, for an infinite time. It is only myth that attempts to say how the universe came to be, either four thousand or twenty billion years ago .... An infinitely old universe, always evolving, may not be compatible with the Book of Genesis. However, religions such as Buddhism get along without having any explicit creation mythology and are in no way contradicted by a universe without a beginning or end.[9]

Cosmologies intuited, or information transferred from a higher source (i. e., divine inspiration) via the Tanakh (the Hebrew Bible), the

---

5. Dhammika, "What Does the Buddha Say about the Origin of the Universe?" line 2.

6. Quantum physicist: one who studies the nature and behavior of matter and energy at the atomic and subatomic levels. Max Planck first proposed quantum theory in 1900.

7. Peat, "Interview," para. 43. See also Öpik, *The Oscillating Universe*.

8. Plasma: the fourth state of matter, differing from solids, liquids and gases. Plasma cosmologists theorize about the electrodynamic nature of the universe; gravity and inertia are not the only forces at work.

9. Cited at http://www.plasmacosmology.net/bb.html "Science and Ideology: The Big Bang," para. 18.

New Testament, or the Qur'an (Islam's holy text)—all these come to us from a prescientific era. But we live in a scientific age, and I address this book to a late modern and postmodern audience that has grown up with scientific explanations of material reality. Unfortunately, many Christians still adhere to a literal interpretation of the early chapters of Genesis on the assumption that there is an inherent contradiction between science and biblical inspiration. They are convinced that if one places one's faith in scientific explanations, then inspired scripture is excluded, and vice versa. In my opinion, this approach generates unnecessary confusion and doubt toward both science and faith.

Further, as my friend and geneticist Bisharah Libbus has reminded me, there are many issues—time, causality, relatedness, change—that take on different meanings by virtue of differences in scale.[10] Many Christians are most comfortable with a scale that implies immediacy and direct causality. But some of the issues I am raising in this book take on different meanings and exhibit different dynamics when the scales are grand: time, infinity, space, eternity. The noted Harvard professor Stephen Jay Gould expressed it neatly: From outer space, even the Himalayas will appear as a minor wrinkle on the surface of the earth.[11]

When David Bohm spoke of a particular pulse coming together, creating our universe, he was referencing the Big Bang. The Big Bang model is currently the prevailing scientific theory of the origin and early history of the universe. The Belgian priest Abbeé Georges Lemaître, who was also an accomplished scientist, first proposed this theory in the years between 1927 and 1931. Sir Fred Hoyle opposed the theory vehemently and sarcastically bestowed the label "Big Bang" on it in 1950. Ironically, the scientific community adopted the label. The Big Bang can be understood as part of the larger theory of evolution, dealing with its earliest phases.

All civilizations, ancient and modern, have constructed myths and metanarratives as explanations of the deeper questions of existence that haunt human beings. The standard theory of evolution itself constitutes a scientific metanarrative.

Responding therefore to my grandson Scott's question posed at the beginning of this introduction, I would say: What we choose to believe will depend largely on our worldview, whether with respect to God it is

10. Bisharah Libbus, e-mail correspondence, January 2008.
11. Lewontin, "The Triumph of Stephen Jay Gould," 41.

fundamentally believing, agnostic, atheistic, or indifferent. Some scientific theories and some quasi-religious worldviews (e. g., Buddhism) posit the "just-is-ness" of the universe. By contrast, the Big Bang theory does not require a creator, but it certainly is compatible with such belief. So you can choose. If you opt for the "just is" scenario, with or without a Big Bang, your choice is rationally viable—but you will find yourself alone in an uncaring universe. For some, such as the oft-quoted author of "Invictus," this option satisfies:

> Under the bludgeoning of chance
> My head is bloody, but unbowed . . .
> I am the master of my fate;
> I am the captain of my soul.[12]

Others will seek a personal, trusting relationship with the Creator of the universe and find it spiritually rewarding. More than that, they find it carries the inner conviction of truth. I myself have found it so.

To me it seems a pity that, as Professor Karl Giberson has written, "One hundred and fifty years after Darwin, many evangelicals continue to reject evolution, even as data from the genome project establishes the near certainty of Darwin's central idea of common ancestry [and] Young Earth creationists reject definitive evidence for the big bang theory."[13]

I do not wish to engage in the creationism-evolution debate. In spite of objections raised by some Christians, the fact remains that the standard theory of evolution is accepted in most contemporary scientific circles.[14] And the special case of theistic evolution is adhered to by many scientists who are devout Christians. Until the theory is replaced at some future date—as perhaps it may be—I accept the premise that our universe began with the Big Bang and has evolved over eons, as postulated by the standard theory. On the one hand, as a layperson I am in no position to assess scientific methods; I reasonably rely on the experts. On the other hand, as a Christian, I choose to believe that God created the universe and therefore also assume that the evolutionary process was God's *method* of creation. This position is what is meant by theistic evolution.[15]

12. William E. Henley (1849–1903). *Invictus* is the Latin word for "unconquered."

13. Giberson, "No Science, Please," 19.

14. Readers who wish to refresh their recollection of the standard theory of evolution from the Big Bang till today may consult the appendix for a concise summation.

15. Theistic evolution: the concept that some form of evolution (though not necessar-

Parenthetically, this position also resurfaces the question: Why would anyone *choose* to believe in God as the uncreated ground of all reality? I suggested above that the desire for a personal relationship with the creator is one reason. But Justin L. Barrett, a senior researcher at Oxford University's Centre for Anthropology and Mind, offers a more scientific explanation. He contends that belief in God is natural, and that theism, not atheism, is humanity's natural condition. Belief in God, he suggests, depends on nonconscious mental tools in our brain that generate universal assumptions about how things are in the world. He calls these mental tools hypersensitive agent detection devices, or HADD. All human beings possess these tools, which have been elaborated through natural and cultural selection—that is, evolution.[16]

"Natural" doesn't equate to "necessarily true," however; our evolved instincts and intuitions may be misleading. Nevertheless, we can begin by accepting that even within an evolutionary context it is not unreasonable to believe in God. In chapter 2, then, we will examine how this evolutionary scenario proves to be compatible with the biblical metanarrative and important aspects of Christian theology. We will also explore the way in which the theory of evolution illuminates some of the problems that have exercised Christian thinkers through the centuries—for example, such questions as free will vs. determinism, the presence of evil in the natural world, and the mystery of what theologians term original sin.

ily the standard theory held by the scientific community) is God's method of creation.

16. Barrett, *Why Would Anyone Believe in God?* The reader is referred to chapters 3, 31–44 and 6, 75–93.

2

Purposeful Creation?

For God chose us in Christ before the creation of the world.

EPHESIANS 1:4–5

WE BEGIN WITH THE affirmation that love is the primary energy in God's relationship with the universe he created. The early church fathers who followed the apostles defined God (though God, by definition, cannot be defined!) as tri-unity: three persons comprising one God. Then they tried to articulate that mystery by the strange-sounding concept of *perichoresis*.[1] The fathers asserted that the three divine persons of the one true God eternally permeate or interpenetrate one another in a reciprocal exchange of love. That is a concept difficult, perhaps impossible to comprehend, but it dramatizes the point that love is God's very essence. God *is* love, the evangelist John wrote (1 John 4:8, 16). And thus in eternity, apart from space and time and what other dimensions there may be,[2] God willed to share that love with us—to extend the triune community, if you will. This love is expressed both in the epigraph above and in its larger context, Ephesians 1:3–14 below. Note the emphases I have added:

> Praise be to the God and Father of our Lord Jesus Christ . . . . For
> he chose us in him before the creation of the world to be holy and
> blameless in his sight. *In love* he predestined us for adoption to
> sonship . . . . In him we have redemption through his blood, the for-

---

1. *Perichoresis*: a Greek term used to describe the relationship between each person of the Trinity. It can be defined as co-indwelling, co-inhering, and reciprocal interpenetration. Cf. Prestige, *God in Patristic Thought*, 291–99. Also see Stăniloae, Vol. 1, *Revelation and Knowledge*, 245ff.

2. Contemporary string theory suggests ten or more dimensions. Cf. Schwarz, "Superstring Theory: Basics: How Many?" para. 3. For a discussion of multiple universes, see Chaikin, "Are There Other Universes?" para. 2.

9

giveness of sins, in accordance with the riches of God's grace that he lavished on us . . . . He made known to us the mystery of his will according to his good pleasure, which he purposed in Christ, to be put into effect when the times reach their fulfillment—to bring unity to *all things* in heaven and on earth under Christ.

In him we were also chosen, having been predestined according to the plan of him who works out everything in conformity with the purpose of his will . . . . And you also were included in Christ when you heard the word of truth, the gospel of your salvation. When you believed, you were marked in him with a seal, the promised Holy Spirit, who is a deposit guaranteeing our inheritance until the redemption of those who are God's possession—to the praise of his glory.

The language of Ephesians is somewhat archaic; even so, it makes clear that God relates to us in love and that this was his intent before the world was ever created. And while Paul's letter is addressed to Christians, it may well be that the "we" and the "us" and the "you" Paul speaks of encompass a far larger audience than even he realized when he wrote. With that in mind, let us preview this chapter.

We will begin by positing that God created the universe as a means of producing a very special entity: the human race. We will discuss God's motive in doing so and the difficulty we commonly have in discerning that motive in nature. We will discuss God's twofold purpose for creating the human race and the role evolution plays in fulfilling that purpose. With that background at hand, we will explore the first three chapters of Genesis to determine ways in which the theory of evolution is not only compatible with the Judeo-Christian tradition but may even illuminate such traditional doctrines as creation, the fall, and original sin.

The End Product

God did not create the universe merely to have toys to play with. Nor did God create it out of idle curiosity, to see what might happen after the Big Bang. Although God truly delights in the universe's exuberant diversity—constantly evolving, ever changing—that diversity is a by-product, not the end product.[3] The notable eighteenth-century divine Jonathan Edwards once wrote:

---

3. Cf. Schörnborn, *Chance or Purpose?* chapter 3, 51–67.

> We must suppose that God, before he created the world, had some good in view, as a consequence of the world's existence, that was originally agreeable to him in itself considered, that inclined him to bring the universe into existence, in such a manner as he created it.[4]

Thus God willed the universe into existence with a certain good in view: the creation of human persons to whom he could manifest his glory and on whom he could lavish his love. In generous love God also willed that these persons should share in the governance of his larger creation. In short, God created the universe to produce *us!*[5]

Not so, said the second-century Greek philosopher Celsus. "The world came into being as much for the sake of animals as for that of man,"[6] he averred, and produced a well-reasoned argument in favor of his contention. Jews[7] and Christians, however, have long held the conviction that the world was specifically created with humankind in view. The *Letter to Diognetus* is one of the very earliest postapostolic writings we have. An anonymous person who described himself as a "disciple of the apostles" wrote it to someone usually thought to be the tutor of the future emperor Marcus Aurelius:

> For God has loved mankind, *on whose account He made the world,* to whom He rendered subject all the things that are in it, to whom He gave reason and understanding, to whom alone He imparted the privilege of looking upwards to Himself, whom He formed after His own image, to whom He sent His only-begotten Son, to whom He has promised a kingdom in heaven, and will give it to those who have loved Him[8] (emphasis mine).

You and I are end products of 13.7 billion years of evolution. Our bodies are composed of elements created eons ago in the explosions of supernovae. Like animals, fish, birds, trees, grains, and flowers, we are carbon-based life forms. Thus we are truly embedded (to borrow a term from battlefield journalism) within the natural world. We are in solidarity with all of nature. And, as Dumitru Stăniloae, the noted Romanian

4. Edwards, "Dissertation," 4.

5. Cf. Colling, *Random Designer,* 187.

6. Cf. Schörnborn, *Chance or Purpose?* 114.

7. Ibid., 111, n. 5.

8. Referenced in the bibliography under Mathetes, X, 2. *Mathetes* is Greek for "disciple."

Orthodox theologian, reminds us, our surrounding universe comes to us as God's gift for "personal interaction and disclosure" of mutuality and reciprocity.[9] That is, as God's gift and word, the world exists as a condition for the development of the human race and for the spiritual growth of individual humans.[10] At the same time, humans are expected to be good stewards of the world. This gift and word from God to humanity is rightly regarded as the creation covenant.[11]

Ambiguity

God's purpose for creating the world for the human race is not evident from evolutionary theory per se. The naturalism of science is method-ological, not metaphysical.[12] Science seeks to explain how things work without resorting to supernatural causes. But that does not mean there is nothing beyond nature, despite what Richard Dawkins (*The God Delusion*), Daniel Dennett (*Darwin's Dangerous Idea*), Christopher Hitchens (*God Is Not Great*), and other ideological evolutionists assert. Nor does it mean that there is no purpose behind evolution, even if that purpose is not dis-cernable within the theory of evolution itself. Purpose is not something that science can address authoritatively.

When we speak of God's creative love, therefore, we are not talking about *eros* (romantic love) or *philia* (friendship or nonsexual affection), but *agape*. *Agape* is generous, unconditional, self-sacrificing, and thought-ful good will that both desires and works for the welfare of the other. Such love is God's essence and provides God's motive for creating *Homo sapiens* in his own image. The centrality of *agape* cannot be overemphasized. Many Christians see deity as bipolar and attempt to set God's holiness or wrath or justice over against his love. This bifurcation is grossly misdirected. Not only grace and mercy but also God's justice and wrath are expressions of God's love; all are filtered through his love. The witness of Scripture in its wholeness amply supports this truth, although at times tension exists in Scripture between God's wrath and God's love. Contemporary minds

---

9. Cf. Miller, *Gift of the World*, 58–60.

10. Cf. Stăniloae, *Creation and Deification*, chapter 2.

11. E. g., Bühlmann, *God's Chosen Peoples*, 11.

12. Metaphysical: that part of physics concerned with ultimate causes and the under-lying nature of things.

continue to wrestle with the tension.[13] We ourselves will have opportunity to wrestle further with this tension in chapters 9 and 10.

Even though God's purposeful love is not self-evident in our material universe, other dimensions of his eternal power and divine nature are (cf. Romans 1:20 and Wisdom 13:1–9).[14] We see the universe as frustratingly ambiguous in its present form. Some might indeed perceive God's love in the beauty of a sunset or a tree[15]—but in a death-dealing earthquake or tsunami? Surely not. Such evils call into question the very existence of a God worthy of worship, or so it seems to many witnesses.

What *is* evident to human observers for the most part is a combination of reassuring natural law and seemingly random events.[16] That "God so loved the world" (John 3:16), or that "God loves the human race"[17] is something that has been *revealed* to certain persons and groups throughout human history.[18]

We do not always recognize that the Hebrew patriarchs—Abraham, Isaac, and Jacob—did not speak of the love of God. Or if they did, it is not recorded in the Bible. Yet by the time of Israel's dramatic exodus from Egypt, Moses and Miriam were singing, "In your unfailing love you will lead the people you have redeemed" (Exodus 15:13). Later David also would sing of God's love: "The earth is full of his unfailing love" (Psalm 33:5). Still later the weeping prophet Jeremiah would testify, "The Lord appeared to us in the past, saying, 'I have loved you with an everlasting love; I have drawn you with unfailing kindness'" (Jeremiah 31:3). Other Hebrew prophets during the period leading up to the exile in Babylon also testified to God's love (e. g., Hosea 11:4 and Joel 2:13).

So what had happened in the interim between the patriarchs and the impending exile in Babylon? What had happened was that God had sought out these tribes and established a personal relationship with them.

13. Cf. Talbott, *Inescapable Love*, especially 32*ff.* and 113*ff.* See also Fristad, chapter 7, 73–88. Fristad's book has a strong pastoral perspective.

14. *Wisdom of Solomon*: one of the books of the Apocrypha.

15. Joyce Kilmer, an American poet of the early twentieth century, wrote, " I think that I shall never see/A poem lovely as a tree/. . . Poems are made by fools like me/but only God can make a tree." Kilmer was killed at the second battle of the Marne in 1918 at the age of 31.

16. Cf. Monod, *Chance and Necessity*.

17. Irenaeus, *Against Heresies*, III: 18:6.

18. Bloesch, *Holy Scripture*, especially chapter 4, 85–130.

In theological terms, God "elected" them.[19] It is in this personal relationship that Israel experienced God's love. This experience carried over into the life of the early Christian churches, and the apostle Paul most eloquently proclaimed it. God's love has been "poured into our hearts," he says, and nothing in all creation "can separate us from the love of God" (Romans 5:5; 8:39). For Paul, God's love in Christ, revealed preeminently in the Christ event, "surpasses all human understanding" (Ephesians 3:19).

Why Human Beings?

This question brings us back to God's double purpose in creating our universe.[20] God's very nature moved him to extend his love to other entities that did not even yet exist! And since it is the nature of love to reciprocate, God purposed to create persons who could and would love as God loves, in radical freedom. This capacity to love unconditionally is inherent in being made "in the image of God" (Genesis 1:27).

Another way of visualizing this purpose is to imagine God willing into existence "an eternal community of mutual love"[21] and allowing this community to share with him in the stewardship of the universe. This is not the precise order in which God's binary purpose is revealed in the Bible—Genesis comes before Ephesians, after all—but it is faithful to the biblical witness in toto. The text from Ephesians quoted earlier speaks of this community of mutual love. The prior Genesis text speaks of shared governance:

> Then God said, "Let us make human beings in our image, in our
> likeness, so that they may rule over the fish in the sea and the birds
> in the sky, over the livestock and all the wild animals, and over

19. In spite of the sole reference to the contrary in Amos 3:2, we cannot conclude that God has not elected peoples other than Israel. We will discuss this question of election at some length in chapter 11 below.

20. The catechisms of Orthodox, Roman Catholic, and mainstream Protestant churches teach that God created the universe and all things in it for his glory. I am not disputing that, for both the communion and stewardship to which I am calling attention contribute to God's glory. Indeed, everything in one way or another contributes to the glory of God; for that reason I am not sure that discourse about the purpose of creation being to glorify God is very helpful. But the reader should also consult Jonathan Edwards's masterful exposition of the meaning of the glory of God in his "Dissertation Concerning the End for Which God Made the World."

21. My preferred description. Others have termed it the "perfected order of integral love," e. g., Stăniloae, Revelation and Knowledge, 66. Some call it the kingdom of heaven.

all the creatures that move along the ground" (Genesis 1:26; cf. 2:19–20).

Clearly, a love coerced would never fulfill this purpose of God. That is to say, God *could* have but *would* not have created by crude fiat beings who must necessarily love him and their fellow humans and rule the world with justice. This is not the style of *agape*. On the contrary, in God's own freedom he graciously endowed the human race with free will. Perfect love demands perfect freedom. Again, it is in this radical freedom with its potential to love that we must understand the phrase that humans are made "in God's image." And perhaps it is in the exercise of free will in their stewardship of earth that human beings experience their highest dignity: "You have crowned them with glory and honor [and] made them rulers over the works of Your hands" (Psalm 8:5).

Evolution: God's Plan

But how to create such creatures if not by fiat? Christians believe that God lovingly, generously, and even humbly in divine *kenosis*[22] made room for the creation of the universe. Before, there was God alone; after, there was God and something(s) else. I propose that in doing so, God impressed into the very structure of the universe the capacity for radical freedom from the Big Bang forward. If love was God's *motive*, and an eternal community of mutual love able to share in the governance of the universe was God's *purpose*, then evolution grounded in free will was God's *plan*.

Note that I distinguish here between purpose and plan, as does the text from Ephesians that we have already read. But the purpose and the plan are tightly integrated. God's plan is love's plan. Evolution is God's way of ensuring that the universe—and human beings especially—are free to be themselves and make themselves.[23]

I am suggesting that every atom, every quark, contains an urge to freedom, an energy that, when we encounter it in animate beings, embodies both free will and self-preservation. It is this urge to freedom—which in the natural world may appear as merely random events—that propels

22. The Greek word *kenosis* means self-emptying or self-limiting. Cf. Stăniloae, *Revelation and Knowledge*, 212.

23. Cf. the words of the philosophical theologian Austin Farrer: "God made the world, but he did not just make it; he made it make itself." Cited in Beckett, "Not a Theory, but a Life," 23.

the essentially selfish drive to survive and reproduce. Yet over eons, that urge also gives rise to the distinctive properties of human consciousness and love.

This freedom paradoxically functions within the limiting framework of gravity, the second law of thermodynamics (otherwise known as entropy), and natural selection. Gravity we are familiar with. Entropy means that anything left to itself tends to deteriorate and fall apart, becoming less organized and less useful than it was before. Natural selection is a built-in quality of nature grounded in freedom. It is a template for environmental adaptation that sorts out the more effective molecules, cells, organs, species, and the like from the less effective ones.[24]

I am not presuming that gravity, natural selection, and the second law of thermodynamics are the consequences of free will, although such a sequence is not impossible to conceive and may well prove to be the case. What I am suggesting is that the radical will to freedom entailed in God's plan of evolution eventually produces consciousness, love, and a host of other uniquely human qualities. These human qualities cannot be accounted for solely on the basis of the properties of the constituent parts of the human brain. They appear rather by way of the well-established phenomenon of emergence. Emergence refers to the way in which complex systems and patterns arise out of multiple and relatively simple interactions. Ice turns into water and water becomes vapor. A butterfly flaps its wings in Tokyo and sets in motion a tornado in Topeka. Emergence is central to the theory of such complex systems as weather structures.[25]

Some young-earth creationists conclude that the second law of thermodynamics is counter to evolution, since that law prescribes that everything in the universe is becoming less organized rather than more so. But that is not quite the case, for the processes of the second law of thermodynamics (processes termed katabolism) cannot prevail uniformly over anabolism, which is the winding-up or storing of energy that can be utilized later for other purposes. Thus certain aspects of the universe continue to develop toward greater complexity even as other parts wind down and die. Anabolism occurs only when a significant source

---

24. For a lucid explanation of the second law of thermodynamics as related to randomness, see Colling, *Random Designer*, 21–26. For a more detailed description of natural selection, see Biology-Online, "Theory of Natural Selection," para 2.

25. For emergence, see Goldstein, "Emergence as a Construct," 49–72. For a book-length account, see Holland, *Emergence from Chaos to Order*.

of outside energy is provided. Obviously God is such an outside energy source, especially in the evolution of the species *Homo sapiens* (hereafter *H. sapiens)* and its associated cultures.

True free will is random, both in the concrete sense that it is unpredictable and in the more abstract sense that in certain circumstances it appears to be without plan or purpose. Yet surprisingly, this randomness produces order out of chaos.[26] Mere mention of chaos brings to mind the Genesis creation story: "Now the earth was formless and empty, darkness was over the surface of the deep, and the Spirit of God was hovering over the waters" (Genesis 1:2).

The free-will-built-into-nature thesis that I am suggesting is a hypothesis, to be sure. But I offer the concept, at least as metaphor, for one of the great mysteries of the universe because it communicates the radical freedom with which I believe God has endowed his creation, and to which Scripture, especially the New Testament, bears witness.[27] And it is not inconceivable that in due time scientific research may confirm the hypothesis. Further, this conjecture is not all that different from that of Pierre Teilhard de Chardin, the famous paleontologist.[28] He argued that every atom has an inner and an outer reality.[29] Says quantum physicist John Polkinghorne:

> The insights of cosmology, evolutionary biology and molecular genetics all bear witness to the astonishing potentiality with which matter is endowed . . . . The world is endowed in its fundamental constitution with an anthropic potentiality[30] that makes it capable of fruitful evolution. The exploration and realization of that potentiality is achieved by the universe through the continual interplay of chance and necessity within its unfolding process. The cosmos is given the opportunity to be itself . . . . [God] is not the puppet master of either men or matter.[31]

26. Cf. Rae, "Chaos Theory: A Brief Introduction," para. 1.

27. E. g., Galatians 5:1.

28. Paleontologists: scientists who study prehistoric forms of life preserved in fossils.

29. Teilhard de Chardin, *Phenomenon of Man,* 57–61.

30. Anthropic principle: posits that the universe is finely attuned to the production and maintenance of carbon-based human life.

31. Polkinghorne, *Science and Providence,* 31, 77–78. Cf. Harrell's *Nature's Witness: How Evolution Can Inspire Faith.* This is a thoughtful book, written in a stream-of-consciousness style that can make the reader impatient at times, but its thoroughness in exploring the ambiguities of both evolution and faith is rewarding.

With this hypothesis in mind, it is time to look more specifically at the relationship between the early chapters of Genesis and the theory of evolution.[32]

Genesis and Evolution

The book of Genesis contains two separate accounts of creation.[33] The first account begins in Genesis 1:1 and extends to the third verse of Genesis 2. The second account begins with Genesis 2:4 and continues to the end of that chapter. Both accounts are assumed by some to conflict with the theory of evolution. But this assumption rests on a faulty understanding of the nature of the accounts and why they appear in the biblical record. They were never intended as scientific records. Rather, their purpose is to announce a specific set of Hebrew beliefs to counter prevailing ancient Middle Eastern mythologies. These Hebrew beliefs include the following:

- There is one God, not a pantheon of gods.

- God created an ordered world by his word; the world was not formed by battles among the gods.

- No part of the physical world is divine. The sun and moon and other celestial objects are not gods controlling the fate of humans.

- All parts of creation are good or very good. It is not the case that some physical structures are related to good deities and others to bad ones.

- God created humans in his image and gave them responsibility to be stewards of creation. It is not true that humans are made as an afterthought from the flesh of a defeated god in order to be slaves of the gods.[34]

Given the fact that the biblical editors were likely to have composed the Genesis accounts from oral traditions *after* elements of Buddhist thought had reached Palestine, I would add one more point. In contrast to the Buddhist concept that the diversity of the universe is illusory (*maya*), Genesis asserts:

---

32. For an excellent presentation of the way in which human life arose from randomness in the universe, see Colling, *Random Designer,* chapter 11.

33. Cf. Kugel, *How to Read the Bible,* 52–56.

34. Cf. Haarsma, *Origins,* 116.

- God created the great diversity we see in the universe and pronounced it good (Gen 1:12, 21).[35]

Thus the Genesis accounts are not to be interpreted as scientific treatises nor are they to be interpreted literally. Like Psalm 104, another creation account, Genesis 1 can be read as a creation poem, for the days and sequence of events are recounted in the manner of Hebrew poetry. Days one, two, and three speak of *forming* and are paralleled by days four, five, and six of *filling*. Parallelism is a characteristic trait of Hebrew poetics.[36]

Taken as a whole, the primeval history recorded in Genesis 1–11 is presented in the language of myth and legend. Some people are put off by the use of the term *myth*. But myth and legend are simply ways the ancient storytellers captured truth—or what they believed to be truth—and conveyed it to subsequent generations. Some of the world's foundational myths are in fact false in the sense that they hide a deeper and inadmissible truth. The biblical authors, while they utilized the language of myth and legend, actually convey truth and unmask the underlying falsity of mythology.[37]

If one reads the creation accounts in Genesis literally, problems arise. For example, the two Genesis accounts present the events of creation in different orders. In Genesis 1, the creation of dry land is followed by the creation of plants; in Genesis 2, the creation of the dry land and rivers is followed by the creation of humans and then plants. In Genesis 1, land animals are created, followed by human beings, male and female; in Genesis 2, land animals and birds are created, then the first woman, created from the first man's rib or side.

35. Scientists count about two million global species. But with recent developments in deep-sea biological research, that number may be doubled or quadrupled. "Such a wanton waste of beauty!" exclaimed the early evolutionary researcher Alfred Russell Wallace (cited in Knapp, "In a Green Light," 12). But from a Christian perspective, these species have delighted God for millions of years.

36. A pastor friend suggests that the Genesis creation account concludes with God "finishing" creation, signifying in the ancient world that God could be trusted, unlike the pagan epic dramas in which the creation stories were reenacted repeatedly in order to maintain power in the universe, for the gods could not be trusted to do so. (Dan Groh, e-mail correspondence, August 2008.) This is true and remains true, but in the context of our time, and with the advent of evolutionary theory, I would prefer the word *initiating* to *finishing*.

37. The admittedly obscure reference here is to René Girard's theory of the mimetic origin of culture and the scapegoat theory it disguises. I defer more detailed discussion of Girard to chapter 8 below.

I do not want to belabor these discrepancies. The point is that the Bible's creation stories serve a theological purpose, not a scientific one. They do not feature *how* God created the world (they are content with "And God said . . ."), only that God *did* create it, and did so for a purpose. There is no reason on the face of it to reject the idea that evolution was God's "how." On the contrary, the concept of evolution illumines important features of the biblical metanarrative, as we shall see.

Good, Very Good, or Perfect?

The Genesis narrative reports that God found his diversified and dynamic creation "good," even "very good." In Aristotelian terms we might say that God found the creation suitable for his intended purpose and that it was proceeding according to plan. How much time would be required for the plan is left unmarked in Scripture. But for now God could "rest" (Genesis 2:2).

Note that Genesis does not say that God found his creation to be *perfect*. Indeed, God could not have found it so because the free will built into the creation necessarily allowed for the possibility of mishaps and even volitions counterproductive to God's binary purpose. Perfection, that is, the capacity to exercise radical freedom in full accordance with God's purpose, existed in Genesis as latent potentiality, not completion.

The essential teleological[38] goodness of creation underlies every other major truth in the Bible. But can we really say that God *loves* every part of his creation? Or is it only the end product—the human race—that God loves and elects? Followers of Jesus know that God cares for creation, for Jesus asserted that not even a sparrow falls to the ground unnoticed by the heavenly Father (Matthew 10:29, cf. Psalm 104:27ff). But if *agape* love is that generous, unconditional, self-sacrificing, and thoughtful good will that both desires and works for the welfare of the other that we spoke of earlier, then it would seem that God indeed loves the whole of his creation—the stars, our earth, sea and rocks, plants and animals, fish and birds. Writing in the first century before Jesus, a sage declares,

> For you love all things that exist, and detest none of the things that you have made, for you would not have made anything if you had hated it (Wisdom 11:24).

38. Teleological: having to do with direction to a final end (meaning and purpose are assumed).

Further, God is passionately involved with the totality of creation. We are not speaking of the God of the deists but the God of the Bible. Providentially, God sustains the universe, possibly though the mysteries of dark matter and dark energy, which together constitute 96 percent of the universe, and which cosmologists are currently trying to verify.[39] When the time comes for the renewal of all things, and for what the early church fathers called "the deification of the world,"[40] we can be sure that "all things" will embrace the manifold diversity of nature, including trilobites and dinosaurs.

In spite of the comment in Genesis about God "resting" after creation, we must note that the earth itself is still evolving. It is *in statu viae* (on the way), as Cardinal Schörnborn reminds us. This evolution is evident in the movement of tectonic plates, volcanic eruptions, tsunamis, and the like. The northward movement of India and Australia continues to raise the Himalayas and trigger eruptions of many volcanoes in Southeast Asian islands and archipelagos. The Atlantic Ocean continues to widen as Africa and Europe drift further from North and South America. Meanwhile the subduction of the Pacific plate under the North American continent has slowed somewhat.[41] Thus God's rest should not be understood as a total and permanent cessation of activity.

Continental drift illustrates the free will dynamic that I suggest is implicit in planet Earth, as well as the unfinished nature of the universe. More importantly, this drift suggests that the planet's unfinished status provides an explanation if not a justification for what we call natural evil—that portion of the evil afflicting the human race that is *not* caused by humans. The evil we experience from natural causes cries out for justification, and this can only be some form of what philosophers call "greater good" theodicy.[42] The apostle Paul, for example, employs the greater good theodicy in Romans 8:18–22.

---

39. Cf. Britt, "Dark Matter Exposed," para 1 *ff.*

40. Cf. Stăniloae, *Creation and Deification*, chapter 7. In Eastern Orthodox thinking, deification does not imply that humans become gods but that they will eventually share perfect communion with God.

41. See MacEvoy, "Geoevolution: Modern," para. 2.

42. Theodicy: the attempt to justify God's goodness and power in the face of the reality of evil. The "greater good" theodicy, in brief, argues that the greater good, or blessing, that will ultimately ensue from the conflict between good and evil justifies the suffering of individuals that is entailed.

N. T. Wright, the scholarly Anglican Bishop of Durham, is impatient with all attempts to explain natural evil. The issue, he insists, is not *why* there is evil in our universe, but rather how God *deals* with it.[43] For many of us, however, the "why" seems important, and theodicy explanations are relevant, so further on in this monograph we will discuss both the why *and* the how of natural evil.

Early Humans

The scientific evidence that humans are composed of star dust evokes Genesis 2:7 (humans made from the dust of the ground) since the ground itself is composed of 112 known chemical elements created in starry explosions more than five billion years ago. Arnold Benz, professor of astrophysics at the Swiss Federal Institute of Technology in Zürich, writes,

> The carbon and the acids in our bodies come from the helium-burning area of an old star. Shortly before and during a supernova explosion, two silicon nuclei fused to make the iron in our blood. The calcium in our teeth was formed from acid and silicon during a supernova . . . and the iodine in our thyroid glands originated through the capture of neutrons in the collapse before a supernova.[44]

Similarly, the poetic description of God's breathing into man's nostrils the breath of life (Genesis 2:7 again), man thereby becoming a living being—or better yet, a true person, suggests the emergence of distinctive human consciousness from common ancestry. That all this complex development, being contingent on God's scheme of random mutation and natural selection, required billions of years to eventuate should come as no surprise.

Over tens of thousands of years the earliest humans emigrated from southern and eastern Africa to the other continents, where they lived in close communion with their immediate natural environments and such other *Homo* species as the Neanderthals. As their brains developed, so did their self-awareness and their increasing intuition of their creator. Adam and Eve represent these earliest humans.[45] Their number is not known,

43. N. T. Wright, *Evil and the Justice of God*, 39.

44. Cited in Schörnborn, *Chance or Purpose?* 117.

45. Cf. the important recent contribution of Livingstone, *Adam's Ancestors: Race,*

but from Genesis 4:14–15, it must be evident to even the most literalist of readers that other human beings besides Adam, Eve, and Cain resided in different parts of the world in significant numbers.

Obviously this account does not preclude the idea that *H. sapiens* began with a single individual or pair. The consensus, however, is that while a hypothetical human population of the present size might have descended from a single pair, the *particular* population that now exists could not have. It includes far more genetic variety than could have been transmitted by a single human couple.[46] According to the geneticist F. J. Ayala, the minimum possible number of individuals in the breeding population at any time in our history was at least four thousand, which would correspond to a total population of fifteen to twenty thousand.[47]

James Stephenson tells the remarkable story of a hunter-gatherer group, the Hadzabe, living around Lake Eyasi in Tanzania, southwest of the Ngorongoro Crater. "Sweet, innocent lovelies, the last of the old people," he writes.[48] The most fascinating thing about the Hadzabe, as I read the account, is their almost total identification with nature. They are, as it were, a throwback to the Garden of Eden.

But then the moment came (and biblical moments can span thousands of ordinary years; cf. 2 Peter 3:8) when women and men became consciously aware of their distinction from nature and other living things. Thereafter *H. sapiens*, in accordance with the twofold purpose of God, assumed authority over the "garden" in which they found themselves, and God "rested."

Biological evolution occurs as entities react or respond for better or worse to their environments. In the Garden of Eden narrative we see God deputizing *H. sapiens* to oversee the future of our planet, and perhaps more. Within the garden environment the human race would have the opportunity to learn to love purely and govern justly. More importantly, with the advent of self-awareness, humans became aware of *God* as their ultimate environment. From this point forward, *H. sapiens* would evolve less with respect to the physical environment (though this factor is never

---

Religion and the Politics of Human Origins.

46. Colling, *Random Designer,* 112. Cf. Domning, "Evolution and Original Sin," 85–86.

47. Cited in Domning, *ibid.*

48. Stephenson, *Language of the Land,* x.

absent nor should it be) than to their new cultural and spiritual environments. Again, this evolution can be for weal or woe.

The Fall and Its Consequences

The apostle John writes that God is light as well as love (1 John 1:5). Within the Christian tradition humanity is portrayed as estranged or alienated from God; and this alienation in turn is presented as the result of humanity's turn to evil: a combination of unrestrained desire and willful disobedience. How this came about is recounted in Genesis 3. The event is traditionally known as the fall, though this designation is not altogether satisfactory, as we shall see.

With the emergence of self-awareness and moral consciousness, symbolized by the tree of the knowledge of good and evil planted in the midst of the garden, *H. sapiens* became acutely aware of its special relationship to its Creator. Instead of a fall as traditionally understood, what we actually have here, from an evolutionary perspective, is an *elevation* of consciousness—most likely associated with the development of language thirty thousand to one hundred thousand years ago.[49] Claude Levi-Strauss, a major figure in post-World War II structuralism, believes that

> [L]anguage can only have arisen all at once. Things cannot have begun to signify gradually . . . a shift occurred from the stage when nothing had a meaning to another stage when everything had a meaning.[50]

Levi-Strauss's hypothesis goes against our ordinary conception of incremental evolution and may or may not prove correct. Yet such an occurrence would reflect the Niles Eldridge-Jay Gould theory of punctuated equilibria[51] or, from a theistic perspective, a direct intervention by God. And with that rise in consciousness human beings became acutely aware of their moral freedom. Soon thereafter they exercised their freedom to exceed the favored but still creaturely limits inherent in their place in the universe. It is in this conscious perversion of freedom that we

---

49. Team C004367, "The Evolution of Language," para. 2.

50. Strauss, *Introduction to the Work of Marcel Mauss*, 59–60, citied in Dawson, "The Magic Word and the Logical Machine: Myth and History in Levi-Strauss, Derrida and Girard." Unpublished paper, 6.

51. Eldredge and Gould, "Punctuated Equilibria," 82–115 . . .

may indeed speak of a fall. In short: an elevation of consciousness but a moral fall.

In the next chapter we shall inquire more closely into the true nature of original sin and actual, everyday sin. Then we will survey the remainder of the Old Testament, asking whether *H. sapiens* is doomed to annihilation or self-destruction morally and physically, or whether God has a way to deal with all evil and its natural consequences, enabling humankind and all creation to be reconciled to its creator and fulfill its intended destiny. After a few preliminaries, God's call to Abraham will be our focal point.

3

East of Eden[1]

All peoples on earth will be blessed through you.

AS THE BIBLICAL NARRATIVE has it, a serpent tempts Eve to taste the forbidden fruit. Adam imitates Eve's action. Their combined disobedience resulted in what Christian theologians call original sin, a constitutionally sinful nature inherited by all subsequent generations. It is worth noting that the doctrine of original sin is not part of Jewish theology, nor does the term *original sin* appear in the New Testament. The apostle Paul introduced the idea, but only indirectly in connection with his teaching on redemption (cf. Romans 5:12). Nevertheless the concept is ensconced in Christian doctrine and we shall have to deal with it.

Who or what, then, is that serpent? Traditionally, the serpent is understood to be Satan or more literally, a snake inspired by Satan. But this notion is a late idea, found only in the later books of the Tanakh[2] and in the deuterocanonical[3] book Wisdom of Solomon (Wisdom 2:14), which was composed about 50 B.C.E.[4] Readers interested in the history of the devil in global perspective can consult the book noted in footnote 5. I suggest that in the Genesis context we do well to think of the serpent as a metaphor for the genetic heritage of *H. sapiens*. This heritage accumulated over a period of nearly one million years. Indeed, it goes back even further, to the origins of life itself. It is deeply ingrained in us.[5]

1. The title of John Steinbeck's epic novel, based on the Genesis story of Cain and Abel.
2. 1 Chronicles 21:1; Job 1:6; and Zechariah 3:1.
3. The reader is referred to the glossary for a complete list of the deuterocanonical books.
4. Cf. Schwager, *Banished from Eden,* chapter 5, 143–65.
5. Cf. Messadié, *A History of the Devil;* also Pagels, *The Origin of Satan.*

During this long period, under the pressures of random mutation and natural selection, humans evolved instincts requisite for survival: sexual drives, aggressiveness, larger brains, and importantly, a capacity for mimesis, or learning by imitating. The seeds of what we recognize as human evil are embedded in this ancient nature (cf. Romans 6:6, "the old self") and are powerful, even assuming the free will that human beings evidence.

The Selfish Gene

Behind the instincts mentioned above, and others as well, lies the primal one: selfishness. From my perspective, we would not be misled in identifying this selfishness with the radical freedom with which God originally endowed the creation. Freedom, as the dictionary has it, is "the absence of necessity, coercion, or constraint in choice or action." Or, as Jonathan Edwards wrote, "The power, opportunity, or advantage, that any one has to do as he pleases."[6] Thus the Howard University paleobiologist Daryl Domning helpfully suggests that instead of speaking about original sin, we learn to speak about "original selfishness."[7]

The free-will bias characteristic of the material universe does not appear to require preservation of all material forms as such. Galaxies collapse and collide, stars explode, rocks are eroded and disappear. But the situation changes with the advent of life. The driving forces of biological evolution are clearly self-preservation and perpetuation, and these forces entail the now-notorious "selfish gene" popularized by Richard Dawkins of Oxford University. In terms of physical survival, selfishness is a positive value; it breeds success. Under some circumstances, genetic selfishness can lead to disaster, as with viruses or cancer cells, but for the most part, selfishness has tended toward the good—the survival—of the particular species.

> For eons . . . the mutation/selection process has successfully formulated the biological background and established the necessary framework for biological synthesis reactions—ultimately paving a pathway for the emergence and endurance of life, and even humankind."[8]

6. Edwards, "Freedom of the Will," I:5.

7. Domning, "Evolution and Original Sin," 56. A paleobiologist is a scientist who deals with the fossils of plants, animals, and other organisms.

8. Colling, *Random Designer,* 133.

But how is sin, thus embedded in human nature, passed on to each successive generation? Drawing on René Girard's mimetic theory,[9] I suggest that human beings in each successive generation imitate their forebears and peers in the exercise of their freedom. After all, imitation is the way all infants learn. In this way sin—which we can understand here as the proclivity to make one's own way in the world independent of God's twofold purpose—becomes *habituated* within the human race. The theory of evolution allows the millions of years required for this habituation to become effective in human beings. And Girard's extensive research into the origins of human civilizations comports well with the story told in Genesis 4–11.

Thomas Aquinas, the theologian *par excellence* of the high Middle Ages, argued that original sin is passed on to following generations not by imitation but by the father's semen.[10] Contemporary evolutionary biologists premise much of human behavior on coded genes that are in fact transmitted from one generation to another through chromosomes present in sperm. So to this extent, Aquinas was right—although he overlooked the reality that human reproduction requires both sperm and egg,[11] so our genetic heritage must come through both male and female. Moreover, one cannot escape the conclusion that specifically sinful acts are prompted not only by genetic disposition but also by imitation and volition, as previously noted.

There is another dimension to sin mentioned in passing in the previous chapter that we should now consider further: *H. sapiens* is programmed by natural selection for survival by way of instincts based in our emotions. Therefore, many or most of our life decisions are made emotionally and only afterward justified rationally. Thus much sin is not associated with true free will but with unintentionality. The Mosaic laws make allowance for unintentional sin; cf. Leviticus 4:2. Our radically free wills have been severely compromised by our selfish genes. It is an error, therefore, to attribute all personal sin to the exercise of conscious free will.

9. The reference is to René Girard, the French-born literary critic, anthropologist, and professor emeritus at Stanford University. Girard is known for his theory that human civilizations are founded on the sacrifice of scapegoats as the way out of mimetic (imitative) violence between rivals. For a brief exposition of this theory, the reader is referred to chapter 8 below.

10 Aquinas lived before the discovery of spermatozoa in semen, first recorded by Anton van Leeuwenhoek in the seventeenth century.

11. The human ovum is the largest cell in the human body, but was not discovered until 1827 by the German anatomist Karl Ernst von Baer.

In any event, and however we express it, we humans are existentially aware that "all have sinned and fall short of the glory of God" (Romans 3:23). Not all cultures express the reality of sin in these terms, however. Buddhism, for example, avers that all life is suffering and argues that the true aim of life is to escape this world and its suffering. Hinduism attributes human suffering to *karma*[12] accumulated by the individual in past lives. In Western culture, sin is related to guilt, whereas in some important world societies, such as Japan and Arabia, for example, sin is grounded in the concept of shame.[13] Whether the emotion felt is guilt or shame, we human beings experience a sense of alienation and estrangement from the divine and simultaneously a longing, a deep yearning, for transcendence. Beyond immediate feelings of guilt or shame, Christians hold that the chief consequence of sin is spiritual death, understood as alienation from the creator God.

Further Reflections on Sin

The protagonists in our story gave in to the unbounded desire to "be like God, knowing good from evil" (Genesis 3:5). For many American evangelicals this sin is thought of as premeditated rebellion against the reign of God[14] I suspect that may be too simplistic an interpretation. Although the narrative has the temptation reasonably culminating in rebellion, thereby incurring guilt, it might just as rationally be thought of as an act of weakness incurring shame. In the long history of humankind sin is actually more insidious than overt. Think for a moment about your own moral experience. Only the most pharisaical among us will deny having misbehaved during his or her lifetime, but relatively few of these instances have been out-and-out volitional. More often than not we have harmed others or offended God by neglect or indifference or ignorance, or under some compulsion we did not fully appreciate at the time.

---

12. Karma: Sanskrit for "action" or "deed." The law of karma is action and reaction. One reaps what one sows, or, what goes around comes around.

13. For a perceptive discussion of shame cultures, see Green and Baker, *Recovering the Scandal of the Cross,* 153–70. Also see Nabeel Jabbour, *The Crescent through the Eyes of the Cross,* chapter 11, 161–72.

14. C. J. H. Wright, *Mission of God*, 164. It may be noted that St. Augustine, by contrast, understood the fall as being the result of *concupiscientia*, or the disordered desire for a lesser good; *Contra duas epistulas Pelagianorum*, I:34–35. Rebecca Frey, personal correspondence, May 2009.

If that is the case, perhaps we should rethink our understanding of the evil we call sin. Recall that God's ultimate purpose in creating the universe was to produce human beings perfected in freedom and love who would then constitute an eternal community of mutual love and partnership with the triune God. I suggest that anything that deviates from that purpose, consciously or unconsciously, willfully or by default, is sin in the broadest sense. The Greek word translated as sin in Romans 3:23 and elsewhere is *hamartia*, which conveys the idea of missing the mark or falling short, as in an archery competition.

By virtue of the radical freedom God granted the universe, by the time hominids evolved, the blind, unconscious exercise of freedom had already caused all creation to deviate from God's purpose, producing what we call natural evil. Hence all creation needs redemption. Within this context *H. sapiens* inherited and developed selfish instincts that work powerfully against pure altruism and love—instances of which have always been present in the human race alongside the evil impulses. In the Genesis story, with the advent of human persons came the possibility of conscious and willful deviation from God's purpose in creation. Human inclination to sin—what medieval theologians called concupiscence or the tinder of sin (*fomes peccati*)—is therefore a subset of the larger phenomenon of evil. It is the selfish gene's entry into the arena of moral consciousness.

Through imitation (mimesis), especially covetous imitation,[15] this deviation, at once both genetic *and* willful, became habituated in the human race. Although the disposition to sin is genetic in origin, the actual *volition* to sin or not to sin transcends our genetic heritage. Sin in this strict sense—culpable choice by a moral agent to act on selfish desires that are harmful, resulting in actual sin and guilt[16]—has decisively impacted the universe for the worse; hence our contemporary ecological crisis. Moreover, spiritual death has come to all people (cf. Ephesians 2:1–3). The coexistence of the will to do right with the disposition to do wrong is powerfully reflected by the apostle Paul in Romans 7:14–25.

Many Christians believe that the theory of evolution assumes inevitable progress. My understanding of evolution does not support this notion. The truth is that evolution, though it appears to generate greater complexity and sophistication in living organisms, and is directed toward

15. Hence the tenth and summary commandment: Thou shalt not covet (Exodus 20:17).

16. Domning, "Evolution and Original Sin," 59.

survival, is also premised in part on random mutation. Therefore evolution cannot guarantee the kind of inevitable "progress" that might save the human race, for some mutations could conceivably lead to the annihilation of humanity. Furthermore, evolution involves the universe, not just the human race. And events in the universe—the collision of an asteroid with the earth, for example—could imperil the human race, as one such collision is said to have extinguished the dinosaurs.

Having said that, I allow for the possibility that God-directed evolution may be the ordained means for achieving God's ultimate purpose. I say *may*, because there is a strong apocalyptic[17] element in the New Testament that Christians cannot discount. On the other hand, Eastern Orthodox Christians have always defined God's ultimate purpose for humankind and creation as a whole in terms of deification, and understand it as the culmination of a gradual spiritual progress, though not without setbacks along the way.

> Thus, God makes use both of the evil and the good forces as he leads history toward higher stages and ultimately toward salvation and deification, for providence implies synergy between God and the conscious creature.[18]

Nevertheless, it seems to me that at this point in evolutionary history human beings have essentially given up trying to eliminate sin. So habituated to sin have we become, so powerful are the effects of inherited original sin, that we are powerless to do so. Instead, we try to civilize ourselves by means of law, art, and religion. We attempt to increase our level of comfort through science, economic activity, and psychological counseling. We strive to protect ourselves and expand our influence through military prowess. While some success may be claimed for these efforts to raise the level of society—indeed, there is always much in civilization to celebrate—civilization does nothing to assuage the intuition we have of being alienated from the transcendent. All religions, primitive and sophisticated, attest in one way or another to this sense of estrangement. As the apostle Paul notes,

17. Apocalyptic: descriptive of the final cataclysm destroying the powers of evil and ushering in the kingdom of God.

18. Stăniloae, *Creation and Deification*, 207.

The sinful mind is hostile to God; it does not submit to God's law, nor can it do so. Those controlled by the sinful nature cannot please God (Romans 8:7).

The Story Continues

Sin carries its own consequences. In true Girardian fashion the Genesis story details how mimetic rivalry ends in violence and murder. Cain slays Abel (Genesis 4).[19] Violence and mayhem escalate sevenfold (Genesis 4:15) and then seventy-sevenfold (4:24). Moral perversion follows the violence (Genesus 6). The more human population increases, the more violence keeps pace with it. Eventually the earth "was full of violence" (Genesis 6:11). God is said to have regretted making human beings. The ecological judgment of the deluge results (Genesis 7–8).

Although all of nature has long been "red in tooth and claw," as the poet Alfred Tennyson surmised, *H. sapiens* has developed violence into a veritable art form. The twentieth century was probably the most violent in recorded history; its death toll is well documented.[20] Our twenty-first century has begun with equal or greater violence.[21] The possibility that the human race may annihilate itself through a nuclear holocaust, excessive global warming, deforestation, biological warfare, or some other criminally perverse behavior cannot be ruled out. The human race continues to play by so-called Darwinian rules, in continuity with the whole sweep of evolution, and will have to be saved from itself or it may perish.

Yet remarkably—and this is a major point in my exposition—after the fall God did not give up on *H. sapiens* or let it reap the extinction that such other species as trilobites and dinosaurs suffered in the long process of evolution. Instead, God *renewed* his covenant with his creation, and more particularly with the human race (Genesis 9–10) through the so-called Noahic Covenant. God made this covenant even though his

19. An astute friend asks, "From where did Cain learn violence?" My response: Like Adam and Eve, Cain may be regarded as a representative figure of all early humans in the Genesis narrative. Also, the mimetic rivalry between Cain and Abel had already been modeled first between Eve and the serpent, and then between Adam and Eve. Cain's violent response was not "learned" from Adam or Eve, but was the inevitable result of the rivalry. It was implicit in his heritage as a member of *H. sapiens*.

20. Glover, *Humanity: A Moral History of the Twentieth Century*.

21. Why is there more violence today than ever? See René Girard's lucid explanation in Girard, *Evolution and Conversion*, 219.

understanding of human nature *after* the flood was precisely the same as *before* the flood! Before the flood God had observed, ". . . even though every inclination of the human heart is evil from childhood" (Genesis 6:5). After the deluge God makes the very same observation in Genesis 8:21!

Genesis 10, which lists scores of nations that emerged after the great flood, is passed over lightly in many biblical commentaries. This oversight is unfortunate not only in view of the rise of new religions during the Axial Age, but also in view of our increasing awareness of religious pluralism in our own day. I take Genesis 10 to be a clear indication that the authors or editors of the Pentateuch believed in God's continuing concern for and involvement with all the peoples of the world in spite of their evil inclinations, and even though, as we shall see, God was about to alter his strategy by focusing on an elect people.

A New Cycle

After the new covenant between God and humankind, evil in the form of human sinfulness began a new cycle, ending with the preposterous image of unbounded desire and arrogance expressed in the tower of Babel (Genesis 11). Human nature had not changed in any measurable degree; evolution is a long, slow process. Human discordance from God is pervasive despite all attempts to ground civilization in religion. Indeed, religion is a major part of the human problem. Over the centuries religion has contributed much evil as well as much good, spiritual bondage as well as freedom, today as surely as in the past. Girard's research referred to earlier[22] demonstrates that religion is complicit in the human effort to conceal the memory of the founding murder that underlies each civilization.

What then in summary does Genesis 1–11 reveal about God's nature and God's relationship to the human race? For one thing, it tells us that God takes sin and sinfulness seriously. The ecological and social consequences of sin (e.g., the flood, the destruction of the tower of Babel) are described as expressions of God's wrath. Yet the same record also reveals that God's love is unfailing; his wrath is penultimate, not ultimate; and God aims at renewal, not vengeful retribution.[23]

---

22. I briefly summarize Girard's thesis in *What about the Cross?*, 127*ff*. For the full exposition see Girard, *Things Hidden* and *I See Satan Fall*.

23. Heschel, *The Prophets*.

In the eighteenth century the famous American clergyman, Jonathan Edwards, preached his equally famous sermon, "Sinners in the Hands of an Angry God." A typical paragraph reads:

> The wrath of God burns against them, their damnation does not slumber; the pit is prepared, the fire is made ready, the furnace is now hot, ready to receive them; the flames do now rage and glow. The glittering sword is whet, and held over them, and the pit hath opened its mouth under them.[24]

This is the same Jonathan Edwards cited earlier, and this is the image of God that dominated the minds of millions during the past millennium. There is no way that this kind of rhetoric can communicate to the late modern or postmodern mentality. The doctrine of the wrath of God properly understood can never override the equally true doctrines of the love and the grace and the mercy of God. This is God's ultimate commitment to the human race. The prophet Habakkuk prayed, "In wrath may you remember mercy" (Habakkuk 3:2). Later the brother of Jesus asserted, "Mercy triumphs over judgment" (James 2:13).

To summarize: the advent of evil, natural as well as human, perverted God's initial gift of freedom. Nature and the human race became spiritually separated in greater or lesser measure from each other, from God, and from God's intentions. God's purpose in creation was checked. Checked, but not defeated. It is impossible that the will of the sovereign God should be defeated over the long run. God's loving will is evident in his commitment to the human race and to the universe as a whole. What is not immediately evident is just *how* God would proceed to fulfill his loving will.

Out of Ur

More than six thousand years ago a Sumerian civilization existed at the head of the Persian Gulf near the confluence of the Tigris and Euphrates rivers. Its main city was called Ur, and its primary deity was the moon god Nannar.[25] The later biblical editors knew it as Ur of the Chaldeans, a group that had arrived in the area about 900 B.C.E. Long before that date, however, a resident of Ur named Terah set out with his son Abram, his son's wife Sarai, and his grandson Lot to go to Canaan, a land we know as modern Israel and Palestine. Why they emigrated, we don't know. Perhaps

---

24. Edwards, "Sinners in the Hands of an Angry God," para. 11, lines 5–10.

25. Pexa, "Ur," para. 5.

it was because they were originally from Canaan or the upper Euphrates. Abram is not a Sumerian name, and another biblical text refers to him as "a wandering Aramean" (Deuteronomy 26:5).

It wasn't feasible to travel directly westward from Ur to Canaan as the crow flies. That route covered eight hundred miles of rocky, parched desert.[26] Instead, Terah's company followed the course of the Fertile Crescent northward along the Euphrates River, then curving around southward into Canaan proper. They never got to Canaan. For some reason they stopped at Haran, near the apex of the arc of the Fertile Crescent. Why Haran? Again, we don't know, although we know the people of Haran also worshipped the moon god. Or perhaps because Terah's recent ancestors had lived in Haran (one of Terah's sons, deceased, was named Haran).

Terah died in Haran. Thereupon his son Abram, now seventy-five years old, gathered "his wife Sarai, his nephew Lot, all the possessions they had accumulated and the people [servants? slaves?] they had acquired in Haran, and they set out for the land of Canaan, and they arrived there" (Genesis 12:5). Why would Abram resume the journey that his father Terah had aborted? Because, we are told, the LORD commanded him to do so:

> The Lord had said to Abram, "Go from your country, your people and your father's household to the land I will show you. I will make you into a great nation, and I will bless you; I will make your name great, and you will be a blessing . . . and all peoples on earth will be blessed through you" (Genesis 12:1–3).

This is a remarkable text, and limns a pivotal occasion in the historical relationship of God with the human race. To begin with, it suggests by virtue of the phrase "had said" that God may have revealed himself to Abram earlier in the idolatrous city of Ur, and that it was Abram who had prompted his father Terah to emigrate. If so, God's plan had been temporarily checked by human free will (what else is new?) when Terah decided to stay in Haran instead of proceeding onward to Canaan. But with his father's death Abram was free to obey what he believed to be God's will.

Further, as the Old Testament scholar Christopher Wright emphasizes, the phrase sometimes translated as "you will be a blessing" is actually an imperative, meaning "Go . . . *be* a blessing."[27] That is to say,

---

26 I have driven the route, and it was not a pleasant experience, even in an Opel station wagon.

27. C. Wright, *Mission of God*, 201.

God was about to fulfill his purpose by adjusting his plan. God is, among other things, the cosmic chess master par excellence. His new strategy entailed the selection of a single individual and his family, not to save that individual and his family from physical destruction as had been the case with Noah, but through that individual to save the human race spiritually. "All peoples on earth will be blessed through you," God promised.

What was new in this novel strategy was the highlighting of the element of faith—faith in the sense of believing in, totally relying upon, or trusting. Abram was being called on to recognize that he, with the rest of humankind, had been unable to achieve happiness or implement the purposes of God through his own strength. Instead he was being challenged to enter into a personal relationship with God and *trust God* to fulfill God's promises to the human race through him.[28] "And he believed the LORD; and the LORD reckoned it to him as righteousness" (Genesis 15:6).

In order to become a blessing to all peoples Abram had to make a radical break with his own Sumerian culture. In other words, his trust in God was no routine evolutionary development in the history of the human race; it is more aptly compared to a divinely instigated mutation. Throughout human evolution, the highest priority of *H. sapiens* has been self-preservation and reproduction favored by natural selection. Beginning with Abram, God progressively revealed that the human race is offered the opportunity to play by a new set of values, no longer Darwinian, but grounded in trusting relationships—first with God and then with other human beings. As St. Maximus the Confessor (580–662 c.e.) wrote:

> But this renewal did not come about through the normal course of things; it was only realized when a wholly new way of being human appeared.[29]

And the Blessing?

The blessing itself is none other than the salvation of the race and the universe: *the renewal of all things*. How that works out is, of course, the

---

28. How did Abram or Abraham conceive the God he met? For a provocative discussion, see how the noted Jewish biblical scholar James L. Kugel contrasts the way God is presented in Genesis and elsewhere with later rabbinic and modern conceptions. Kugel, *How to Read the Bible*, chapter 7, 107–18.

29. Maximus the Confessor, *Cosmic Mystery*, 70.

theme of this book. Christopher Wright describes in depth the biblical meaning of blessing.[30] In briefest summary it is:

- *Creational.* In Genesis 1 God's blessing of creation brings fruitfulness and fullness on the one hand and rest and harmony on the other.

- *Relational.* Those who are blessed know Who is blessing them, and in turn reach out to bless others.

- *Missional.* Genesis 12:3 is the Old Testament version of the New Testament's Great Commission (Matthew 28:19). The command to be a blessing indicates a purpose that extends into the distant future.

- *Historical.* The blessing is fulfilled in the course of world history as it is carried to all peoples.

- *Covenantal.* (Genesis 15). Although God continues to bless all peoples, symbolized by his subsequent promise regarding Ishmael (Genesis 21:13), there will be a special relationship with Abram and his physical and spiritual descendants. Abram's name is changed to Abraham, "father of many."

- *Ethical.* Israel is called to respond to God's command and promise by faith and obedience. This response is holistic and entails a commitment to social justice, seen most clearly in Genesis 18:19: "For I [God] have chosen him [Abraham] so that he will direct his children and his household after him to keep the way of the Lord by doing what is *right and just.*"[31]

- *Multinational* or universal. "All peoples on earth" are destined to share in the blessing promised to Abraham and through Abraham's mission to be a blessing.

- *Christological.* We are of course "jumping the gun" at this point, but the New Testament witness is that "if you belong to Christ, then you are Abraham's seed, and heirs according to the promise"(Galatians 3:29).

---

30. C. Wright, *Mission of God,* 213–20.

31. Emphasis mine. Hebrew: *tsedeqah wa mishpat,* a technical phrase used throughout the Old Testament for social justice; cf. Scott, *Bring Forth Justice,* 49. Wright does not draw attention to this text until late in his book (367), but I consider it of major importance and include it here.

Israel's Relationship with God

The Hebrew patriarchs were nomads. Eventually they left Canaan under the pressure of prolonged drought and settled in Egypt. There they were exposed to a high civilization[32] equal or superior to that of the Sumerians, but their descendants also endured a prolonged period of abject slavery. Their personal relationship with God nearly faded from memory until God [Hebrew: *Elohiym* = God Almighty] "heard their groaning, and remembered his covenant with Abraham, Isaac, and Jacob. God looked upon the Israelites, and God took notice of them" (Exodus 2:24–25).

God took notice by revealing himself to Moses at the famous burning bush, this time as *YHWH* or Yahweh.[33] The name *Yahweh* means something on the order of "I Am Who I Am" or "I Will Be What I Will Be"—in other words, "the self-sustaining, self-sufficient One," as defined by the *Jewish Encyclopedia*.[34] According to Exodus 6:1–3, the patriarchs knew God as *Elohiym*, not Yahweh. There are indications that Moses' father-in-law Jethro, the priest of Midian, may have been instrumental in helping the Hebrews recapture the memory of Yahweh. Some scholars believe that YHWH was the tribal God of the Midianites.

In any event, under Moses' leadership the Hebrews escaped—or more precisely were liberated from—their bondage in Egypt. This is the well-known exodus event that became Israel's paradigm of redemption. During a generation of wandering in the wilderness God made a new covenant with this loose conglomeration of tribes, the chief feature of which was the comprehensive Mosaic law; 613 commandments are recognized by Jews today. Some of these laws were designed to regulate religious experience; others were aimed at the social welfare of the families of Israel and foreigners who sojourned with them. The law of Jubilee is a good example

---

32. That Israel absorbed a measure of the wisdom of Egypt is indicated by the fact that Proverbs 22:17–23 (or possibly up to 24:22) is a translation or paraphrase of an older Egyptian text. Cf. Kugel, *How to Read the Bible*, 509. With reference to the anthological character of Proverbs, Kugel notes: "To be a [Hebrew] sage was to know, not to compose. In a sense, Wisdom's true author was God . . . . The sage's job was thus to collect and transmit the received wisdom to those eager to study it . . . . [T]he apparent intention of the Bible's mention of Solomon *speaking* 'three thousand proverbs' is not that he composed them (although this is how the verse is sometimes mistranslated) but that he had mastered them" (ibid.).

33. The sacred name is pronounced Yahweh, not Jehovah, and rendered as LORD in English translations.

34 Jewish Encyclopedia, "YHWH," para. 3.

of the latter (Leviticus 25:8ff). This Mosaic covenant was a serious attempt at social justice.

Included in the new covenant was the requirement of a tabernacle—a portable tent sanctuary or shrine—and a system of sacrificial offerings to God. Interestingly, the dimensions of the tabernacle seem to match those of an ancient Canaanite temple unearthed at Arad in northern Syria that predates the exodus. Similarly Solomon's famed temple, patterned on the tabernacle, seems to have had a floor plan typical of such West Semitic temples as those excavated at Ein Dara or Tel Ta'yinatin Syria. And the different classes of sacrifices offered by Israel used some of the same names found in ancient Canaanite texts; the priests were designated by the same word, and so forth.[35]

These similarities are significant, for they reveal that the *forms* of Israel's religion were in large measure adapted from the surrounding culture. Yet in spite of similarities, the particularity of Israel's religion is striking. In New Testament idiom, the Israelites were in the world but not of the world. "Indeed, the whole earth is mine," God tells Israel, "but you shall be for me a priestly kingdom and a holy nation" (Exodus 19:5–6). As Christopher Wright correctly comments, "The particularity of Israel here is intended to serve the universality of God's interest in the world. Israel's election serves God's mission."[36]

Eventually the tribes made their way to the promised and. This entry inaugurated a new era in Israel's relationship with God. Reestablished in Canaan through violent battles, some of which were genocidal and marked by ethnic cleansing, the Israelites lived for several centuries in tension with the other peoples of the region. During this time they were greatly influenced by the latter's religious practices; at the same time they witnessed in greater or lesser degrees of faithfulness to the one true God.

During this period God raised up judges who were at one and the same time saviors—military champions in the ongoing competition with the other inhabitants of the land. Thanks to the leadership of the judges, Israel survived and in due time was able to make the transition from a loose confederation of tribes to a monarchy, "like the nations around us" (1 Samuel 8:5). Recall René Girard's mimetic theory previously noted. David and Solomon were the most idealized of their early kings. David

---

35. Kugel, *How to Read the Bible*, 288.

36. C. Wright, *Mission of God*, 257.

established Jerusalem as the religious and political center of Israel. His son Solomon brought the holy ark to Jerusalem and built an elaborate temple for the worship of the LORD. He understood that it would serve as a magnet for the nations. In his dedication of the temple, Solomon is reported as praying:

> Likewise, when a foreigner, who is not of your people Israel, comes from a distant land because of your name—for they shall hear of your great name, your mighty hand, and your outstretched arm—when a foreigner comes and prays toward this house, then hear in heaven your dwelling place, and do according to all that the foreigner calls to you, so that all the peoples of the earth may know your name and fear you, as do your people Israel ..." (1 Kings 8:41–43).

For almost a century Israel was dominant in the region. Yet after a hundred years the monarchy split into two kingdoms: Israel in the north and Judah in the south. Neither Israel nor Judah was able to maintain their exclusive devotion to the LORD and to the mission the LORD had assigned to them in the midst of the idol worshippers. Their poets and prophets clearly understood Israel's mission to the world, however, as the following two texts illustrate:

> May God be gracious to us and bless us and make his face to shine upon us, that your way may be known upon earth, your saving power among all nations ... Let the nations be glad and sing for you, for you judge the peoples with equity and guide the nations upon earth" (Psalm 67:1–2, 4).

> [God says,] "It is too light a thing that you should be my servant to raise up the tribes of Jacob and to restore the survivors of Israel. I will give you as a light to the nations, that my salvation may reach to the ends of the earth" (Isaiah 49:6).

Interestingly, during these years the people of Israel's conception of God's relationship with them evolved. Early on, particularly after the exodus, their monotheism emphasized God's power and sovereignty. They interpreted the misfortunes they suffered as punishment for rebelling against God's kingship, particularly in reference to their own indulgence in idolatry. But as time went on, particularly during after their forced exile, they began to see defeats and exile as fatherly chastisement with restoration to God's favor and return to the land as the promised assurance.

From time to time, under the kings Joash, Hezekiah, and Josiah, there were brief national revivals. During Josiah's reign, for example, a copy of the Mosaic law, long vanished, was "discovered" (2 Chronicles 34:14*ff.*). But each revival was followed by decline and, as the later priest-editors of the Old Testament concluded, these resurgences of devotion were ephemeral and the nation was judged a spiritual failure. One would be justified in believing that once again God's plan was doomed.

But no; during these dark days God maintained contact with Israel through the prophets, such major prophets as Isaiah and Jeremiah, and such minor (so called only because their writings were shorter) ones as Hosea, Joel, and Amos. One should also note the fact that during its days of exile, Israel was exposed to religious insights from the East, particularly ideas about the afterlife. These notions would surface in the Apocrypha[37] and dominate discussion during the century prior to the birth of Jesus. It was in these days that the seeds of messianism, the messianic age, and the expectation of a Messiah[38] were planted.

Messianism is the Jewish belief in a Messiah or "anointed one" who would redeem Israel and usher in a more perfect era. This new era would be the messianic age prophesied in Isaiah 2:1–4 and 11:1–6. The Messiah[39] would be a descendant of King David (Jeremiah 23:5). Announced by the prophet Elijah (Malachi 4:5) at the end of days, the Messiah would be a great political leader, well versed in Jewish law; an outstanding military commander who would win battles for Israel; and a great judge who would make righteous decisions. During the messianic age Israel would be redeemed, its Diaspora[40] gathered in from exile. The law of Jubilee would be reinstated, the temple rebuilt, and the sacrificial system reestablished— though with only thanksgiving, not expiatory, offerings. All nations would be subject to Israel. The whole world would recognize God as the only true God, and Judaism as the only true religion. All peoples would live in harmony with one another and with nature.[41] This vision was only incipi-

---

37. Apocrypha (= deuterocanonical books): books included in the Septuagint and Vulgate versions of the Bible, but not in the *Tanakh* and Protestant versions of the canon of Scripture.

38. Heb: *moshiach*, pronounced muh-shee-akh.

39. Note that the term "The Messiah" is not an Old Testament expression. It occurs for the first time in apocalyptic literature. Cf. Jacobs and Buttenwieser in *Jewish Encyclopedia*, "Messiah," para. 1*ff.*

40. Diaspora: the scattered colonies of Jews outside Palestine after the Babylonian exile; today, those Jews living outside Israel.

41. Rich, "Moshiach: The Messiah," para. 6. Cf. Joseph Telushkin, cited in Jewish

ent during the centuries I am writing about. It did not flower until later in Israel's history, in the era of the Maccabees[42] and in the years of the Roman occupation.

Like all peoples, Israel was guilty of a variety of moral transgressions. But it was because of their idolatry, the prophets assure us, that the peoples of the northern kingdom were dispersed among the nations and disappeared from history. Again for the sin of idolatry, so the *Tanakh* testifies, most of the population of the southern kingdom was exiled to Babylon, though some, like the prophet Jeremiah, managed to escape to Egypt. The period of exile in Babylon was relatively short but apparently cathartic, for the evidence indicates that upon their return to the promised land the Jews no longer were tempted to worship the gods of other nations alongside Yahweh.

Life continued to be difficult, however. The fourth and third centuries B.C.E. were the great age of Hellenism inaugurated by Alexander the Great (356–321 B.C.E.). After Alexander's premature death Israel came under the domination of various Hellenic rulers, the Seleucids of Syria and the Ptolemies of Egypt, who attempted to impose Hellenic culture upon the Jews. Under the priestly Maccabees, as noted above, the Jews rebelled and Israel was, again, but only for a century, independent. Once more they were conquered, this time by Rome in 64 B.C.E.

For many it seemed that their exile had become a permanent condition even in their own land.[43] Many devout Jews were left wondering whether God would ever fulfill his promises to the patriarchs and the prophets. In the year 70 C.E. the Romans destroyed the Jewish temple, and it was in the post-70 C.E. period that Judaism as we know it today emerged, built on strong foundations laid by such great rabbis as Hillel, Shammai, and Akiba ben Joseph.

Roman rule, then, was the context in which Jesus of Nazareth appeared on the scene. But before we consider the Christ event, we must take note of what was occurring in the world at large beyond the nation of Israel.

Virtual Library, "The Messiah," para. 1*ff*.

42. Maccabees: a priestly family that led a Jewish national liberation movement in the second century b.c.e. and founded the Hasmonean dynasty. The contemporary Jewish feast of Hanukah celebrates the victory of Judah Maccabee over the Seleucids. The story of the movement is recorded in the deuterocanonical books of 1 and 2 Maccabees.

43. N. T. Wright, *People of God*, 284–86.

4

The Axial Age

Blessed be Egypt my people, Assyria my handiwork,
and Israel my inheritance.

ISAIAH 19:25

THE PREVIOUS CHAPTER TRACED the long slow evolution of Israel's special relationship with God, which continues to this day (cf. Romans 11:5). Meanwhile, what about the other nations of the world? Did God maintain a relationship with them? The epigraph above would suggest that God did, though from a Judeo-Christian perspective it is difficult to speak definitively about just what that relationship was. Consider also the following questions from God to Israel through the prophet Amos:

> Are you not like the Ethiopians to me, O people of Israel? says the LORD? Did I not bring Israel up from the land of Egypt, and the Philistines from Caphtor and the Arameans from Kir? (Amos 9:7).

Or consider this promise of the Lord through Isaiah:

> In a very short time will not Lebanon be turned into a fertile field, and the fertile field seem like a forest? In that day the deaf will hear the words of the scroll, and out of the gloom and darkness the eyes of the blind will see (Isaiah 29:17–18).

These texts confirm that God was interacting with other nations in ways not unlike the way he interacted with Israel The influential twentieth-century philosopher and theologian Karl Jaspers developed the fruitful concept he termed *Achsenzeit*, the Axial Age. The Axial Age, according to Jaspers, covered the six-hundred-year period from 800 to 200 B.C.E. During this time unique religious developments occurred in Greece, the Middle East, South Asia, and East Asia. As Mark Muesse comments, "Just the mention of some of the individuals who lived during this period in these localities alerts us to the importance of the age: Pythagoras, Plato and Aristotle, Isaiah and Jeremiah, Zoroaster, the Buddha, Confucius and Lao Zi."[1]

Actually, Zoroaster, or Zarathustra, probably lived before the stated beginning of the Axial Age, and both Jesus and Muhammad lived afterward. But Zoroaster contributed important concepts to Hebrew religion (see below), and both Christianity and Islam have close links to Judaism. So for our purposes we can accept Jaspers's dates for the Axial Age.

Greek science and philosophy were born in this age, but of equal or greater significance is the fact that all the great world philosophies and religions as we know them today also emerged during the Axial Age: Hinduism, Buddhism, Jainism, Confucianism, and Daoism.[2] It seems presumptuous to attempt to summarize these great systems in just a single chapter, but I will try.

Prior to the Axial Age, religion and religious rituals served essentially to guarantee peoples' abilities to attain the goods necessary for a prosperous and stable life on earth. Gods were entreated to help maintain productivity and harmony in the here and now rather than to secure otherworldly salvation. Systems of sacrifices ensured the maintenance of the cosmic and moral order necessary for human survival. "The central purpose of religion at this time was co-creation with the gods in the processes and functions of life."[3] This observation would seem to apply to the nomadic Hebrew patriarchs as well.

Zoroastrianism

Zoroaster, the founder of Zoroastrianism, was a precursor of other Axial sages in that they linked human destiny with moral behavior as he did. Of course, one might say that Moses did the same. Zoroaster imagined human history moving in a linear fashion toward a final conclusion in which good would triumph over evil.[4] At the last day, persons whose lives

---

1. Muesse, I:4. For this chapter I am indebted to Professor Mark Muesse of Rhodes College, Memphis, Tennessee, and his course on Religions of the Axial Age. Hereafter, references to a page number without mention of the source refer to Muesse's course guidebooks.

2. Sometimes spelled Taoism.

3. Muesse, I:12.

4. We have no evidence that this understanding of history was a feature of Moses' worldview.

had been aligned with Ahura Mazda, the god of goodness, would achieve everlasting life, while those who served Ahriman, the god of evil, would be annihilated. Zoroaster's rituals were intended to help individuals cultivate moral qualities and a spirit of goodness. This emphasis on morality appears to be a new development in the religious evolution of *H. sapiens*. Legend has it that Zoroaster was killed by leaders of the ancient sacrificial system because he was hostile to the practice of ritual sacrifice.

Not all agree, but most scholars believe that Judaism integrated certain aspects of Zoroastrianism, probably during Israel's exile in Babylon, though perhaps even earlier. These aspects include the concept of the devil, the day of judgment, heaven and hell, angels, and the concept of *saoshyant*, a universal redeemer appearing at the end times. One might compare the apocalyptic figure of the Son of Man, who appears in the books of Daniel and Enoch, and who himself was connected in the biblical record with Babylon and Persia (Daniel 7:1, 13–14; *1 Enoch* 19–20).

Where did Zoroaster get all these ideas? Is it possible that God revealed them, or some of them, to him? Or did he intuit them on his own? We will explore these possibilities in more detail later in this book. But according to Zoroaster himself, at the age of thirty he had a remarkable experience not unlike those of Moses, Isaiah, and Muhammad, wherein he was led into the presence of Ahura Mazda, from whom he received his revelation.

Hinduism

For several centuries prior to the Axial Age, an impressive civilization existed in the Indus River Valley in what is now Pakistan. Some of its cities contained as many as fifty thousand people.[5] This civilization came to an end about the time of Moses, in 1900 B.C.E. The Indo-Aryans[6] who then came to dominate the region produced the beginnings of what would become Hinduism in the Axial Age. Their religion, which we learn about from their sacred scriptures, the Vedas, centered on ritual and sacrifice. These ensured the proper functioning of the world.[7]

The Indo-Aryans expanded eastward into the Ganges plain of northern India. Although they maintained some Vedic traditions during the

---

5. Khan, "Ancient Indus Civilization," para. 11.

6. Indo-Aryans: peoples who originated in the area north of Afghanistan-Pakistan and later spread eastward to India.

7. Muesse, I:23, 26.

Axial Age, they also initiated a number of distinctive changes, the most important of which had do with growing doubts about the value of ritual. In a new set of writings, the Upanishads, which were written squarely within the Axial Age, the Aryans began to reevaluate Vedic practices. Like the Vedas, the Upanishads are regarded as *śruti*, revealed knowledge.[8]

Primary elements of the emerging religious outlook included the belief in *samsara*,[9] that is, the belief that beings endure a beginningless series of births, deaths, and rebirths—that is, reincarnation. The moral principle of *karma* (see below) governs these births, deaths, and rebirths. The sages of the Axial Age devalued the preoccupation with material wealth and longevity that had characterized previous generations. Concerns about death and the afterlife became more prominent. Whereas the earlier Vedas are concerned above all with ritual and sacrifice, the Upanishads—Hindu scriptures belonging to a later period—are more contemplative.

As the South Asian Axial Age progressed, the concept of reincarnation became more refined, particularly with regard to the role of karma. The belief that the events of a person's life are neither random nor predestined by realities outside the self but rather by how one behaves in this present life is karma. No god metes out karma; it acts inevitably with perfect justice. The gods themselves are subject to karma.

The conviction that one's future incarnation depends on one's conduct in this life is central to Hinduism. As in Zoroastrian religion, the Upanishads make one's moral behavior the decisive element in one's destiny. Israel's prophet Ezekiel, who also lived during this period, made the same point (cf. Ezekiel 18). All this indicates "a growing focus during the Axial Age on the interiority of the spiritual life," Muesse notes.[10] The fact that similar developments were occurring not only in Israel but also in other parts of the world suggests that YHWH's election of Israel was not at the expense of his relationship with other peoples. Perhaps all the peoples of the world are "God's chosen peoples," as the title of Bühlmann's book suggests. This is a matter we will explore in greater depth in chapter 11.

Many observers regard India as the most religious place on earth. The endless cycle of birth and rebirth—*samsara*—was always considered

---

8. Muesse, I:30–31.

9. Sanskrit: wandering.

10. Muesse, I:31.

undesirable, however. Developments during the Axial Age led thousands to renounce the material world and seek final liberation from *samsara* through ascetic discipline. This final liberation is known as *moksha*, the end of reincarnation. People who sought moksha were known as *samanas*. So numerous were these *samanas* that they became a virtual fifth caste, alongside priests, warriors, agricultural producers, and servants.[11]

How did these *samanas* hope to achieve liberation, or salvation? I have mentioned ascetic practices, but these were mere means to an end. What the early Hindus were after was knowledge of the deepest principles of reality, or *Brahman*. Recall the philosopher Leibniz's query: Why is there anything at all? *Brahman*, or ultimate reality, is absolute unity, with no parts or divisions. Such a concept of knowledge is very un-Western, and hard for the average Westerner to grasp. Yet "the trend to view the world, not as a collection of unrelated objects and beings, but as an integrated totality that could be understood . . . was so pervasive that this effort is seen as one of the salient characteristics of the Axial Age."[12] *Brahman* is not the same as God, however, for *Brahman* is absolute being itself. As such it is incomprehensible.

Gradually the Aryan sages began to see that esoteric "knowledge" of reality was actually the knowledge of the self or the soul, an immortal substance that they termed *atman*. In time they concluded that *atman* was in fact identical with *Brahman*. Why then is the soul still subject to endless reincarnation? They concluded that endless reincarnation is the consequence of our misunderstanding of reality. This misunderstanding or ignorance they called *maya* (illusion), a veil over reality that causes us to think of ourselves as separate entities. This misguided thinking in turn creates the illusion of separateness and generates fear and hatred, greed, and fear of death.[13] Once we truly "know" that our soul is identical with ultimate reality we will experience moksha, liberation from the cycle of reincarnations, and salvation, the attainment of equanimity toward the world.

Ascetic practices, chief of which is meditation, are the key to knowledge of the *atman-Brahman*. Serious meditation can bring about visions, ecstasy, awareness, and transcendence. Other practices include vows of silence, poverty, fasting, celibacy, and mortification of the body. All are

11. The so-called untouchables—modern Dalits—were not considered a caste, nor were the tribal groups of northeast India.

12. Muesse, I:35.

13. Muesse, I:38.

meant to help the individual relinquish all selfish desires, for it is selfish desires that generate karma, which ties one to endless reincarnation.

As Professor Muesse observes, most Hindus found this path of knowledge too demanding. Ordinary Indians preferred a piety focused on worshipping personal gods and goddesses, each one a manifestation of and conduit to ultimate reality. The best resource for understanding the popular Hindu religion that emerged from the Axial Age is the Bhagavad-Gita, scripture written at the end of that age. According to the Bhagavad-Gita, devotion to a particular god is the best practice of all. "Do everything with faith in a god." What matters is not the object of faith but its quality and sincerity.[14]

Buddhism

Siddhattha Gotama (or Gautama) was born during the Axial Age into a privileged Hindu family. At the age of twenty-nine—compare Zoroaster, Ezekiel, Jesus, and others—he came face to face with suffering for the first time, or perhaps realized for the first time that he himself was subject to the inescapable cycle of *samsara*. In consequence he became a *samana*, a searcher after true knowledge. Several of his early attempts failed. During this time Mara, the demonic tempter, accosted him and tried to lure him away from his quest (cf. Jesus' temptations as recorded in Matt 4). Finally, at age thirty-five, Gotama achieved enlightenment and adopted the title of the Buddha, the "Awakened One."

One could say that Buddhism is a reinterpretation and extension of Hinduism in much the same way that Christianity and Islam are reinterpretations and extensions of the Hebrew religion. The Buddha's teaching, or *Dhamma*,[15] centers on the Four Noble Truths, the first of which is that the essence of life itself is suffering (*dukkha*). There is the ordinary *dukkha* of sickness and death, of course. And there is the broader *dukkha* of change, including especially the disappointment we experience when reality does not conform to our expectations. The world is in constant flux. Change by itself does not cause suffering but our unwise or unskilled responses to change do.

The second noble truth is that a principal cause of suffering is *tanha*—desire or literally thirst. Muesse says that this truth "is at the

14. Muesse, I:43–44.
15. Also spelled *dharma*.

heart of the Buddha's vision and is what most distinguishes it from other religious perspectives."[16] Desire leads to attachment or clinging, which is one driving mechanism of *samsara*. Or it can lead to aversion, which is just as difficult to relinquish. The answer is equanimity, the middle way between these two extremes. At the root of our misguided thirst is *avijja*, ignorance, especially the failure to understand that everything is impermanent. For the Buddha, everything is in constant flux (cf. the modern science of quantum physics). The cosmos is a complex array of processes, not a set of material objects. Change is the only thing there is. Therefore, contrary to Hinduism, Buddhism posits no permanent, immortal, or substantial soul. Similarly there is no God.

The third noble truth is that no one needs to suffer. By ending one's craving, attachments slip away and one ends the cycle of suffering and rebirth. This end of suffering is *nirvana*. Nirvana is the point at which one stops thirsting for reality to be other than what it is and achieves a radical acceptance of the way things are. By ending one's craving, the illusion of a separate substantial self is annihilated.[17]

The Buddha's method for quenching thirst is detailed in the fourth noble truth. Freedom from suffering is not a grace or a gift from a god. We are the cause of our own suffering; only we can free ourselves from it, which requires discipline and effort. These disciplines are outlined in the Noble Eightfold Path. The path includes right understanding, right intention, right speech, right action, right livelihood, right effort, right mindfulness, and right concentration. All eight limbs of the path must be pursued concurrently. Near the end of the Axial period the conversion of the brutal Emperor Ashoka—overwhelmed by guilt at the slaughter he had initiated at the battle of Kalinga in 265 B.C.E.—was instrumental in making Buddhism acceptable in India. Gradually Buddhism spread throughout central and eastern Asia. Unfortunately, the invasion of India by Islam, climaxing between the tenth and twelfth centuries C.E., destroyed Buddhism in India itself.

Jainism

Jains are disciples of *jina*, a spiritual conqueror. One particular conqueror was Vardhamana Mahavira, whose name means "great hero." He was born

16. Muesse, II:4.
17. Muesse, II:8.

in India about 600 B.C.E., became a *samana* at the age of thirty, and endured a decade of severe asceticism before achieving enlightenment at the age of forty-two. Mahavira accepted many of the basic assumptions circulating in the Ganges Valley during the earlier part of the Axial Age, but in almost every case he reinterpreted these ideas—including time, conceptions of the world's structure, the nature of the soul, and karma—to fit his emerging worldview.[18] Perhaps the distinctive religious contribution of Jainism is that of absolute nonviolence, which has had a significant influence on other major religious figures, including Albert Schweitzer and Mahatma Gandhi. Jains refrain from harming any living being, even insects, and eat a vegetarian diet. Jains also reject sacrifice and, being against the sacrificial order, they themselves were often scapegoated. Because, like Zoroastrians, but unlike Hindus and Buddhists, they are not numerous today, I will limit my description of them to this paragraph.

Confucianism

The Chinese worldview prior to the Axial Age comprised two realms—a divine realm that included a heavenly court and an earthly realm that included an earthly royal court. The latter was assumed to be modeled on the former. Shang Di was the lord supreme of the divine realm who presided over many lesser divinities. Within the earthly royal court, divination was the chief ritual, utilized for both religious and political purposes. Ancestors mediated between human beings and the gods. Virtue, the term used to refer to a power or force generated by compassionate deeds, was extolled.[19]

The Axial Age in China largely coincided with the Zhou Dynasty (1122–256 B.C.E.). The Zhou rulers worshipped a high god they called Tian. The main difference between Tian and Shang Di of the pre-Axial age was that Tian cared about moral behavior. This belief generated the concept of Tianming, the Mandate of Heaven. Under the Mandate of Heaven, a ruler's legitimacy was contingent on his virtue or righteousness.[20] As the Zhou Dynasty, the longest in China's history, progressed,

---

18. Muesse, II:18.

19. Ibid., II:23*ff*.

20. A Chinese professor who had fled from the communist takeover of his homeland back in 1950 taught a sophomore course I took in Chinese philosophy. The professor's mastery of English was imperfect. He continually emphasized the importance of "recklessness" in Chinese philosophical thought. This usage mystified me—until I finally realized he was speaking of "righteousness."

deteriorating relations between the rulers and the ruled and among the ruled themselves preoccupied the Chinese.[21]

Kong Zi, or Confucius, was born about 550 B.C.E. His main interest was in ethics and morality. He had little to say about gods, souls, or spirits; however, he was very interested in rituals, especially those performed for the welfare of the state, but also with respect to all human interactions. His ideal person is the *junzi*—a word usually translated as "gentleman" or "superior man." The *junzi* is distinguished from others by the quality of *ren*, which involves kindness, benevolence, or goodness. Occasionally Confucius refers to *ren* as "love of others." *Ren* must be carefully culti- vated by following the principle of reciprocity—loving others as one loves oneself—or more often, in not inflicting on others what one doesn't want imposed on oneself. The key to developing *ren* is *li*, the proper perfor- mance of rituals at the level of everyday life. "Although his vision centered on the individual, Confucius believed that the cultivation of goodness would have salutary effects throughout society."[22] Unlike the Buddha, Confucius did not guarantee the possibility of achieving goodness; one cultivates goodness for its own sake, not with the expectation of reward. Confucianism was destined to become the basis of Chinese education up to the era of present-day communism.

Daoism

Dao means "the way" or "the path."[23] Daoism originated in the third or fourth century B.C.E. in opposition to Confucianism. The *Daodejing*[24] is one of the principal texts of Daoism; in it, "the way" really means "the way of nature."[25] For Daoists, to follow the way is to participate in the changes and rhythms of the universe and the natural world. Neglecting the way of nature is the root of society's misery. For instance, water flows around obstacles in a stream. What appears weak is really a powerful force, for water ultimately erodes the rocks. Thus the weak and flexible conquer the strong and unyielding.

21. Muesse, II:29.

22. Ibid., II:34.

23. Cf. the early Christian assumption of the same name: see Acts 9:2 and five other references in Acts.

24. Sometimes spelled *Tao Te Ching*.

25. Muesse, II:43.

Like Buddhism, Daoism began as a form of philosophical reflection. But after the formal close of the Axial Age, the Daoist "church" came into being in the second century C.E. This development took place during the Han Dynasty, when Confucianism had just been established as the state religion and Buddhism had arrived in China. The legendary founder of Daoism, Lao Zi, was deified, as were the Buddha and Confucius at the popular level. Temples were built and sacrifices made in his honor. Over time Daoism, Buddhism, and Confucianism all blended into present-day Chinese folk religion, which involved divination, ancestor worship, and magical practices.[26]

Summing Up

The Axial Age brought with it the concept of selfhood. The self was now recognized as a separate individual with agency and moral responsibility. It thus became incumbent on individuals to transform themselves. As Muesse observes, "Every Axial sage . . . had a solution, making the function of religion one of personal transformation."[27]

- For Zoroaster, the solution was for people to orient their lives to the power of good.

- For the Upanishad sages of Hinduism, one solution was to recast the self as eternal and one with all reality.

- For Buddha, the solution was to eliminate the concept of selfhood as just an illusion.

- For the Jains, it was to stop the accumulation of karma and eliminate old karma that weighed down the soul.

- For Confucius, it was subduing the self and its wishes to the greater human community.

- For Daoists, the solution was blending into the world and giving up the need to control.

In addition to the concept of selfhood, the Axial Age gave rise to changes in thinking about ultimate reality: the concepts of *Brahman, nirvana,* and *Dao.*

---

26. Muesse, II:50.
27. Ibid., II:52–53.

So, back to the question with which we opened this chapter: Was YHWH present to peoples outside Israel in the Axial Age? Was it the Spirit, Word, or Wisdom of YHWH who prompted all these religious developments that have shaped even our modern world? Or were these philosophies and religions simply the result of human intuition and reasoning? On the surface, the latter would seem to be the case. After all, how could belief in a myriad of Hindu gods be prompted by YHWH, the sole Deity? And how could the Buddhist belief in no-god have been provoked by YHWH? On the other hand, the Hebrew concept of Wisdom (Proverbs 8, *Wisdom* 6–8, *Sirach* 1), and the Christian concept of the Word, "the true light that enlightens everyone" (John 1:9) hint at further possibilities we shall have to explore further on in this monograph—notably the concept of call and response, God's call and human response. In any case, whether or not we conclude that the Axial Age religions and philosophies were directly inspired by Yahweh, there is first the Christ event to consider.

Part Two

Good News

5

The Christ Event: A "Bottom-Up" Perspective

He came to what was his own, and his own people did not accept him.

JOHN 1:11

JESUS OF NAZARETH APPEARED on the world scene—or more precisely, in "Galilee of the Gentiles" (Matthew 4:15, cf. Isaiah 9:1) a few centuries after the close of the Axial Age. The great philosophical and religious systems described all too briefly in the previous chapter had had time enough to shape their respective cultures. Worldviews had been formulated. Within the Jewish culture, the Tanakh (Old Testament) had been defined by the rabbis[1] who would eventually produce modern Judaism, and a particular way of interpreting it had been codified. The rabbinic hermeneutic[2] was based on four assumptions:

- The Tanakh is fundamentally a cryptic text; that is, the written word conveys a hidden meaning for which interpreters are necessary.

- The Tanakh is a book of lessons directed to readers of the present day. It is not fundamentally history; it is instruction, telling people how to live in the present.

- The Tanakh contains no contradictions or mistakes. It is perfectly consistent.

- The Tanakh is a divinely inspired text in which God speaks to humans directly or through his prophets.[3]

1. Rabbi: Hebrew for "my master" or "my teacher." In Jesus' day, it was the title of a spiritual leader well versed in interpreting the Torah. Jesus was known as a rabbi.

2. Hermeneutics: the art or science of interpreting texts, often sacred scriptures.

3. Kugel, *How to Read the Bible*, 14–15. The perceptive reader will recognize that

Although the canon of the Tanakh had been defined, Hebrew religious writing continued during the centuries immediately preceding the Christ event. This period, which actually extended to 70 C.E., a generation after the Christ event, is known as the Second Temple period.[4] It produced the deutero- and noncanonical books we call the Apocrypha as well as the Septuagint (the Greek translation of the Hebrew Scriptures) and the Dead Sea scrolls.[5] Some of these writings are fanciful legends; some are the product of sages; some are historical; and some are apocalyptic.

It was during the Second Temple period that the Maccabees, later styled the Hasmonean Dynasty, revolted against the Seleucid rulers who followed Alexander the Great but then succumbed to conquest by the Roman Empire. During the time of Jesus, Galilee was ruled by a puppet king. Southern Israel (Judea), including Jerusalem, was governed directly by a Roman procurator. Throughout this period Hellenistic culture[6] prevailed in both Galilee and Judea and was a source of severe tension within the Jewish community, creating rifts among the Sadducees, Pharisees, and Essenes.[7] At the end of the Second Temple period in 70 c.e., a generation after the Christ event, rabbinic Judaism as we know it today began to be formulated.

---

many Christian readers of the Bible hold these same four assumptions today.

4. Second Temple period: the period in Jewish history roughly between 515 B.C.E. and 70 C.E. Returning from exile in Babylon, the Jews built a second temple—the first having been destroyed by the Babylonian invaders. This second temple was itself completely renovated and rebuilt by King Herod around 20 B.C.E. Herod's temple was the one Jesus knew. The Romans destroyed it in 70 C.E.

5. *Septuagint* (commonly designated LXX): The Hebrew Bible as translated into the Greek language by Alexandrian Jews between the third and first centuries B.C.E. *Dead Sea scrolls*: Documents discovered around the Wadi Qumran near the Dead Sea. The scrolls contain Old Testament texts that predate 100 B.C.E. as well as texts related to Essene rituals.

6. Hellenistic culture: A culture representing a fusion of Greek civilization with the cultures of the Near East and India that arose after the conquests of Alexander the Great at the end of the fourth century B.C.E. It was pervasive in Palestine during the time of Jesus.

7. *Sadducees*: members of the aristocratic Jewish priestly sect that flourished in the Second Temple period. They rejected the Pharisees' oral tradition. Pharisees: members of a Jewish religious party that flourished in Palestine during the latter part of the Second Temple period. They insisted on the binding force of oral tradition ("the unwritten Torah"). *Essenes*: a Jewish religious group that flourished from the second century B.C.E. to the first century C.E. (the Second Temple period).

All this material is the background for the apostle Paul's declaration that "when the fullness of time had come, God sent his Son" (Galatians 4:4).

Jesus' Early Years

We are fortunate to have four historically reliable records of Jesus' life and ministry.[8] Three of the accounts—the gospels of Matthew, Mark, and Luke—are similar enough to be designated the Synoptic[9] Gospels. Though each is written from a particular perspective, they are all overviews of the same general series of events in Jesus' life. The Synoptic Gospels were based on eyewitness testimony and short-term oral traditions, together with minimal collections of written material.[10] It is generally thought that Mark's gospel was the first composition, written before the destruction of the temple in 70 C.E. The gospels of Matthew and Luke were likely composed in the decade following the destruction of the temple, though some scholars think they were written earlier. The fourth account—John's gospel—was written perhaps a decade later than Matthew and Luke and is more overtly theological in its perspective and narrative structure.

Most of the New Testament authors, including the apostle Paul (the earliest New Testament writer) and the gospelers Mark and John, pay little or no attention to the early years of Jesus' life. But Matthew and Luke provide genealogical background, tracing his lineage back through David and Abraham to "Adam, the son of God" (Luke 3:23ff.).[11] This interest in genealogy is derived from their concern to confirm Jesus' messiahship. For the same reason Matthew and Luke also record unusual occurrences surrounding his birth and infancy, such as the appearance of angels at Bethlehem, King Herod's slaughter of infants and toddlers, and the escape of Jesus' family to Egypt.

Luke informs us that the baby was christened Jesus (i.e., Joshua, meaning "The Lord saves") and was circumcised and dedicated to the

---

8. Cf. Bauckham, *Eyewitnesses*, 30–38.

9. The English word *synoptic* is derived from two Greek words meaning "together" and "sight."

10. Bauckham, *Eyewitnesses*, chapters 10, 240–63, and 11, 264–89.

11. Hereafter no further references (with very few exceptions, including quotations from outside the Gospels) will be given in this chapter in order to keep the narrative flowing smoothly. All quotations and observations are from the four gospels, primarily the Synoptic Gospels. The reader may consult a concordance for confirmation if desired.

Lord shortly after his birth.[12] "And the child grew and became strong; he was filled with wisdom, and the grace of God was on him." Presumably he was apprenticed as a carpenter, his father's trade. And there is ample evidence from the way he quoted Scripture later that he was well educated in the Hebrew Bible. Apart from this information, we know little about his experiences until approximately age thirty, when he began his ministry.

A few months earlier Jesus' slightly older cousin, John the Baptizer, had initiated his own prophetic ministry, "preaching a baptism of repentance for the forgiveness of sin." All four gospels tell us that Jesus approaches his cousin John to be baptized and on that occasion receives a strong personal affirmation of his calling. Jesus sees the spirit of God descending upon him and hears a voice from heaven saying, "You are my son whom I love; with you I am well pleased." The Spirit then leads him into the wilderness for a prolonged time of inner testing. Soon thereafter his cousin John is imprisoned by King Herod. This event becomes the signal for Jesus to officially begin his own mission.

Public Ministry

Much of what Jesus did was self-consciously new. One pours new wine into new wineskins, he said. Unlike most rabbis of his time, Jesus was indiscriminant in his public associations. His disciples were a motley group drawn mostly from the working classes. Chief among these was Simon Peter, a fisherman. Jesus' entourage also included a number of loyal women (Luke 8:2–3). He had no compunction about dining and drinking with "tax collectors and sinners," claiming "I have not come to call the righteous, but sinners." Yet he also entertained a prominent Pharisee, a member of the Sanhedrin,[13] and counseled a rich young man of the ruling class. Jesus made a special point of embracing children.

He conversed with the despised Samaritans,[14] spoke with women of questionable reputation, and did not hesitate to become ritually impure in the process of healing someone with leprosy or abnormal menstrual

12. Jesus (Joshua) was the sixth most popular male Jewish name in the first century c.e. Bauckham, *Eyewitnesses*, 85.

13. Sanhedrin: the Jewish court system in the Second Temple period. The Great Sanhedrin in Jerusalem consisted of seventy-one ruling elders.

14. Samaritans: an ethnically mixed group living in the area between Galilee in the north and Judea in the south. They were held in contempt by the Jews of Jesus' time. The feeling was probably mutual.

bleeding. He disregarded the rite of fasting practiced by both the disciples of John the Baptizer and the Pharisees: the arrival of the reign of God is a time for feasting, not fasting, he said. On one occasion, when seated in a circle of disciples and told that his mother and brothers were looking for him, he replied, "*Here* are my mother and my brothers!" Jesus assumed that his open-arms attitude reflected God's own attitude, as indicated by his story of the Prodigal Son. Yet his openness aroused resentment and opposition from the religious leaders of the time.

Jesus' public ministry could be described as tripartite: "Jesus went throughout Galilee, *teaching* in their synagogues, *proclaiming* the good news of the kingdom, and *healing* every disease and sickness among the people."[15] His teaching, preaching, and healing attracted followers, and from among these "he appointed twelve that they might be with him and that he might send them out to preach and to have authority to drive out demons." This "training of the twelve" (the title of A. B. Bruce's seminal book on the subject) was quasi-public in nature and was motivated by Jesus' eschatology[16] (Luke 22:29–30). Some scholars have regarded Jesus' discipling of the Twelve as the most important part of his mission strategy.[17] In his relationship with the Twelve Jesus was most concerned to convey both the cost of his own messiahship and the cost of their discipleship.[18]

TEACHING

In years to come it was Jesus' teaching, or segments of it, that would be memorized by the Twelve and other disciples and passed on, first orally and later in writing. One of these collections is the putative Sermon on the Mount recorded in Matthew 5–7. This discourse contains much of what we characteristically think of as Jesus' teaching. Like Socrates and the Buddha, Jesus employed metaphors and parables effectively—such as salt, light, lost sheep or coins, sowers and seeds. His aim was to provoke his listeners to consider the nature of God and the kingdom of God from new perspectives. "You have heard that it was said . . . but I say to you . . ." Much of his

15. Emphasis mine.

16. Eschatology: beliefs related to the final events in the history of the world or humankind.

17. Coleman, *Master Plan*, 21.

18. Cf. Ligon, *Bonhoeffer's Cost of Discipleship*. Dietrich Bonhoeffer was a Christian pastor-theologian of the 1930s who was executed by the Nazis in April 1945 for conspiracy in plotting the assassination of Adolf Hitler.

teaching was countercultural. "The meek shall inherit the earth." "Love your enemies; pray for those who persecute you." "If anyone demands your coat, give him your shirt as well." Against the dominant ethos of his day, Jesus argued:

> You know that those who are regarded as rulers of the Gentiles [i.e., the Romans] lord it over them, and their high officials exercise authority over them. Not so with you. Instead, whoever wants to become great among you must be your servant (Mark 10:42–43).

Jesus seemed intent on convincing his listeners that God is generous beyond all expectation—as in the parable of the workers in the vineyard. He was amazed whenever he encountered genuine faith, especially among the Gentiles, and often challenged his disciples for their lack of the same. He presented himself as a role model, "instructing by example."[19] Matthew reports that "the crowds were amazed at his teaching, because he taught as one who had authority and not as their teachers of the law." Understandably, this style of instruction did not sit well with those teachers of the law.

PREACHING

Jesus began his mission by quoting Isaiah 61:1–2a:

> "The Spirit of the Lord is on me,
>   because he has anointed me to proclaim good news to the poor.
> He has sent me to proclaim freedom for the prisoners
>   and recovery of sight for the blind,
> to set the oppressed free,
>   to proclaim the year of the Lord's favor."

He followed up this quotation by announcing, "Today this scripture is fulfilled in your hearing." Although Jesus did not openly proclaim himself as the Messiah until very late in his mission (Luke 22:67–68), this introduction to his inaugural sermon in Nazareth certainly suggested it. Proclamation was a major part of Jesus' mission. "Repent, for the kingdom of heaven has come near." Matthew identifies Jesus mission with that of the servant of Isaiah 42:1–4:

---

19. Peter Abelard's phrase. Cf. Scott, *What about the Cross?*, 85–86. Abelard was a prominent twelfth-century theologian; see chapter 7 below.

Here is my servant, whom I uphold,
   My chosen one in whom I delight;
I will put my Spirit on him,
   and he will *bring justice* to the nations.
He will not shout or cry out,
   or raise his voice in the streets.
A bruised reed he will not break,
   and a smoldering wick he will not snuff out.
In faithfulness he will *bring forth justice*;
   he will not falter or be discouraged
Till he *establishes justice* on earth.
   In his teaching the islands will put their hope.[20]

Jesus initially focused on the larger towns and cities of Galilee. But they were not as responsive as he had hoped.

Then, in an effort to reach the widest possible audience, Jesus sent out his disciples—first the Twelve and later, seventy others—to preach in the villages. Jesus fully expected a positive response. When the seventy (or seventy-two) others returned, excited by the response they encountered, Jesus, just as thrilled, replied, "I saw Satan fall like lightening from heaven."

> At that time Jesus, full of joy through the Holy Spirit, said, "I praise you, Father, Lord of heaven and earth, because you have hidden these things from the wise and learned, and revealed them to little children" (Luke 10:21).

Jesus' proclamation of the nearness or "at-handness" of the reign of God prompted some to perceive him as the prophesied Messiah. Andrew, Simon Peter's brother, for example, came to the latter with the news, "We have found the Messiah." This acceptance was not universally the case, however. Midway through his ministry Jesus asked his disciples, "Who do people say I am?" They replied, "Some say John the Baptist; others say Elijah; and still others, one of the prophets." "But what about you? Who do you say I am?" Peter answered, "You are the Messiah." Notably it was as Israel's Messiah that Jesus was greeted by the public when he entered Jerusalem on what would be his final visit.

No evidence exists that those who believed Jesus was the promised Messiah thought of him in other than the centuries-old terms. Recall the earlier description of the anticipated Messiah, here slightly condensed:

20. Emphasis mine.

One who would redeem Israel from its oppressors and usher in a more perfect era ... a descendant of King David ... a great political leader, well versed in Jewish law; an outstanding military commander who would win battles for Israel; a great judge who would make righteous decisions. ... During the Messianic Age ... the Diaspora would gathered in from exile. The law of Jubilee would be reinstated, the Temple rebuilt, and the sacrificial system reestablished .... All nations would be subject to Israel. The whole world would recognize God as the only true God, and Judaism as the only true religion. All peoples would live in harmony with one another and with nature.[21]

There is no evidence, however, that Jesus ever proclaimed the kingdom of God—and the messiahship and messianic age associated with it—in these terms. On the contrary, when on one occasion he was asked when the kingdom of God would come, his reply was startling: "The coming of the kingdom of God is not something that can be observed, nor will people say, 'Here it is,' or 'There it is,' because the kingdom of God is in your midst [or, within you]." On the other hand, there was a clear apocalyptic dimension to Jesus' preaching, the so-called "little Apocalypse" of Mark 13 being an example.

HEALING

Jesus is reported to have performed a variety of miracles, including such marvels as turning water into wine, feeding five thousand people, walking on water, calming a storm at sea, even raising the dead. John's gospel features these miracles as seven "signs" of his messiahship, for the kingdom personified in Jesus aimed at *shalom*, wholeness, the renewal of all things. One person's miracle is another's coincidence, of course, and there were some in Jesus' day who questioned his miracles, just as there are today.[22]

Far and away the most important of these miracles for ordinary folk were his healings. It was as a healer and exorcist that Jesus initially created a reputation. "News about him spread all over Syria, and people brought to him all who were ill with various diseases ... and he healed them. Large crowds from Galilee, the Decapolis, Jerusalem, Judea and the region across

21. A recent advertisement by the Jewish Hasidic sect, the Lubavitchers, calls on God to reveal the Messiah, "that he may immediately build the Third Holy Temple in Jerusalem, complete the ingathering of the exiles of Israel, and bring the entire world to recognize the Creator with the Final Redemption now," *New York Times*, April 19, 2008, A6.

22. For a rational discussion of miracles by a quantum physicist who is also a Christian, see Polkinghorne, *Science and Providence,* chapter 4, 53–68.

the Jordan followed him." Jesus understood that his extraordinary ability
to heal pointed to the imminent presence and power of the reign of God.
"But if it is by the Spirit of God that I drive out demons," he said, "then
the kingdom of God has come upon you." Much later the early Christians
would understand these healings as the fulfillment of Isaiah 53:4, "He took
up our infirmities and bore our diseases." Whatever the case, it is clear that
the salvation Jesus associated with the reign of God included release and
deliverance from the sicknesses that plague humankind.

The Wider World

Jesus' ministry was more extensive than one might think. From his opera-
tional base in Capernaum, Galilee, he traveled north to Tyre in Lebanon and
then east into Gentile-populated areas of Syria, including the Decapolis.[23]
During these excursions he interacted with Gentiles. He traveled south
into Samaria and Judea, and across the river into what is today's kingdom
of Jordan. John's gospel records Jesus as saying, "My Father is still working, and I also am working."[24] It may well be that Jesus was referring to
the fact that God had been working in the cultures and religions beyond
Israel for centuries; recall our brief survey of the Axial Age. And Jesus
wanted to participate in the Father's work, at least symbolically. Although
he conceived his primary mission as directed to Israel, his forays into
Lebanon, the Decapolis, Samaria, and Jordan indicate his awareness of his
own and Israel's larger mission to be "a light to the nations" (Isaiah 49:6).
And though as a Galilean he was regarded as an outsider, he knew that he
must necessarily take his message of the reign of God to Jerusalem, the
nation's religious and political center. And this he did.

Jesus' Inner Life[25]

The earliest indication we have of Jesus' self-awareness is when, at the age
of twelve, he responded to a question from his parents by asking, "Didn't
you know that I had to be in my Father's house?" (or, "Didn't you know

23. Decapolis: a group of ten cities, centers of Greek and Roman culture at the eastern
edge of the Roman Empire. All but one of the cities were located in what is the contemporary state of Jordan.

24. John 5:17.

25. For a helpful elucidation of Jesus' self-awareness with respect to the Father, see
Dupuis, *Religious Pluralism*, 268–71.

that I had to be about my Father's interests?") At his baptism, as previously noted, he heard a voice saying he was God's beloved son.[26] Prior to the inauguration of his public ministry, also as previously noted, Jesus endured a forty-day spiritual testing during which he conquered inner temptations, especially those associated with the high visibility of leadership. During this wilderness trial Jesus relied on previously memorized passages from the Tanakh to fortify his resolve. Later, as he launched his mission, he found it necessary to withdraw frequently from the public in order to spend extended time in prayer, though he did not favor lengthy prayers in public.

Jesus' chosen personal identification was "son of man." What did he understand by this expression? Jesus was able to read Hebrew but spoke Aramaic, the lingua franca of his day, and perhaps some Greek, since as a carpenter from Nazareth he had probably done business in nearby Sapphora, where the Greek language prevailed. Was "son of man" just the common Aramaic idiom for a human being? (It was.) Or did he borrow "son of man" from the prophetic book of Ezekiel, where throughout it seems equivalent to "mere mortal"? (Possibly). Or did he take it from Daniel 7 or *Enoch* 48,[27] where again it suggests a human being, but one with a messianic mission? (Likely.)

> I saw one like a human being, coming with the clouds of heaven. He approached the Ancient of Days and was led into his presence. He was given authority, glory and sovereign power; all nations and peoples of every language worshiped him. His dominion is an everlasting dominion that will not pass away, and his kingdom is one that will never be destroyed (Daniel 7:13).

In any event—and I suspect Jesus employed the title in each of the meanings citied above, depending on the occasion—Jesus associated "son of man" with his authority. Having healed a paralyzed man, for example, Jesus forgave the man his sins. The reaction of onlookers was, "Who can forgive sins but God alone?" To which Jesus replied, "I want you to know

26. English-language Bibles capitalize the phrases "Son," "Son of Man," and "Son of God." In this section I will not do so, for during the time period covered in the Gospels the phrases carried several meanings. The capitalizations reflect the conclusions of the New Testament writers as they interpreted the Christ event, and I wish to postpone this discussion to chapter 6.

27. *Enoch*: a noncanonical scripture written around 200–150 B.C.E., popular in Jesus' day.

that the son of man has authority on earth to forgive sins." Later he would clearly use the title with messianic intent (as in Matthew 26:64, in which instance it could be properly capitalized), but in the early stage of his mission he was more ambiguous. Perhaps he did not wish to attract the attention of King Herod prematurely. If so, in the instance of the paralyzed man he may merely have meant, "Human beings indeed have the power to forgive the sins of others" (cf. Matthew 16:19).

More problematic is the title "son of God," or "Son of God" and its implications for Jesus. Apart from one instance (Matthew 11:25ff.) the Synoptic Gospels do not record Jesus as identifying himself openly as the son of God. It is worth noting that the Chinese people customarily referred to their emperors as "sons of Heaven."[28] And Roman emperors in Jesus' day deified themselves while the Greeks dignified their heroes as "sons of God." In this context the comment of the Roman centurion in charge of Jesus' crucifixion (Matthew 27:54) is ambiguous.

Nevertheless, Jesus clearly thought of God as his Father. The perception by the Hebrews of God as Father had been present as early as the exodus,[29] and appears again in the Song of Moses: "Is he not your Father, your Creator, who made you and formed you?"[30] The Psalmist calls God "the father to the fatherless."[31] The name of Joab, King David's general, means "God is father"; and the name of Abijah, one of Israel's kings, means "father is God." God promised that he would be a father to King Solomon (2 Samuel 7:14). But the idea doesn't really take hold until the era of the prophets. The later Isaiah besought God to restore his people with these words: "You, LORD, are our Father, our Redeemer from of old" and again "Yet you, LORD, are our Father . . . we are all the work of your hand."[32]

God himself addresses Israel just prior to their exile: "Have you not just called to me, 'My Father, my friend from my youth, will you always be angry?'" and complains that though they speak in such intimate terms, they continue to do evil. Again, plaintively, "How gladly would I treat you like my children . . . . I thought you would call me 'Father' and not turn

---

28. Cf. Wills, Jr., *Mountain of Fame*.

29. Exodus 4:22.

30. Deuteronomy 32:6.

31. Psalm 68:5.

32. Isaiah 63:16 and 64:8.

away from me."[33] In the final book of the Tanakh God speaks to Israel, "A son honors his father . . . . If I am a father, where is the honor due me?" The prophet Malachi himself then addresses Israel: "Do we not all have one Father? Did not our God create us? Why do we profane the covenant of our ancestors by being unfaithful to one another?"[34]

In Jesus' day and in the century thereafter, Jewish worshippers commonly affirmed God's fatherhood. The famous Jewish saint Onias (first century B.C.E.) did so, as did the Alexandrian philosopher Philo, the historian Josephus, the sage Yochanan ben Zakkai, and the martyred rabbi Akiba.[35] I give this background because it is sometimes taught in Christian circles today that the fatherhood of God was one of Jesus' innovations. It was not; nevertheless, most scholars agree that the fatherly relation of God to Israel was only gradually recognized and expressed by Jewish worshippers.[36] It was Jesus who brought it to the fore.

For Jesus of Nazareth, God's fatherhood was central, so much so that in private he would address God as "Daddy."[37] This form of address had practical implications. It meant that his disciples could trust God absolutely, whether in connection with the mundane cares of daily life or for spiritual needs.

> So do not worry, saying, "What shall we drink?" or "What shall we wear?" For the pagans run after all these things, and your heavenly Father knows that you need them. But seek first his kingdom and his righteousness, and all these things will be given to you as well (Matthew 6:31–33).

> If you then, though you are evil, know how to give good gifts to your children, how much more will your Father in heaven give the Holy Spirit to those who ask him? (Luke 11:13).[38]

33. Jeremiah 3:4–5, 19.

34. Malachi 1:6; 2:10.

35. Cf. *Jewish Encyclopedia*, "Abba," para. 1*ff.*

36. Dalman, cited in "Abba," ibid, para. 10.

37. Abba: The Hebrew word for father is *Av* [or *Ab*]. The suffix *ba* signifies intimacy.

38. A Russian Orthodox theologian comments on the opening sentence of the Apostles' Creed: "The divine omnipotence is qualified immediately as *paternal*. Before everything else, and essentially, God is Father, and only after is he Creator, Judge—and what lies at the heart of the Christian hope: Savior and Comforter. And he is all these because he is Father." Paul Evdokimov, *La femme et le salut du monde*, 147, cited in Stăniloae, *Revelation and Knowledge*, 192.

Jesus' parable of the Prodigal Son (Luke 15) highlights God's fatherly attitude. God can be trusted to embrace the repentant sinner and forgive his or her sins, no questions asked.

All four gospels are replete with references to God the Father—172 references. This intimacy carried over into the first-generation Christian community. The apostle Paul wrote, "When we cry 'Abba! Father!' it is that very Spirit bearing witness with our spirit that we are children of God" (Romans 8:15–16). Again, "And because you are children [of God], God has sent the Spirit of his Son into our hearts, crying, 'Abba! Father!'" (Galatians 4:6).

As part of his inward journey as the son of man and son of God, did Jesus ever reflect on the possibility that his mission might end in outward failure and that he himself might suffer death in the process? As we shall see, he did.

The Wheel Turns

During the first part of Jesus' mission all went well. Crowds responded enthusiastically to his proclamation that the reign of God was immanent. His teaching intrigued them and the miracles he performed left them awe-struck. John's gospel reports that at one point they were prepared forcibly to make Jesus king of Israel. Yet behind this euphoria trouble was brewing. The superstitious King Herod who had beheaded John the Baptizer wondered whether Jesus was John raised from the dead. A delegation of Pharisees and teachers of the law arrived from Jerusalem to observe the putative Messiah personally and were not happy with what they saw. Jesus prudently decided it was time to withdraw from the public for a while. He and the Twelve disappeared into the northernmost region of Israel. It was there at Caesarea Philippi that Peter confessed Jesus' messiahship, and it was there that Jesus warned them not to speak about this to anyone. And it was there that, for the first time, he predicted his death to the incredulous disciples.

What seemed incredible to the Twelve was that the Messiah (the "son of man," Jesus said) "must suffer many things and be rejected by the elders, the chief priests and the teachers of the law, and that he must be killed and after three days rise again." This prediction was not at all implicit in the prevailing vision of a Messiah who would usher in the reign of God, as we have noted twice before.

It seems most likely that Jesus' own study of the Tanakh, particularly the prophets, and most particularly Isaiah 52:13—53:12, led him to this conclusion. Heretofore the rabbis had interpreted such passages as the four "Servant Songs" of Isaiah,[39] which suggest humiliation and death before ultimate vindication, as referring to the nation of Israel; so too the vision of Ezekiel about the valley of the dry bones and their resurrection (37:11). But Jesus—in an extension of his inner pilgrimage discussed above—apparently saw himself as embodying and fulfilling the fortunes and destiny of Israel and applied the texts to himself.[40] Other texts, for example the story of Jonah (three days in the belly of the great fish), suggested the same to him.

How long it took Jesus to mentally revise the traditional concept of messiahship and what spiritual anguish the revision may have entailed for him, we do not know. But as Jesus and the Twelve pursued their long final trek to Jerusalem, Jesus spoke twice again to them about his impending death and resurrection. Between the second and third prediction a conflict about status arose within the group of disciples. In this context Jesus remarked, "Even the son of man did not come to be served but to serve, and to give his life as a ransom of many" (Mark 10:45). Voluntarily giving up his life would be the final expression of his serving others. Then, as if to reassure the disciples of his ultimate vindication, the gospel writers tell how Jesus took three of the disciples with him to a "high mountain" where they witnessed a glorious transfiguration (transformation) of his outward appearance. This event would later become paradigmatic in Eastern Orthodox theology.

As previously noted, Jesus entered Jerusalem with the crowd shouting *hosannas*, Salvation has come! He entered the temple area, the heart of Jewish life, where famously he disrupted routine commercial transactions. This action was the proverbial straw that broke the camel's back, inciting the chief priests to plot to kill Jesus. From their perspective, his messianic pretensions were likely to inspire revolution and bring down the wrath of the Roman Empire upon the nation (John 11:49).

While the rulers were plotting against him—not for the first time, as John's gospel emphasizes—Jesus predicted the destruction of the temple and followed this by a lengthy prophecy concerning the circumstances

---

39. Isaiah 42:1-4; 49:1-6; 50:4-9; 52:13-53:12.

40. This is the theme of Bishop N. T. Wright's voluminous writings.

surrounding such destruction. It was Passover time, so Jesus gathered together the Twelve and perhaps some of the women and other disciples to share the *Seder*, the Passover meal. Again, John's gospel provides the most detailed description (John 13–17) of Jesus' conversation and prayers on this occasion. During the Seder he predicted Judas' betrayal and Peter's denial. Jesus also took bread and distributed it to the disciples, saying, "Take it; this is my body." It is unclear why he did not use the Passover lamb to make this point, unless he was deliberately dissociating his passion from the established sacrificial system. He also distributed the traditional cup of wine among them, saying, "This is the blood of the covenant, which is poured out for many" (Mark 14:22–24).[41] At the conclusion of the Seder the group sang a hymn and adjourned to Gethsemane, a site on the Mount of Olives just outside the city.

Here Jesus experienced understandable anguish as he contemplated what was about to happen. "My soul is overwhelmed with sorrow," he told the Twelve (now the Eleven, for Judas had left their company in order to meet with the high priests with the intent of betraying Jesus). And how could it be otherwise? He had come to inaugurate the reign of God and instead was about to be crucified, all hope for a glorious messianic age dashed to pieces. With sweat falling from his face like drops of blood, he prayed, "Abba, Father; everything is possible for you. Take this cup from me. Yet not what I will, but what you will."

Judas appears with a crowd of armed thugs and Jesus is hauled off to the Sanhedrin to face trial. The high priest asks, "Are you the Messiah, the son of the Blessed One?" And Jesus answers, "I am. And you will see the son of man [Son of Man] sitting at the right hand of the Mighty One and coming on the clouds of heaven." "Blasphemy!" they respond, and condemn him as worthy of death.[42]

The Sanhedrin was not actually permitted to execute anyone, however, so Jesus must stand trial again before Pontius Pilate, the Roman governor. "Are you the king of the Jews?" Pilate asks. "You have said so," Jesus replies—an affirmative answer. Such a reply could be understood as a threat to the empire, though Pilate does not seem to take it seriously. He hesitates for a time, not finding an overt crime to question Jesus

---

41. For the significance of this act with respect to the atonement, see Scott, *What about the Cross?*, 197.

42. Cf. the alternative account of Reb Yakov Leib HaKohain, *To Die for the People: A Kabbalistic Reinterpretation of the Crucifixion of Jesus*, para. 16*ff*.

about, then turns to the crowd. "What shall I do then?" he asks, hoping to appease the crowd. But now the mob has turned against Jesus. "Crucify him," they shout back.[43] Pilate concedes, and orders Jesus to be flogged and crucified. Crucifixion was a common form of execution at this time; the Romans had adopted the practice from the Carthaginians, who had copied it from Alexander the Great, who had learned it from the Persians. Like all crucifixions, this one was slow and agonizing; it was also meant to humiliate the victim. Onlookers derided Jesus: "He saved others, but he can't save himself! Let this Messiah, this king of Israel, come down now from the cross, that we may see and believe." Sooner than normal—a fact that surprised Governor Pilate—Jesus breathed his last breath.

Joseph of Arimathea, "a prominent member of the Sanhedrin, who was himself waiting for the kingdom of God," obtained permission from Pilate to bury Jesus and did so, placing the body in a rock tomb. That should have been the end of the story. One would have to have been a Jew of Jesus' generation, I suspect, to fully grasp the gut-wrenching impact of his shameful death. "Anyone who is hung on a pole is under God's curse" (Deuteronomy 21:23). One could only conclude that God himself had put an end to this would-be Messiah's pretensions. All the hopes and expectations of Jesus' followers were now in smithereens.

But the day after the Sabbath three female disciples of Jesus came to the tomb to anoint the body in order to assuage the stench following death, only to find the tomb empty. Again, it is impossible to overestimate the impact of this disclosure on Jesus' followers. Upon his arrest those he had named apostles quite naturally had fled the scene. One, Simon Peter, stayed in the high priest's courtyard for a while before fleeing; another, John the beloved, appears briefly at the crucifixion. But for the most part they all laid low; it was the women of Jesus' entourage who witnessed the crucifixion in full, it was the women who saw where he was entombed, and it was the women who later found the tomb empty and became the initial witnesses of his resurrection.

The women shared this news with the Eleven. Peter and "the disciple Jesus loved," later known to us as John the elder, confirmed it by visiting the site themselves. Soon thereafter the Eleven, and other disciples as well, reported a number of occasions in which Jesus appeared to them, alive and well, with explanations and instructions, including what

43. This entire scene exemplifies René Girard's scapegoat theory perfectly. See the detailed discussion of Girard in chapter 8.

Christians have come to call the Great Commission (Matthew 28:18–20). Apparently Jesus had indeed been resurrected, just as he had predicted. (The authorities published an alternative explanation: Jesus' disciples had stolen his body and hidden it.) Not all of Jesus' disciples were immediately convinced of his resurrection, however—hence the well-known story of "doubting Thomas."

Despite initial doubts the Eleven came to believe and were totally reinvigorated. The reality of the resurrection served to contravene the shame of the crucifixion. Everything now must be rethought. How would the Eleven and the other eyewitnesses interpret the Christ event, which had turned out so differently from what they had anticipated? We will explore their interpretations in chapter 6.

6

The Earliest Gospels

There is no other name under heaven . . . by which we must be saved.

ACTS 4:12

Iɴ ᴛʜᴇ ᴀғᴛᴇʀᴍᴀᴛʜ ᴏғ Jesus' crucifixion the eleven remaining apostles, along with certain women and other disciples, numbering about 120 altogether, were understandably in a state of bewilderment. On the one hand, the kingdom proclaimed by Jesus of Nazareth seemed not to have materialized, and the proclaimer himself had been ignominiously executed as a blasphemer and threat to public order. On the other hand, by virtue of the empty tomb and Jesus' subsequent appearances to them, they were convinced that he had been raised from the dead. What then was the meaning of his messiahship, especially in the light of his shameful crucifixion? At this point, while Jesus was still presenting himself to them in post-resurrection form, their focus returned to the kingdom of God.

The imminent reign of God had always been at the heart of Jesus' ministry, so it was the only framework the disciples had in which to try to make sense of all that had happened. Thus they had a compelling need to understand the "why" of his crucifixion and the significance of his resurrection in the light of the reign of God.[1]

Luke, the author of both the gospel of Luke and the Acts of the Apostles, tells us that "after his suffering [Jesus] presented himself to them and gave many convincing proofs that he was alive." Further, "he appeared to them over a period of forty days and spoke about *the kingdom of God*" (Acts 1:3, emphasis added). The apostles in turn questioned him: "Lord, is

1. For stylistic reasons I use the phrases, "kingdom of God," "reign of God," and "dominion of God" interchangeably. They all refer to the same reality.

this the time when you will restore the kingdom to Israel?" (Acts 1:6). It is apparent from this inquiry that the disciples were still thinking about the reign of God in traditional terms; that is, the restoration and preeminence of the nation of Israel. True, Jesus had not ushered in the kingdom before his premature death, but surely now that he had been resurrected he would do so. Consequently during these forty days Jesus set about to help them understand more clearly the nature of God's reign and his own mission. This new understanding involved five mental and spiritual adjustments on their part.

The first had to do with the vital connection between the ancient Hebrew theme of the righteous sufferer (as in Job, Psalm 22, and Isaiah 50 and 53)[2] and the kingdom of God. On the final journey from Galilee to Jerusalem, Jesus had tried to convince them of the necessity, according to the Scriptures, that the Son of Man must suffer, die, and be vindicated on the third day. Now he explained it again with his own passion fresh in their memory.

Second, during these forty days Jesus instructed his followers to "wait for the gift my Father promised" (Acts 1:4–5). This was the gift of the Holy Spirit. The presence and power of the Spirit in their lives would be powerful prophetic evidence that the reign of God through Jesus had in fact been inaugurated though not yet consummated. A new order in history was now under way, though imperceptible to most observers.

Third, the outpouring of the Spirit, Jesus told them, was initially for the purpose of empowering them to be effective witnesses for him. As Jews, the apostles believed that at the end of the age, when God's dominion had come, the Gentiles would flock to Jerusalem (cf. Zechariah 8:23). Now Jesus reverses that trajectory. Instead of the nations coming to Jerusalem to experience the true God, Jesus will send his disciples out to the nations (Acts 1:8). The centripetal has become centrifugal; the inward-oriented has become outward-bound.

Fourth, Jesus disappears from their sight; and in his place, Luke tells us, appear "two men dressed in white" (Acts 1:10). We are meant to understand them as angels, messengers from God. They assure the disciples that "this same Jesus, taken from you into heaven, will come back" (Acts 1:11). He would come back presumably as the Son of Man in great power and glory, as Jesus himself had prophesied (Mark 13:26). So now the

---

2. Cf. Green and Baker, *Recovering the Scandal of the Cross*, 17–18.

disciples have received a twice-repeated challenge to wait—to wait for the outpouring of Jesus' spirit and to wait for Jesus' return. Both implied that the kingdom is in some sense already present, but in another sense, not yet. Thus they became aware that the coming of the kingdom, contrary to their previous expectation as devout Jews, is a two-stage process with an intervening time gap of indefinite length. During this hiatus they were expected to carry the good news of God's salvation to the nations.

Fifth, Jesus was "taken up" (Acts 1:9) and exalted to a position of universal authority. From this event they would understand that "God has made him both Messiah and Lord, whom you crucified" (Acts 2:36). Messiah is not a new title here—but Lord is. Caesar is not lord; Jesus is. Lord of the universe, Lord of life, Lord of history, Lord of the nations, Emperor of emperors—the One to whom judgment is committed at the end of the age (Acts 10:42).

From these five mental revolutions would come a sixth and greater one. Very early on it became evident to these fervent monotheists— though they would have difficulty articulating it—that they could not evade associating (equating is too strong a word at this early stage) Jesus of Nazareth with Deity. Not that he was God: in his early sermons Peter refers to Jesus as "a man accredited by God" and "God's servant"—but that he had been exalted to a position next to God. In Jewish tradition the Messiah had never been thought to be Deity itself. Yet within a decade an early Christian poem—a hymn, perhaps, incorporated by the apostle Paul in a letter he was writing, evoked the incredible idea that Jesus was equal with God.

> Who, though he was in the form of God,
>   did not regard equality with God
>   as something to be exploited,
> But emptied himself,
>   taking the form of a slave,
>   being born in human likeness.
> And being found in human form,
>   he humbled himself
>   and became obedient to the point of death –
> even death on a cross.
> Therefore God also highly exalted him
>   and gave him the name
>   that is above every name
> So that at the name of Jesus

> *every knee should bend,*
>   in heaven and on earth and under the earth,
> *And every tongue should confess*
>   that Jesus Messiah is Lord,
>   to the glory of God the Father
>   (Philippians 2:6–11, emphasis added)

The significance of the second stanza above is that while referencing Isaiah 45:23 (see italics above), the hymn substitutes the name of Jesus for that of YHWH! This conviction of Deity became ever stronger as time went on and a full-fledged theology of incarnation developed rather rapidly. The prologue to the gospel of John, generally thought to have been written in the last decade of the first century C.E.—that is, within two generations of the Christ event—reads:

> In the beginning was the Word,[3] and the Word was with God, and the Word was God. He was with God in the beginning. Through him all things were made; without him nothing was made that has been made .... The Word became flesh and made his dwelling among us. We have seen his glory, the glory of the one and only Son, who came from the Father, full of grace and truth (John 1:1–3, 14).

The exact nature of Jesus as the Second Person of the Trinity would not be formalized until much later, and then only within the context of Greek thought patterns.[4] It remains to be seen whether these patterns can be successfully reformulated in the thought patterns of the twenty-first century in other parts of the world.

Peter's Early Gospel

With that background, let us return to the specifics of the apostle Peter's early understanding of the Christ event. It is uncertain whether Luke knew Peter personally; thus it is impossible to know whether Luke is quoting Peter exactly when he records Peter's early "sermons." Presumably Luke is giving his readers brief summaries. Yet there seems no reason to doubt that Peter's speeches as recorded by Luke present credible instances of

---

3. Word (Greek *logos*): a Greek concept of universal divine reason, first used by the philosopher Heraclitus the Ephesian (circa 500 B.C.E.). It creates, governs and reveals the cosmos to the human mind; it is sometimes referred to as "the mind of God." The idea is comparable in most respects to the Hebrew *dabar* and the Old Testament concept of Wisdom (Proverbs 8 and elsewhere).

4. Cf. Prestige, *God in Patristic Thought,* chapter IV, 76–96.

how Peter and his colleagues understood the Christ event in the weeks
and months immediately following Pentecost. And we can assume that
Peter's apostolic companions, their number now restored to twelve, and
the other disciples shared his understanding in varying degrees.

The first thing we note is that Peter's messages were directed to his
fellow Jews and to their ruling elders. He begins by asserting that the
Christ event was indeed coincident with the long-expected "day of the
LORD" prophesied by Joel and other prophets (Acts 2:16ff.)—a day of
wrath, to be sure, but also the day of salvation (Acts 2:21). He notes the
crucifixion, but places greater emphasis initially on the resurrection of
Jesus (Acts 2:24 and following). He calls on his audience to repent. "Save
yourself from this corrupt generation" (Acts 2:40). Very likely Peter was
recalling Jesus' own prophecies of destruction (cf. the "little Apocalypse"
in Mark 13). By repenting and being baptized in the name of Jesus, Peter's
hearers will receive forgiveness of sins and the gift of the Holy Spirit—that
is, they will begin to participate in the reign of God. That was Peter's "good
news"—the first concrete definition we have of the gospel.

Peter preached another sermon (my word, not his) at Solomon's
colonnade in the temple area. He highlights the people's and their leaders'
ignorance in having rejected and crucified Jesus but assures them that the
prophets had foretold the Messiah's passion. Again he calls for repentance,
"so that your sins may be wiped out, that times of refreshing my come
from the Lord, and that he may send the Messiah who has been appointed
for you—even Jesus." "Heaven" has received Jesus "until the time comes
for God to restore everything." Jesus is the one in whom all the promises
of God to Israel will be fulfilled; these promises are the "restoration" Peter
is describing (Acts 3:18–21).

In Acts 4 Luke gives us a third exposition by Peter, this one directed
again to the rulers and elders of Israel in Jerusalem. It follows the same
line as the previous two, citing Jesus' rejection, crucifixion, and resurrection, and concluding with the assertion that "Salvation is found in no one
else, for there is no other name given under heaven by which we must be
saved" (Acts 4:12).

Who is the "we" in this text? And just what did Peter mean by
"salvation"? Peter is addressing a group of individuals, but the salvation
he speaks of is certainly not the individualized, otherworldly concept
many Christians assume. There is no mention of life after death in these
sermons, much less of heaven or hell. Peter interprets the Christ event in

the light of the reign of God. He addresses the nation of Israel as a whole. Salvation for him meant forgiveness of sins for Israel, especially the sin of rejecting God's Messiah. It meant receiving the Holy Spirit—presence and power for a new age. It meant escape from the impending fate of a corrupt generation. And it meant participating in the dominion of God when the Messiah will return and God will restore everything.

It is clear that the crucifixion and resurrection of Jesus are prominent in Peter's mind. It is less clear that Peter understands the crucifixion, or the crucifixion and the resurrection, as God's particular means of saving the nation. Rather, God's salvation is proclaimed as consisting of inclusion in God's kingdom; and Peter's good news is that Jesus is the promised Savior, God's agent, whose messiahship is confirmed by his suffering and vindicated by his resurrection as foretold by the prophets.

Peter's special apostolic mission was to the Jews (Galatians 2:7). But very early on he had a pivotal experience with a Gentile group, which Luke also records in Acts 10–11. Peter's conversation with the centurion[5] Cornelius and the members of his household reveals a significant expansion in his comprehension of the Christ event, though still within the framework of the kingdom of God. To these Gentiles—and Luke presents Cornelius as one who is a devout Godfearer[6] and already familiar with the ministry of Jesus—to them Peter emphasizes the way in which Jesus "went about doing good and healing all who were under the power of the devil" (Acts 10:38). That is, for Peter the saving Christ event begins with the life and ministry of Jesus. He then goes on to speak of Jesus' crucifixion, resurrection, and personal appearances, and Jesus' special command that the disciples testify to the fact that God has appointed Jesus "judge of the living and the dead .... Everyone who believes in him receives forgiveness of sins through his name" (Acts 10:42–43).

While Peter was speaking these words the Holy Spirit "fell upon" these Gentiles. The circumcised believers who had accompanied Peter heard the uncircumcised Romans "speaking in tongues and extolling God." Peter's reaction: "So if God gave them the same gift he gave us [Jews] who believed in the Lord Jesus Christ, who was I to think that I could

---

5. Centurion: Originally, the commander of a century—a company of a hundred soldiers in the Roman army. By the time of Jesus, however, the usual number of soldiers under a centurion's command was eighty.

6. "Godfearer" or "one who fears God" were terms used to describe Gentiles who believed in the one true God of Israel and denied the idols and gods of the Gentile world.

stand in God's way?" (Acts 11:17). Cornelius and his household would participate in the kingdom of God just as surely as the Jewish Christians. Peter's spiritual horizon now encompasses more than the nation of Israel; it extends to the whole world. Peter would eventually travel widely, visiting Jewish communities throughout the Mediterranean world, spending crucial years in Rome itself where, it is said, he was crucified upside down by Emperor Nero.

To see just how the apostles understood and proclaimed the Christ event in the earliest days of the Way[7] (as the Christian community was known in the years immediately after Pentecost), it is helpful to note the Old Testament texts they cited when interpreting the great events of which they were eyewitnesses and active participants.[8] These texts speak of the prophesied "day of the Lord"; of resurrection, ascension, and exaltation; of the coming of a Moses-like prophet who would restore the nation; of the promise of blessing to all nations through Abraham's offspring; and of the rejection of the "cornerstone." In Psalm 109:8 they found what appeared to be a prophecy of Judas' defection, and in Psalm 69:25 they found a directive for the election of someone to take Judas' place as an eyewitness to the Christ event.

Thus there is no overt doctrine of the atonement in the early gospel proclamations. Forgiveness of sins was central, but it was associated at this point not with the death of the Messiah per se but with the reception of Jesus as Messiah and the gift of the Spirit.

After Peter and John were released from prison (Acts 4), the believers gathered together to pray. Within their prayer they recited Psalm 2:1–2, "the rulers band together against the Lord and against his anointed one." On another occasion the deacon Stephen, brought before the Sanhedrin, made a long statement (Acts 7), referring to or quoting from ten different passages in the Tanakh to illustrate that the rejection of Jesus was further proof of an established pattern of persecution of prophets.

That Isaiah 53 was significant in helping the earliest believers understand the so-hard-to-accept death of Messiah is clear from the apostle (or deacon) Philip's encounter with the Ethiopian official, a man who was a Godfearer, perhaps even a Jewish proselyte. Philip found the Ethiopian reading Isaiah 53. So, "Starting with this scripture, he proclaimed to him

7. See Acts 9:2; 19:9, 23; 22:4; 24:14, 22.

8. E. g., Genesis 18:15; Deuteronomy 18:15ff.; Psalms 2:1–2, 16:8–11 (Septuagint), 110:1, and 118:22; Joel 2:28–32.

the good news about Jesus" (Acts 8:35). The significance of Isaiah 53 to Philip and the other disciples was its support of Jesus' insistence that the Messiah had to suffer and die. Whether at this point the disciples understood in full measure *why* the Messiah must suffer and die is not clear.

Paul's Gospel

Scholars believe that Saul of Tarsus (renamed Paul) was converted to Jesus within a few years after the Messiah's crucifixion, resurrection, and ascension. He wrote his first epistle or letter (that is, the first that has been preserved) around 52 C.E. So we have in Paul's writings early testimony— earlier than any of the gospels—about the ways in which some followers of the Way who were not part of Jesus' original entourage understood the Christ event. Before discussing the specifics of Paul's interpretation of the Christ event, we should note that Paul is distinguished from the Twelve in that unlike them—they were "unschooled, ordinary men" (Acts 4:13)—he was a Roman citizen, a well-educated Hellenistic Jew with formal training in the Pharisaic Judaism of the day. "I studied under Gamaliel,"[9] he told one audience," and was thoroughly trained in the law of our ancestors" (Acts 22:3). It is not surprising, therefore, that Paul became Christianity's first creative theologian as well as its paradigmatic missionary.

Upon his conversion Paul began to proclaim in the synagogues of Damascus that Jesus is the Son of God (Acts 9:20). This is the only time in the entire book of Acts that the phrase "Son of God" appears, so we cannot be certain just what Paul meant by it in this particular instance. My judgment is that he was simply saying that Jesus was the long-awaited Messiah. Paul was not an eyewitness of the Christ event; he learned the essential facts from those who were, as he himself acknowledged:

> For I handed on to you as of first importance what I in turn had received: that Christ died for our sins in accordance with the Scriptures, and that he was buried, and that he was raised on the third day in accordance with the Scriptures, and that he appeared to Cephas [Peter], then to the Twelve. Then he appeared to more than five hundred brothers and sisters at one time, most of whom are still alive ... (1 Corinthians 15:3).

---

9. Rabban Gamaliel, a noted teacher of the law and member of the Sanhedrin in the late Second Temple period. Cf. Acts 5:34*ff.*

This, Paul insisted, was "the gospel . . . which you in turn received, in which also you stand, through which also you are being saved."[10] The only hint provided in this creed as to *why* Jesus died is the ambiguous phrase "for our sins." The preposition *for* obviously has a variety of meanings, ranging from but not limited to "the reason for," to "on behalf of," to "in place of."[11]

In what many believe to be Paul's oldest surviving letter, his letter to the church at Thessalonica, Paul proclaimed this good news in the context of the kingdom of God in much the same manner as the Twelve (cf. Acts 20:28 and 28:31). He writes to the Thessalonians, a church he founded, "how you turned to God from idols, to serve a living and true God, and to wait for his Son from heaven, whom he raised from the dead—Jesus, who rescues us from the wrath that is coming" (1 Thessalonians 1:9–10). Here "the wrath that is coming" is the judgment associated with the day of the Lord and the restoration of all things, just as Peter had preached. Paul, like Jesus and Peter, had a decidedly eschatological orientation. But as a theologian he went further than the Twelve in thinking through the implications of the gospel as it related to the Jews, to the Gentiles, and to both groups. This process becomes increasingly evident in his subsequent letters.

Paul knew himself to be a missionary to the Gentiles. He said his commission was founded on Isaiah 49:6 (see Acts 13:37). For Paul, the crucial impact of the Christ event was that the hour had come for the inclusion of the Gentiles. He claims that he received this understanding directly from the Lord Jesus (Galatians 1:12), but he understood that he would need to present the Christ event in a way that would apply equally to Jews and Gentiles. And from this insight he developed his famous gospel of justification by faith (Romans 5:1).[12] He presented and defended this message first in his letter to the church of Galatia and later in more depth in his letter to the Christians at Rome. In essence, this gospel posited that human beings are made righteous or justified before God not by adhering to Jewish law—or any law, for that matter, including the inner law of

10. 1 Corinthians 15:1–2.

11. Cf. Scott, *What about the Cross?* 19–20, for a list of twenty-six possible meanings of the preposition *for*.

12. Paul's doctrine of justification by faith was taken up by Martin Luther in the Reformation of the sixteenth century. Although Lutheran ideas spread into Eastern Europe, the specific theme of justification did not attract much attention, for it was deemed irrelevant to the Orthodox tradition. Cf. Hsia, ed., *Cambridge History of Christianity*, Vol. 6: *Reform and Expansion 1500-1600*. Cited in the *Times Literary Supplement*, July 18, 2008, 32.

conscience–but simply by exercising faith in God's grace as promised to Israel, fulfilled in Jesus, and revealed in the cross. The cross was above all an implement of shame, and Paul saw in the cross God's mystery of salvation. In fact, the cross exemplified the very shame and suffering that Paul himself endured as God's servant (cf. 1 Corinthians 4:8–13).

But justification by faith was not the only strand in Paul's gospel. One important strand Paul discerned was that the Christ event had introduced a new world order (1 Corinthians 5:17). The spiritual powers that rule and enslave the world had been conquered on the cross (Galatians 1:3–4; Colossians 2:15). A third strand Paul drew upon was the Old Testament sacrificial system. Paul declared that "God presented the Messiah as a sacrifice of atonement, through the shedding of his blood" (Romans 3:25). A fourth strand was that in Christ God was reconciling the world to himself and was simultaneously reconciling Jew and Greek—that is, all nations, all classes, all genders, to one another.

> For in Christ Jesus you are all children of God through faith . . . .
> There is no longer Jew or Greek, there is no longer slave or free,
> there is no longer male and female; for all of you are one in Christ
> Jesus (Galatians 3:26, 28).

Indeed, in Christ God would ultimately reconcile the whole cosmos (Romans 5:10; Ephesians 2:16; and Colossians 1:20). A fifth and perhaps surprising strand in Paul's various expositions of the gospel is his marked tendency toward an affirmation of universal salvation:

> Consequently, just as one trespass [Adam's] resulted in condemna-
> tion for all people, so also one righteous act [Jesus'] resulted in
> justification and life for all (Romans 5:18).

And again,

> For as in Adam all die, so in Christ all will be made alive (1
> Corinthians 15:22).

As an aside, we may note that Paul is not alone in announcing the inclusiveness of salvation. His colleague John the elder attests that Jesus said, "And I, when I am lifted up from the earth, will draw all people to myself" (John 12:32). And again: "He [Jesus] is the atoning sacrifice for our sins, and not only for ours, but also for the sins of the whole world" (1 John 2:2).

Returning to Paul, it is evident that he had no single fixed theory of the atonement. Rather, he expounded at length various implications of the gospel of God's salvation, creatively drawing on a variety of images and metaphors depending on the particular audience at hand. Because of the number of epistles Paul wrote and their obvious influence in the early church, some have imagined that he, not Jesus, was the true founder of Christianity.[13] This is not necessarily a heretical statement, for Jesus came to inaugurate the reign of God, not to found a new religion. At the same time, the claim is something of an overstatement, for what Paul really did was simply place the Christ event in a context that non-Jews could understand. Contextualization[14] is a task familiar to every missionary.

The Loaves Multiply

Thousands of books have been written explicating Paul's gospel, so I will take the matter no further here; many useful books are readily available.[15] As Green and Baker admonish us, by focusing too much on Paul, Christians "are in danger of turning a choir of New Testament voices into a solo performance."[16] The main point to note here is that within a single generation after the Christ event, its meaning was being worked out not only by the Twelve but also by numerous other disciples. By the end of that first generation, at least one of the four gospels (Mark) was available and the letters of Paul were circulating. By 90 c.e., the gospels of Matthew, Luke, and John were being read as well as epistles by Peter, James, John, Jude, and other leaders in the Christian community. The seeds of future interpretations of the Gospel were being planted. They would sprout in the second century c.e. and for twenty centuries thereafter.

13. Cf. Wenham, *Paul*. Also Ludemann, *Paul: The Founder of Christianity*.

14. Contextualize: to place an idea in a particular context. In missiology it usually refers to a specific ethnic group or culture. Shoki Coe pioneered the use of the word *contextualization* (Cf. Coe et al, *Ministry in Context: The Third Mandate Programme of the Theological Education Fund, 1970–77*). Contextualization goes beyond the notion of indigenization, which refers to utilizing select aspects of a local culture in church development. Contextualization goes beyond indigenization also by taking into account the processes of secularity, technology, and the struggle for human justice. Cf. Nicholls, "Contextualization," 164. Muchee suggests seven contextual principles utilized by New Testament writers. See Muchee, "Contextualize," 51–59.

15. Examples include Becker, *Paul*; Dunn, *Theology of Paul*; and N. T. Wright, *Paul: In Fresh Perspective*.

16. Green and Baker, *Recovering the Scandal*, 69.

Take the first epistle of Peter, for example. Peter wrote this letter from Rome not long before Emperor Nero crucified him. The epistle reflects nearly three decades of Peter's pondering the meaning of the Christ event and reads quite differently from the early "sermons" we looked at in Acts. He still thinks in terms of Jesus the cornerstone (1 Peter 2:4–7; cf. Acts 4:11). But he has also come to think of the Christ event in the context of the ancient sacrificial system of the Jews (1 Peter 1:18–19), in the context of the Servant Songs (1 Peter 2:24–25), in the context of releasing prisoners in Hades (1 Peter 3:18–22), and in the context of an exemplar to those enduring persecution (1 Peter 4:12–13, 16). Nevertheless, for Peter the good news remains "the salvation that is ready to be revealed in the last time" (1 Peter 1:5) and which is a never-fading inheritance reserved for persecuted believers.

Or again, consider the letter to the Hebrews, written by another scholarly believer whose theological acumen in some respects rivaled Paul's. While Peter and Paul both focus their attention on Jesus' death, the author of Hebrews focuses more on Jesus' *life*, both before and after his crucifixion. And while Peter and Paul see Jesus as a sacrifice, a sin offering, the writer of Hebrews sees Jesus as the high priest who *offers* the sacrifice (Hebrews 2:14–18; 7:24–27). This is a crucial distinction. Hebrews understands Jesus as the fulfillment of the Old Testament sacrificial *system*, which is no longer necessary now that it has been fulfilled in Jesus. The writer was so immersed in the Jewish tradition that he could not conceive of the sacrificial system as being illegitimate in any way. However, with René Girard I believe that Jesus did not legitimatize the sacrificial system by fulfilling it; rather, by his death on the cross he unmasked its illegitimacy. Although Jesus unmasked the sacrificial system, he did so precisely by offering himself as a voluntary victim of mob violence. We can dispose of the ancient system—for it is based on a lie—but we cannot dispose of sacrifice.

Believing that Jesus fulfilled the Old Testament sacrificial system, in Hebrews the good news is that now Jesus "is able for all time to save those who approach God through him, since he ever lives to make intercession for them" (Hebrews 7:25). From a different perspective, similar to that in Luke's gospel, the author of Hebrews sees Jesus as the mediator of the new covenant long promised by God (Hebrews 8; cf. Jeremiah 31:33–34).[17]

---

17. Matthew and Mark also emphasize Jesus as the initiator of the new covenant; see Matthew 26:27–29 and Mark 14:22–25.

Then there is John the elder, a disciple and eyewitness of the Christ event who wrote the gospel of John[18] and three short letters bearing his name, and possibly the book of Revelation as well. As mentioned earlier, John's gospel has a strong theological tone, indicating that the writer had thought long and hard about Jesus as Messiah. It is John who uses the phrase "Son of God" as a synonym for "Messiah," but who, lest there be any misunderstanding of the significance of the title, also in his prologue asserts Jesus' divinity in the boldest possible way: "The Word was with God and *the Word was God*" (emphasis added). By contrast, this same John takes great pains to insist on Jesus' true humanity. "Every spirit that acknowledges that Jesus Messiah has come in the flesh is from God" (1 John 4:2). And it is this John who, like Paul, reveals God's motive in sending the Son: "For God so loved the world . . . ." (John 3:16). John also attaches strong ethical consequences to Jesus' death: "Jesus Christ laid down his life for us, and we ought to lay down our lives for one another" (1 John 3:16).

Finally, the seer who penned Revelation, who may or may not have been John the elder, portrays the Christ event in graphic terms as an apocalyptic cosmic conflict and sees the ultimate triumph of God over the malignant forces headed by Rome that rule his age. His good news is the prospect of a new heaven and new earth: no more tears, no more death or mourning or crying or pain, "for the old order of things has passed away" (Revelation 21:4).

Summation

The earliest followers of Jesus felt little need to develop a high theology of the gospel; they were completely enthralled by the reality of their salvation. They knew they had been forgiven. They were experiencing new life in the Spirit. They believed that Jesus Messiah could return at any moment to consummate the reign of God in its fullness. On the other hand, while they had no sharply defined or agreed-upon interpretation of the Christ event, they developed a myriad of ideas and images and metaphors for it, as we have seen.

As decades passed and Jesus did not return as expected, and the world did not come to an end, and the persecution of believers intensified, and the power of Rome seemed greater than ever, questions arose in the minds of the believers about the meaning of their salvation and how

18. Cf. Bauckham, *Eyewitnesses*, chapters 14–17, 358–471.

Jesus of Nazareth had achieved it. In short, their experience was being challenged by the realities of daily life. Thus their questions became the preoccupation of the church fathers and doctors (teachers) of the second to fourth centuries C.E., and again in the eleventh and twelfth centuries, and again in the sixteenth-century Reformation. All these believers pondered at length the many dimensions of the Christ event. One of these dimensions is the means by which human beings have been reconciled to God (2 Corinthians 5:19), or what we have come to think of as the doctrine of the atonement. In the next chapter we will examine three different models that Christians proposed and demonstrate how different worldviews shaped alternative models.

7

Other Gospels

And so we know and rely on the love God has for us.

1 JOHN 4:16

IN THIS CHAPTER WE exit the New Testament environment, leaving be-hind a predominantly Jewish worldview,[1] and enter a Hellenistic one. Initially the distinction between the two is not watertight. Most Greek-speaking Christians of the second century C.E.—and we are speaking only of Christians here—were endowed with a Hellenistic worldview that had been modified significantly by what they had absorbed from the Hebrew Bible and the apostles' writings. Thus their understanding of reality was similar to that of Christians from first-century Jewish backgrounds. But gradually over the next two or three centuries the Christian worldviews of Jewish and Gentile believers diverged. Gentile converts had little interest in a Messianic king of the Jews, but they could relate by virtue of their own religious heritage to the incarnate god who died and rose again to become Lord of the universe. It is unlikely that the philosophical theoriz-ing about the Trinity that we encounter in the Greek-speaking Christian communities during the third and fourth centuries after the Christ event would ever have occurred among the dwindling numbers of Jewish be-lievers in Judea, Samaria, and Galilee.

Further divergences within the expanding Christian community appeared in the fourth and fifth centuries when the Roman Empire, invaded by Huns, Goths, and Visigoths, split into two parts, eastern and western. By 800 the western Latin-speaking worldview differed markedly from the Eastern Orthodox Greek-speaking worldview. Later still, begin-

---

1. For an overview of worldviews, see Smart, *Worldviews: Cross-Cultural Explorations of Human Belief.*

ning with the Renaissance, an early modern Western worldview emerged with vastly different features from those of the preceding medieval worldview. Looking back, we cannot say that the Jewish Christian worldview was sacrosanct and the Hellenistic Christian worldview was wrong, or that the Hellenistic Christian worldview was correct and the subsequent Latin Christian worldview was in error; or that the medieval worldview conveyed reality whereas the Renaissance worldview did not. What we can say with assurance is that the varied worldviews produced different Christian conceptions of salvation and atonement. And it is these—or the most influential of these—that we shall survey in the present chapter.

In the preceding chapter, as we explored the way the New Testament writers communicated their varied understandings of the gospel, we did not distinguish sharply between salvation and atonement, for the New Testament writers themselves did not do so. Even today few Christians distinguish the two, so perhaps we should pause a moment to illustrate the difference between salvation and atonement:

> Imagine a recently convicted drug dealer. While out on bail and awaiting sentencing, he decides to go swimming down at the New Jersey shore. There he is caught up in a rip tide and is about to drown. At that moment the prosecuting attorney, also enjoying a day at the beach, spots the drowning man. Being both decent and strong, the prosecutor goes to his rescue. Having succeeded, however, in this instance the prosecutor wants nothing more to do with the felon. He is satisfied to await the man's incarceration. Salvation has occurred, but no reconciliation. No at-one-ment has been achieved between the two parties. They are not friends, though the felon has indeed been saved.[2]

In this scenario, as in the Christian gospel, salvation is the larger concept. In the gospel atonement is achieved within the greater framework of salvation, which is God's renewal of the human race—and in fact the renewing of the whole universe.

In this chapter and the next we shall be looking at a fascinating array of presentations of the atonement that Christians have formulated down through the centuries. They are many, and they are diverse (again, something that few Christians today seem to be aware of), but for that very reason I offer them to you though not in as much depth as I have

---

2. Scott, *What about the Cross?*, 3.

elsewhere.[3] At the conclusion of chapter 8 I will present my own model of the atonement and its place in the larger scheme of God's salvation.

Atonement is not the whole of the gospel, but traditionally it has been its central feature. Christians have long thought of the atonement as being the very essence of the gospel. Whether one believes that to be true or not, the atonement is important to the larger story, for the atonement is the means by which God reconciles human beings to himself, to one another, and to their natural environment. So in this chapter the atonement will be our focus. But as it was with the apostles, so it is with the writings of later Christians: they did not always make the distinction between salvation and atonement to which I have drawn our attention.

A. Competing Paradigms: Irenaeus, Anselm, and Abelard

IRENAEUS AND THE COSMIC CONFLICT MODEL[4]

Irenaeus' life covers most of the second century after the Christ event. He was a disciple of Polycarp, who in turn was a disciple of John the elder, the presumed author of the gospel of John.[5] Thus it can be fairly inferred that Irenaeus' understanding of the gospel traces back to those who were eyewitnesses of Jesus and participants in his mission. In midlife Irenaeus became bishop of Lyons, the chief city of Gaul (modern France).

In briefest summary, Irenaeus' cosmic worldview included Satan and a host of fallen angels—which the apostle Paul had termed principalities, authorities, powers, thrones, and dominions that rule "this present evil age." Irenaeus believed with the other church fathers that humanity as a whole is in bondage to sin and death as a result of the fall. Beyond that, human beings are captive to Satan, for in Adam they succumbed to Satan's lure in the Garden of Eden. The human race therefore became Satan's rightful possession and must be ransomed or redeemed. This redemption is what God effected through Jesus:

---

3. This chapter and chapter 8 following are a rather severe condensation of my earlier book, What _about_ the Cross? Readers who wish substantially more biographical, biblical, and contextual background on the models of the atonement presented in this chapter may consult that earlier book.

4. The cosmic conflict model is variously known as the patristic, classical, ransom, and more recently, the _Christus victor_ model of the atonement.

5. Cf. Bauckham, _Eyewitnesses_, chapters 14–17, 358–471.

For the Word of God fought and conquered; for He was man contending for our ancestors, and through obedience doing away with disobedience completely. For He bound the strong man, and set free the weak, and endowed His own handiwork with salvation, by destroying sin. For He is a most holy and merciful Lord, and loves the human race.[6]

"Contending for our ancestors," he says. Irenaeus was a Gentile, writing here on behalf of countless prior generations of pagans. Satan is the strong man and Jesus is the stronger. Jesus exercised his strength not by brute force but by obedient submission to his heavenly Father, thereby negating Adam's disobedience. The victory was won by steady conflict with the devil from Jesus' birth onward. It culminated but did not end in the crucifixion. When Satan conspired to have the innocent, obedient Jesus killed, he overstepped his rights over humankind and consequently forfeited them forever. In this way, God acting through his Son liberated the human race and united them with himself.

Among the chief Eastern Fathers who held to this model are Origen, Athanasius, Gregory of Nyssa, and Gregory Nazianzen. Among the chief Western Fathers are Ambrose, Augustine, Leo the Great, and Gregory the Great. Some of these church fathers developed variations on the model, and contemporary Eastern Orthodox Christians still embrace it.

The strengths of the cosmic conflict interpretation of the gospel are apparent. It is based solidly on New Testament scripture. It is less concerned with the salvation of individuals per se than with the restoration or renewal of the world as a whole, a process that Irenaeus referred to as recapitulation.[7] Individuals are saved as a part of this total renewal. The cosmic conflict model's understanding of the atonement was contextually relevant, for persecution by the Roman Empire was severe up through the early fourth century c.e. In our time the model is also contextually relevant because its basic theme of liberation appeals to oppressed peoples everywhere.

---

6. Irenaeus, *Against Heresies*, III:18.6, lines 12–17.

7. Recapitulation: Irenaeus' teaching that Jesus Christ, as the Second Adam, recapitulates, or sums up, the entirety of human experience in his own life of perfect obedience, thereby setting right on behalf of the human race what Adam got wrong.

Anselm and the Satisfaction Model

Anselm, born about 1030 C.E., was an Italian Benedictine monk sent to England and eventually appointed Archbishop of Canterbury. He was the foremost Christian theologian between Augustine in the fifth century and Thomas Aquinas in the thirteenth. And after a thousand years, Anselm was the first to articulate an alternative to the cosmic conflict model of the atonement. In his book *Cur Deus Homo* (Why God became man), Anselm elaborated what has become known as the satisfaction theory. Anselm sets out to answer this question:

> For what cause or necessity, in sooth, did God become man, and by his own death, as we believe and affirm, restore life to the world; when he might have done this by means of some other being, angelic or human, or merely by his will?[8]

Anselm lived in a feudal society based on honor and characterized by relationships of loyalty, obedience, and mutual protection among nobles and vassals. He envisioned God as the great monarch of the universe. Like any sovereign, God cannot overlook dishonor of his Name. But in fact, humanity has dishonored God by flouting his will. It follows that some kind of satisfaction is required to pay the human debt to God's honor. That debt must be paid to balance the scales and restore the broken relationship between human beings and God. Although Anselm acknowledges the love and mercy of God, he thinks primarily in terms of the justice of God. If you do not understand the need for satisfaction, he declares, you grasp neither the holiness of God nor the awfulness of sin.

Sinful humankind is unable to undo the dishonor done to God and make sufficient satisfaction, however. The debt is something far greater than any individual can pay. The only way in which proper satisfaction could be made and humans forgiven their sins would be the coming of a redeemer who is both God and human.

So God became human in Jesus of Nazareth in order that a perfect man might offer the perfect sacrifice (of himself) and make perfect satisfaction to God's abused honor. The God-man Jesus volunteers himself as this sacrifice, becoming a substitute for humankind and satisfying God's honor by his own infinite merit. Once God's honor has been satisfied, he is free to forgive our sins, which he does.

---

8. Anselm, *Cur Deus Homo*, I, 1.

In the satisfaction model, to atone or to reconcile is to make amends for an offense or injury. It is assumed that God cannot simply forgive humanity's sins; that would fail to do justice to God's honor. The success of Anselm's interpretation of the Christ event may be measured by the fact that many Christians today, Roman Catholic and Protestant alike (though not Orthodox), not only accept some version of this model but also are unaware that there are alternative explanations of the meaning of the life and death of the Messiah.

For whatever reason, human beings value justice. Any doctrine that is rooted in God's justice, as Anselm's is, is likely to be regarded as worthy of serious consideration. Similarly human beings instinctively believe in retribution, "an eye for an eye." We feel that life must be balanced; if we do not see or experience a fair balance in this life, we look for it in the next. Further, the sacrament of penance as practiced and well understood in the Latin-speaking churches of the West served as solid grounding for the satisfaction model in Anselm's day and continues to provide support for it in Roman Catholic circles today. The fact that the apostle Paul's epistle to the church in Rome employs forensic (legal) terminology makes it easy for Protestants to interpret the atonement forensically, even though it cannot be concluded that Paul himself was arguing for a concept of satisfaction. Finally, Jesus' offering himself to God as a sacrifice finds ample support in the New Testament, though not necessarily as a sacrifice of satisfaction, much less penal substitution.

ABELARD AND THE SUBJECTIVE MODEL

Within a generation after Anselm had introduced his new understanding of the gospel, Pierre Abelard, the preeminent philosopher-theologian of the early twelfth century, challenged it. A Frenchman, Abelard was born just forty-five years after Anselm, so in large measure he and Anselm inherited the same worldview. Yet in some respects Abelard is a very modern person, far ahead of his time.

We learn Abelard's theory of the atonement from his *Commentary on the Epistle to the Romans*. For Abelard, the direction the atonement takes is neither toward Satan (as with the cosmic conflict model) nor toward God (as with the satisfaction model). Rather, it is toward the individual person in need of wholeness. Abelard's interest lies in showing how God makes human beings whole by "kindling truest love" in them, not by paying a ransom or demanding satisfaction for their sins. Abelard teaches in his commentary on Romans 3:23–26 that when we contemplate the cross we see the greatness of divine love. This contemplation delivers us from fear and ignites in us an answering love (cf. 1 John 4:18–19). Reflecting on Romans 3:26, Abelard says:

> It, however, seems to us that we have been justified in Christ's blood and reconciled to God in this: [that] God has bound us more to himself through love by this *unique grace* held out to us—that God's own son has taken on our nature and in that nature persisted unto death in *instructing* us through word as well as example—to that the true love of anyone kindled by so great a gift would not longer shrink from enduring anything for the sake of God.[9]

In speaking of reconciliation Abelard is speaking of atonement; the two words are virtually synonymous. But what is this unique grace held out to us? The grace is that, having assumed our human nature, Jesus experienced every aspect of human existence, including that which humans live in dread of: death. Abelard speaks of Jesus *instructing* us by word and deed. The word *instructing*, for Abelard, means "to effect life-change by a reconstruction of the human interior."[10] For Abelard the atonement deals not only with past sin but also with present and future sin, and it does so by kindling a great love within us, a love that casts out fear. Abelard continues:

> Our redemption, therefore, is that highest love in us through Christ's Passion that not only frees us from the slavery of sin but also obtains for us the true liberty of the children of God, so that we do all things out of love, rather than fear, of him who has shown us such grace than which no greater can be found.[11]

Many have mistakenly suggested that Abelard is saying that atonement is achieved when the example of Jesus inspires us to be righteous. This, however, is too facile an interpretation. The power of Jesus' example stems from the fact that it is not the life and death of just any innocent victim, but of God in the flesh. It is *God's* love that is being revealed. The death of an innocent victim might well arouse pity and compassion but would not be likely to arouse love. For Abelard, God is uniting humanity with Godself in Jesus' life and death. The love that is manifest in the

---

9. Bond, "Another Look at Abelard's Commentary on Romans 3:26," 2. Emphasis mine.

10. So Bond, Ibid.

11. Ibid.

Messiah's death is not just revealed to us, however, but is made present in us. Atonement, therefore, is God's love residing in us.

Abelard and his concept of the gospel remained controversial throughout his lifetime. A church trial initiated by Bernard of Clairvaux declared Abelard a heretic in 1142. After his death, however, he was rehabilitated, and his subjective model of the atonment remains powerful in limited circles today.

Both the cosmic conflict and satisfaction models acknowledge the love of God as motivating the atoning act. But Abelard goes much further: God's active love *is* the atonement. God's love is what brings the alienated parties together and keeps them together. Abelard's model is leaner than either Irenaeus' or Anselm's but is in some ways more suggestive.

B. Riffs on the Main Themes

AQUINAS AND PENAL SUBSTITUTION

Thomas Aquinas (born 1225) was the greatest of the medieval philosopher-theologians. So far as the atonement is concerned, our main interest is in the fact that Aquinas modified Anselm's presentation by interpreting satisfaction not as a debt of honor as Anselm had, but as a debt of *punishment*. That is, on the cross Jesus bore the wrath of God due to humankind, for which the only just expression is punitive retribution.

Punishment per se was not a new idea. Although Anselm did not emphasize it, the idea was in the air and as we have seen, Abelard reacted against it. But Thomas Aquinas was the first to formally incorporate punishment into atonement theory. Punishment is good for two reasons: it is just; and it is from God.[12] God does not delight in punishment for its own sake, but he does delight in the cosmic order of his justice, which requires it. Sin incurs a debt of eternal punishment insofar as it causes an irreparable disorder in the order of divine justice. Aquinas sees God as offering this remedy:

> Through Christ's Passion we have been delivered from the debt
> of punishment in two ways. Directly, inasmuch as his Passion was
> sufficient and superabundant satisfaction for the sins of the whole

12 Aquinas, *Summa theologiae*, Q. 87, art. 1. For a well thought-out contemporary exposition of punishment, see the New Zealand scholar, Christopher D. Marshall, *Beyond Retribution*, especially chapter 3, "Punishment that Fits: the Purpose and Ethics of Punishment," 97–144. Also Scott, *What about the Cross?*, 193.

human race. Indirectly, insofar as his Passion is the cause of the
forgiveness of sin, upon which the debt of punishment rests.[13]

At Calvary Christ was our substitute, paying the penalty for our sins.[14]
This notion of substitution is Aquinas' special contribution to models of
the atonement. He does not deny Anselm's insistence on the honor of
God. Nevertheless, in his model taken as a whole, he has shifted the focus
to the wrath of God and to punishment as necessary satisfaction.

Aquinas' model, like Anselm's, treats sin with utmost seriousness.
Justice in the West is commonly understood as balancing the moral scales
of the universe. Any atonement model that utilizes this framework is
easily comprehended. In many societies the concept of *lex talionis* (just
deserts) is present. The idea that a god should punish sinners and that
the punishment, which many envision as never-ending hellfire, seems
reasonable. The idea that God's Son suffered punishment vicariously as a
substitute for sinners is both appealing and seems rational to many. New
Testament texts that feature the words *for*, *for us*, and *for our sins* appear
to support the concept, particularly if one reads them through the lens of
penal substitution.

CALVIN AND LIMITED ATONEMENT

Although not the initiator of the Protestant Reformation, John Calvin was
its major systematic theologian. Born in 1509, he was a younger contemporary of Martin Luther. In Calvin's day, Anselm's satisfaction model of
the atonement had been in existence for five hundred years. It had been
contested by Abelard and both defended and modified by Aquinas, who
incorporated the idea of penal substitution within it. Calvin in turn un-
critically embraced penal substitution. Consequently the belief that the
gospel includes the belief that "Christ died to pay the penalty for my sins"
has become *the* atonement model for both Roman Catholics and the majority of Protestants.[15] Today's typical Protestant is unaware of the roots of
the penal substitution idea in medieval Roman Catholic theology.

In spite of Calvin's general agreement with the satisfaction model
as modified by Aquinas, his role as a reformer meant that he necessarily modified it. Working from Scripture and the writings of Augustine,

13. Aquinas, *Summa theologiae*, Q.49, art. 3.

14. Aquinas, *Summa theologiae*, Q.48, art.5.

15. Eastern Orthodox churches still hold to the cosmic conflict model.

Calvin adjusted the doctrine of penal substitution in at least three important respects. First, *contra* Roman Catholics, Calvin denied that penance was an authentic sacrament, but he held that the absolution expressed by the minister of the church was helpful to the penitent's sense of forgiveness. The believer makes amends for sins committed after baptism simply by making his or her individual confession directly to God. Second, while Catholic scholars tended to apply the atonement to the human race at large, Calvin emphasized that Jesus bore the punishment directly for the sin of *each* (though not every) individual. Third, he focused on the limitations of the atonement. God has predestined[16] an elect group from the human race to be saved. It follows, then, that Jesus died to remit the sins of *only* these chosen ones, and that the saving effects of the atonement are limited to them. The doctrine of limited atonement is the unique contribution of Calvin to atonement theory.

Anabaptists and the Transformational Model

Lutherans, Reformed (Calvinists), Anglicans, and Anabaptists emerged from the Protestant Reformation in Europe. Menno Simons (born 1496) is probably the best known of the early Anabaptists. Anabaptists viewed the atonement differently from the other reformers.[17] They spoke of the atonement in terms of liberation and divinization of human beings. By liberation and divinization they meant character transformation through participation in the nature of God. In this they were echoing the emphases of the early church fathers, particularly Irenaeus. And by asserting that the atonement effects a real change in human beings they were echoing Abelard.

To Anabaptists, the atonement meant much more than a legal transaction in the heavenly courtroom as envisioned by Anselm, Aquinas, and Calvin. It meant true "at-one-ment" with God in multiple ways through the reconciling work of Jesus. The work of the Messiah includes the actualizing power of his Spirit whereby people are enabled to appropriate Christ's saving work. The gospel for Anabaptists was not only the good news of salvation but also a series of directives for the Christian on how to live, how to follow Christ. Atonement is the transformation of the believer's life.

---

16. Predestination: (a) the actual divine decree foreordaining each individual to either salvation or damnation; or (b) the doctrine that expounds that decree.

17. Here I follow Finger, "Anabaptist Theology of Atonement."

GROTIUS AND THE MORAL GOVERNMENT MODEL

The Dutchman Hugo Grotius (born 1583) was the outstanding jurist of his day; today he is renowned as the father of international law. Like everyone else from Anselm to Calvin, with the notable exception of Abelard, he viewed the world in forensic categories.

The sole ground of God's administrative justice, according to Grotius, is the "demerit" of sin, but the end purpose is to maintain moral government. God cannot *justly* punish sinless persons, not even Jesus. Against Aquinas, Grotius asserts that even if a sinless person volunteers to accept the punishment due another, this acceptance cannot be construed as an act of justice. With respect to penalty and punishment, Grotius the jurist maintains that there are larger issues involved, for justice must promote virtue and protect the rights of all parties. Thus there are reformatory aspects to consider, as well as the matter of deterrence and the value of making an example. To say that justice consists only of ensuring retributive punishment is too narrow an approach. In fact, judges may, and often do, remit the penalty for a crime if doing so will in fact maintain the integrity of the system as a whole.

This approach opens the way to consider the possibility of a kind of substitution other than the actual infliction of punishment for sin. Grotius suggests that Jesus' suffering (not punishment) on the cross fulfilled the larger purposes of God's moral government by manifesting (a) the divine holiness, justice, and love; (b) the evil of sin; and (c) the certainty of penalty if the offer of forgiveness is rejected.

The question naturally arises: Why is Grotius so concerned to eliminate the punishment aspect? The answer is that if our debt of sin has been fully paid by being fully punished, there can be no genuine forgiveness. Think about it: With no debt, what is there to forgive?

The moral government model shares the strengths and weaknesses of the underlying satisfaction model while providing an alternative to the notion of penal substitution and problems associated with punishment. It takes sin seriously; it asserts unlimited atonement; and holds that atonement is conditional. All this is in contrast with the more common Reformed model and is the basis for contemporary Arminian theology.[18]

---

18. Arminians are a cluster of Protestant groups rooted in the teachings of Arminius, a sixteenth-century Dutch theologian who emphasized, over against Calvin, conditional election, unlimited atonement, and resistible grace.

CAMPBELL'S AND MOBERLY'S PERFECT PENITENCE MODEL

The perfect penitence model of the atonement has never gained much of a following but is worth reviewing briefly. Its creators, the Scot J. McCleod Campbell (*The Nature of the Atonement*, 1856) and his younger disciple, the Englishman R. Campbell Moberly (*Atonement and Personality*, 1901) were eminent theologians of the Victorian era.

In Luke's version of the Great Commission (Luke 24:42), Jesus asserts that repentance is a prerequisite for forgiveness. Campbell and Moberly agree that sinners cannot be perfectly penitent, however, because sin deadens one's conscience and will, making genuine repentance difficult if not impossible. Jesus, being sinless, offered himself as the perfect penitent on behalf of all humankind. Jesus exercised vicarious repentance on behalf of humankind in the following respects:

- In his incarnation he identified himself intimately with the human race.

- At his baptism he identified himself specifically with sinful humanity.

- In the Lord's Prayer he also identified himself with the trespassers.

- By a life of perfect obedience he recapitulated on behalf of humankind what was originally expected of it.

- By submitting to mocking, scourging, and crucifixion he was effectively saying to God on behalf of us all, "This is what sin deserves." He was becoming, in Martin Luther's words, "the one sinner."

At this point we have the atonement as an objective fact: Jesus, as representative man, repents and God forgives. But in order to actually save individuals the atonement must become subjective and transformative. This necessity leads directly to Pentecost (Acts 2). "Apart from Pentecost no intelligible link unites man with Calvary."[19] Pentecost is the perpetual extension of the incarnation. Additionally, these writers note, Jesus embraced the role of high priest. In the ancient Hebrew system the high priest, after confessing the sins of the people, turned to them with these words, "Peace be with you." These were also the first words of Jesus to his disciples following his resurrection (Luke 24:36). Moberly observes that the book of Hebrews makes no mention of Christ's resurrection; it moves directly from the cross to the heavenly sanctuary.

---

19. Moberly, *Atonement and Personality*, 153.

Critics maintain that penitence (humble recognition of one's own faults or sins, with appropriate sorrow) could not be really true of Jesus if he were indeed sinless. I personally doubt that assessment. Empathy was a quality Jesus had in abundance; and empathy, I suspect, makes it possible for a person to share what others feel even when the respective situations of the two differ.

KIERKEGAARD'S EXISTENTIAL MODEL

At this point in our survey we are well into the modern Western environment with its emphasis on individualism and subjectivity. As Christians move within the modern culture we can expect them to develop new thinking about the atonement. Campbell and Moberly were examples of this innovation; Søren Kierkegaard is another. Kierkegaard (1813–55) is the Danish Christian philosopher who is regarded as the founder of existentialism, a way of thinking that became very influential in the twentieth century.

Kierkegaard believed that human existence has a set of underlying themes and characteristics: anxiety, dread (German: *Angst*), freedom, awareness of death, the consciousness of existing. He asserted that "truth is subjectivity," that is, human beings can be truly understood only from the inside, in terms of their own experienced reality and dilemmas—not from the outside, in terms of biological, psychological, or other scientific theories of human nature. A key theme in his writings is despair, which he equates with sin, most clearly in *The Sickness Unto Death*. A person is in despair when she or he is alienated from God. In this state one loses one's true identity. This self is the lifework that God judges for eternity. It is recovered only in reconciliation with God, which comes about as God grants the gift of faith. This gift must then be exercised repeatedly and habitually.

Applied to the atonement,[20] Kierkegaard's existential approach means that Jesus' torture-death (and his life's experience leading up to it) achieves two things. First, Jesus enables us to hear him when he speaks to us with *authority* because he has experienced the full range of life experiences, including suffering and death, which we ourselves face. Second, Jesus enables us to hear him when he speaks words of *comfort and encouragement*—the "help" in the quotation following:

---

20. I am relying here on William McDonald, "Kierkegaard," *Stanford Encyclopedia of Philosophy*.

> Because he himself suffered when he was tempted [tried, tested],
> he is able to help those who are being tempted (Hebrews 2:18).

In Kierkegaard's view, the atonement is achieved and we are reconciled to God because we are helped through Christ's life and death to see and respond in faith to God's love in the midst of life's absurdities. Kierkegaard did not, however, address the broader array of questions that we have found to be requisite to a full-blown theory of the atonement. I have included his central concept here because of its obvious connection with Abelard's subjective model and because existentialism has been so influential in Christian circles during the past century.[21]

---

21 For a fuller exposition, see Scott, *What about the Cross?*, 119–20; also the *Stanford Encyclopedia of Philosophy* article referenced above.

8

Contemporary Models

And through him God was pleased to reconcile to himself all things.

<small>COLOSSIANS 1:20</small>

IN THIS CHAPTER, WHICH the reader will find mercifully brief, I want to describe the way some notable contemporary Christian thinkers interpret the atonement and to a lesser extent, the larger topic of God's salvation. I am focusing here on the last third of the twentieth century as it eased its way toward the twenty-first. This is the era in which postmodernism[1] has muscled its way to the forefront, at least in the Western world. How can we communicate the gospel to this new generation?

RENÉ GIRARD'S SCAPEGOAT MODEL

The renowned French anthropologist, literary critic and cultural theorist, René Girard, has proposed a highly original interpretation of the atonement. It is a logical application of his well-known but still controversial mimetic theory of the origin of religion and culture, and of the scapegoat mechanism that is an integral part of the theory. Girard's theory grew out of his research into the modern novel,[2] and then into primordial culture, which, he contends, originated in an act of collective violence, specifically a founding murder afterward covered up. The secular presentation of Girard's theory is found in his *Violence and the Sacred* and *The Scapegoat*.

---

1. Postmodernism: a wide-ranging term applied to literature, art, architecture, philosophy, and cultural and literary criticism. Postmodernism is "post" because it denies the existence of ultimate principles, and lacks the optimism derived from a scientific, philosophical, or religious truth that can explain everything to everybody—a characteristic of the so-called "modern" mind. (Definition supplied by www.pbs.org/faithandreason/gen gloss/post m-body.html, para. 1–2).

2. See his *Deceit, Desire, and the Novel: Self and Other in Literary Structure.*

In the course of his scientific research Girard became a Christian. The application of his theory to Christian faith is found in his *Things Hidden Since the Foundation of the World* and *I See Satan Fall Like Lightning*.

We begin with mimesis. Mimesis is the Greek word for imitation or re-presentation. According to Girard, individuals from birth onward obtain their desires by picking them up from or patterning them after the behavior of other people. This imitation is something that occurs instinctively, a product of the evolutionary process. Because of the mimetic nature of desire—especially acquisitive desire (i. e., covetousness)—rivalry and violence inevitably occur between individuals (cf. James 1:14–15.). Parenthetically I should note that Girard's mimetic theory has found substantial support in recent years from the so-called hard sciences.[3]

Sooner or later the rivalries intensify and spread to all members of the society. Social violence reaches crisis proportions: all are set against all. When this crisis happens, social order is restored by fingering an innocent scapegoat who is murdered. Thereupon the community is reunited and peace is restored. This initial murder is the basis of each civilization, including that in the biblical narrative of Genesis 4:17–24. In order to control ongoing violence and in gratitude for the restitution of civil order, societies redefine the scapegoat as a god,[4] and establish taboos and rituals—the primary ritual being an reenactment of the original murder, as with the Christian Mass. This repetitive scapegoating is the origin of sacrifice as a religious ritual as well as the origin of culture.

Since mimesis is endemic to human nature, however, the cycle inevitably renews itself. For the scapegoat mechanism to work effectively, the community must convince itself that the scapegoat really is guilty of a crime. Consequently, social order depends on concealing both the innocence of the victim and the scapegoat mechanism itself. The trial and crucifixion of Jesus is a perfect example of this process. Although Jesus was clearly innocent, a trial judge pronounced him guilty. According to Girard's model, Jesus' life and death as recorded in the gospels saves us

---

3. Cf. Depoortere, *Christ in Postmodern Culture,* 64–74.

4. Girard sees this scapegoating mechanism as the origin of polytheism. "Polytheism is a product of the victimary mechanism, the result of the many foundational victims which produce more and more false gods, but are nonetheless able to protect the community of believers because of the sacrificial order they enforce. In the archaic world, every time the scapegoat mechanism works, a new god emerges." Girard, *Evolution and Conversion,* 198.

by *unmasking* the mechanism of victimage and making it apparent to all. That is, the gospel narratives expose the falsehood inherent in Jesus' trial and conviction.

Once the unmasking has occurred, we are free—impelled, in fact—to construct a different social order, one based on nonviolence, one built by identifying with the self-giving victim rather than by excluding and lynching the victim. Through imitating Christ and others who are following Christ, we learn to receive our identities as human beings through an entirely nonrivalous, nonenvious, nongrasping practice of life.

Observing the course of history, Girard notes that because people in the time of Jesus were living within the framework of sacrificial religion, Jesus' death on the cross was inevitably understood as just another bloody sacrifice. Consequently a "sacrificial" Christianity emerged and God was thereby "reinfused with violence." And thus a "Christian" culture evolved, with a new sacrificial order and such new scapegoats as Jews and witches. In this way, Jesus' unmasking of the violent basis of culture has itself been masked. "Many centuries must elapse before the subversive and shattering truth contained in the gospels can be understood worldwide," Girard says.[5]

I am embarrassed by trying to convey in a few paragraphs the essence of a theory about which scores of symposia have been convened and hundreds of articles and books have been written during the past half-century. I presented a fuller description in *What about the Cross?* But the limits I have imposed on *The Renewal of All Things* require this present brevity. In the chapters ahead we will have more than one occasion to refer back to Girard and his atonement model.

Robin Collins's Incarnational Model

Robin Collins is professor of philosophy at Messiah University, an Anabaptist institution in Pennsylvania. Building on Girard's theory, Collins offers an alternative model of the atonement that, he claims, has a stronger basis in Scripture and church tradition. Collins begins by postulating that salvation consists in "an ongoing participation in the life of God as it exists in Christ."[6]

The life of Christ is both divine and fully human. Because it is human, we can participate in it. We do this by participating in Christ's

---

5. Girard, *Things Hidden*, 252.

6. Collins, "A New and Orthodox Theory," lines 3–4.

"subjectivity." Subjectivity is a central concept for Collins. He means by it the attitudes, orientations, perspectives, commitments, and values that make Christ who he is as an individual and us who we are as individuals. According to Collins, the "fallen" human subjectivity characteristic of the world-system is based on the denial of the subjectivity established by Christ on the cross. That is to say, the godly qualities Jesus revealed in voluntarily submitting to an unmerited crucifixion are the opposite of the qualities promoted in our fallen world order. By mimetically participating in the new subjectivity established on the cross we are redemptively transformed (always an Anabaptist theme). Christ's subjectivity is integrated into our own subjectivity. This integration in turn undercuts the entire world-system of psychological, social and spiritual bondage in our personal and social lives, liberating us for transformed lives.

J. Denny Weaver's Nonviolent Model

Weaver, author of *The Non-Violent Atonement*, is professor emeritus of history and religion at Bluffton University in Ohio. That the atonement models of Girard, Collins, and Weaver are all nonviolent in character should not surprise us, given the horrific violence of the twentieth century, continued now into the twenty-first. This violence has caused many Christians, including myself, to question the violence implicit in traditional portrayals of the atonement.

Weaver's model is a revisioning of the very early cosmic conflict model, which he renames "narrative Christus Victor."[7] Surprisingly, he begins his exposition with the book of Revelation. There Jesus is portrayed as both Lamb and Lion, the nonviolent victim of evil and its conqueror. In spite of the violent battle scenes depicted in Revelation, which Weaver considers metaphorical, the victory of the reign of God is not achieved by divine or churchly violence. The Lamb-Lion conquers through his own self-giving and the selfless witness of the church's martyrs (Revelation 12:11). Weaver turns next to the gospels, wherein he finds the true nonviolent character of God revealed in the life and ministry of Jesus:

> Jesus was ready to die and he was willing to die. It was not a death, however, that was required as compensatory retribution for the

---

7. Weaver, *Non-Violent Atonement*, 7.

sins of his enemies and his friends. Rather, it was a death that resulted from fulfillment of his mission about the reign of God.[8]

Continuing his survey, Weaver discusses the relevance of the Jewish
sacrificial tradition, a tradition critiqued by the Old Testament prophets
and subverted by the New Testament book of Hebrews. In his final chapter
Weaver evaluates various defenses of the satisfaction model, traditional
and contemporary, and finds them inadequate.

In addition to his own work, Weaver makes a valuable contribution to our exploration of models of the atonement by devoting three
substantial chapters in his book to liberation theologies of the atonement.
To these we now turn.

JAMES CONE AND BLACK LIBERATION MODELS

Cone, author of *God of the Oppressed*, insists that the gospel has a different
meaning for black people than it has for white people. That meaning centers on freedom or liberation from domination. When black people read
the Bible, Cone says, they do not find a docile Jesus teaching a spiritual
salvation. They discover Jesus the liberator, calling his people to freedom
and working for their liberation. Jesus' salvation is not so much a matter
of inner feeling as an actual liberation from the conditions of oppression
in which African Americans live.[9]

Applied to the atonement, this concept of freedom means that
true friendship and fellowship with God is now possible because Jesus,
through his death and resurrection, has freed us from the "principalities
and powers and rulers" of this present world.[10] Liberation is what God
does to effect reconciliation; and without the former the latter is impossible. From this recital it is clear that Cone's black atonement model is a
reformulation of the ancient Christus Victor or cosmic conflict motif.

Weaver next draws attention of a second generation of black theologians exemplified by Garth Kasimu Baker-Fletcher, who writes:

---

8. Ibid., 42.

9. These pages are being written during the American presidential campaign of 2008,
during which Dr. Jeremiah Wright, the pastor of one of the candidates, is being widely
reviled as a "liberation theologian."

10. "Principalities, powers, and rulers" in contemporary theology includes the social,
economic, and psychological forces that shape our corporate cultures.

Our Afrikanity [*sic*] is theologically based on an Xodus [*sic*] doctrine of Atonement, which affirms God's colorfulness as an aspect of spiritual joy. Christ's death and resurrection were not to display the redemptive power of unmerited suffering, but to open up the possibilities for human beings to become God's "new creation" (2 Corinthians 5:17), for peace to be made between formerly warring peoples (Ephesians 2:11-22), and for genuine reconciliation to occur. Christians ought to be joyful about these things, not about the suffering, pain, torture and death of Jesus on a Cross.[11]

ROSEMARY RUETHER AND FEMINIST ATONEMENT MODELS

Just as black theologians criticize the traditional "white" interpretations of the atonement for accommodating violence and slavery, feminist theologians criticize the traditional expositions for accommodating patriarchy and male supremacy.[12] Rosemary Ruether argues that the image of Christ on the cross has been used by preachers to suggest that in order for women to be of value, they should likewise sacrifice themselves. This interpretation in turn has conditioned women to suffer in silence when sexually abused and to remain in marriages in which they are battered. Children too become victims of abuse. All three major traditional doctrines of the atonement are complicit in shaping this passive acceptance of abuse, Ruether argues.

She concludes that Jesus did not come to suffer and to die. Rather, he saw his mission as one of good news to the poor, the liberation of the captives. Jesus' method was not to kill the powers but to convert them into solidarity with those they had formerly despised and victimized. Suffering and death are not redemptive; rather, suffering is "the risk that one takes when one struggles to overcome unjust systems whose beneficiaries resist change."[13]

Feminist theologians, for the most part, pattern their understandings of the gospel and atonement after Abelard's model, reformulating it in various ways. The majority of them focus on redemption through relationship and highlight the role of Christian community in this regard.

11. G. K. Baker-Fletcher, *Xodus*, 188, cited in Weaver, *Non-Violent Atonement*, 118.

12. Patriarchy: social organization marked by the supremacy of the father in the clan or family and the reckoning of descent and inheritance in the male line (New Britannica-Webster Dictionary).

13. Ruether, *Women and Redemption*, 125, cited in Weaver, 125.

Delores Williams and Womanist Theologies of Atonement

Womanist theologians are African-Americans. Consequently they have a historical experience that differs significantly from both their black theologian brothers and their white feminist sisters. In her book *Sisters in the Wilderness*, Williams employs Hagar, Abraham's concubine, as her central image, and focuses on Hagar's role as surrogate to reflect on African-American women's historic role.

As understood by black women, Hagar's story is that of female slaves, the women whose destiny is and has been shaped by the problems and desires of their owners. For Sarah, Abraham's wife, motherhood is a privilege that will grant her status in the world. For Hagar, her concubine motherhood is a coerced experience, forced upon her by another woman, no less! After the birth of Ishmael, Hagar and her son escape into the wilderness, making herself "the first female in the Bible to liberate herself from oppressive power structures.[14]

In the wilderness, Hagar and Ishmael were facing death when God came to them. As a matter of survival, God told Hagar to return with Ishmael to the tent of Abraham and Sarah. The second time Hagar left the house of bondage, God provided Hagar with a new vision so that she could use her own resources to survive. Womanist theologians, therefore,

> ... must show that redemption can have nothing to do with any kind of surrogate or substitute role Jesus was reputed to have played in a bloody act that supposedly gained victory over sin and/or evil .... Rather, it seems more intelligent and more scriptural to understand that redemption had to do with God, through Jesus, giving humankind new vision to see the resources for positive, abundant relationship life.[15]

Caleb F. Heppner's Covenantal Model

Heppner, an Anabaptist theologian, presents an intriguing model of the atonement. According to Heppner, the gospels, if read through the lens of a covenantal relationship between God and God's people, suggest that Jesus' passion was neither substitutionary nor exemplary but mediatorial.

14. Williams, *Sisters,* 19, cited in Weaver, 161.
15. Ibid., 165, quoted by Weaver, *Non-Violent Atonement,* 165.

Jesus was the great mediator of a promissory covenant[16] that had existed for all time between God and humankind:

> For there is one God and one mediator between God and human beings, Christ Jesus, himself human, who gave himself as a ransom for all people (I Timothy 2:5–6a).

This covenant was fulfilled not by the Mosaic law but by the gracious promise made to Abraham before the law was ever given (Galatians 3:16–18; cf. Genesis 12:2–3). Heppner cites with approval Australian theologian Robert Brinsmead:

> God's justice is based on God being true to what he promised in his gracious covenant . . . . This biblical idea of justice, first presented in the Old Testament, is beautiful and powerful in its simplicity. Nevertheless, Western theology insists that justice must somehow be related to what a person deserves.[17]

God's promissory covenant is a unilateral commitment or promise to act toward God's chosen partner with overwhelming kindness and generosity. Jesus is God carrying out what divine love had pledged to do.

> In the case of a will [= covenant], it is necessary to prove the death of the one who made it, because a will is in force only when somebody has died . . . this is why even the first covenant was not put into effect without blood (Hebrews 9:17–18).

The author of Hebrews is referencing the Mosaic covenant, which was a covenant of mutual obligation. By dying, Jesus bore the curse due to the transgression under the first covenant. Heppner asserts that in Jesus' resurrection God fulfilled the covenant promises to restore all people to a right relationship with God and with one another.

For Heppner, the meaning of the atonement is that God has executed the promised liberation justice for everyone—and especially those who are forsaken, destitute, and excluded. The cross symbolized an ancient

16. Covenant: a binding agreement between two or more parties. It is a concept used in the Bible to describe the relationship between God and humankind. Some covenants are based on the ancient "royal grant" model. They oblige only the superior party, and are called promissory or unconditional covenants. The covenants God made with Noah, Abraham, and David fit this model. In these cases, God alone binds himself by a solemn oath to keep the covenant. Heppner assumes that such an unconditional promissory covenant was made by God with Adam (Roberts, "Covenant," para. 1–4).

17. Heppner, "A Covenantal View of Atonement," para. 18.

covenantal transaction familiar to all Hebrew people (Genesis 15). Jesus' death put the covenant, or will, into effect. His resurrection confirms that he is the eternal mediator of reconciliation with God achieved apart from the Law, that is, human effort, and entirely by grace.

Michael Winter's Intercessor Model

Winter is a professor at the London campus of Notre Dame University. He defines reconciliation or atonement not in terms of legal concepts but as the rebuilding of a relationship of love and trust that has been destroyed by some form of infidelity or exploitation. The definition applies not only to the breach between the human race and God but also to the ruptures between estranged parties within the human family. Thus his model has affinities with a number of those we have heretofore discussed, including Abelard, Campbell and Moberly, feminist theologians, and Heppner.

Winter actually begins with Campbell's and Moberly's perfect penitence model, and their emphasis on the need for sincere repentance. "Repentance and conversion is the first stage in rebuilding a shattered relationship," he says.[18] He then posits that in the process of rebuilding the shattered relationship between God and humans, neither ransom nor compensation nor satisfaction nor anything similar is required but one thing only:

> On this matter the teaching of Jesus is unambiguously clear: forgiveness must be asked for. Nothing more or less is required than the sinner's requesting readmission to the love of God, or reconciliation with his brother.[19]

Winter claims that practically the whole of the gospels could be cited in support of this assertion. He himself cites numerous passages,[20] and concludes, "Every instance in the teaching and activity of Jesus where forgiveness is sought shows that individuals are welcomed back to the love of God if there merely ask for it sincerely." Theoretically, this petition might be made to God by each of the countless millions of human beings, past and present. In reality, it has been made by Jesus, acting as spokesperson or intermediary for the human race.

18. Winter, *Atonement*, 88.
19. Ibid., 89.
20. Ibid., 102–14.

A UNIVERSALIST MODEL OF ATONEMENT

This is my own model. Strictly speaking, it is not new, of course; but perhaps the way I am framing it has some originality. Because I will be elaborating on it in Part III following, I will present it here in précis fashion, forgoing the associated biblical references and other supporting arguments. I apologize if this brevity fails to convey the model's inherent passion.

In a nutshell: All members of *H. sapiens,* the human race, who have ever lived or ever will live have been reconciled to God. This reconciliation has taken place in spite of our having become spiritually distanced from God by a sinful nature acquired through long evolutionary history as well as by volitional acts personally committed during our lifetimes. The reality of the atonement is expressed in this way as a doctrine. Our actual *experience* of the atonement is one of guilt forgiven, shame erased, moral pollution cleansed, and peace with God. It is received by faith as a gift from God. It does not require a detailed explanation (that is, a theory or model); nevertheless, a rational explanation of just how this atonement is achieved adds to our appreciation and enjoyment.

In broadest terms, the universalist model posits that the election of the human race for atonement and salvation in Christ had been made from "before the foundation of the world" and achieved in the Christ event. In the Christ event God united himself to humanity and humanity to himself. But if one requires a specific occasion within the total Christ event[21] in which atonement was revealed as such, one might point to the moment on the cross when the Messiah, the Son of God and Second Adam, asked the Father to forgive. Unquestionably, the Father did just that. The Father would not have done otherwise, if we are to believe Jesus' own testimony:

> Which of you, if your son asks for bread, will give him a stone? Or
> if he asks for a fish, will give him a snake? (Matthew 7:9–10).

Reflecting on the text above in the light of Jesus' crucifixion, the English poet John Donne (1572–1631) asked and answered his own question:

21. For me, the Christ event includes, within the context of this discussion of the atonement, the life, ministry, death, resurrection and ascension of Jesus of Nazareth. I reserve discussion of the second coming of Christ to a later discussion of the larger theme of salvation and the renewal of all things.

What if this present were the worlds last night?
Marke in my heart, O Soule, where thou does dwell,
The picture of Christ crucified, and tell
Whether that countenance can thee afright.
Tears in his eyes quench the amassing light,
Blood fills his frownes, which from his pierc'd head fell.
And can that tongue adjudge thee unto hell,
Which pray'd forgivenesse for his foes fierce spight?
Holy Sonnet XIII [22]

Some individuals responding to the proclamation of the Gospel experience the reality of the atonement during their earthly lifetimes. The remainder will experience it at the day of judgment or on some other postmortem occasion unknown to us. Atonement as part of the larger scheme of salvation is assured by Jesus' resurrection as the firstfruits of the renewing of the human race and all creation; also by his ascension to "the right hand of God," where he continues to intercede for humankind; and by the gift of his Spirit. Meanwhile, the Spirit is working to renew the human race and the whole creation in line with the Creator's original purposes. The vindication of this model will be revealed in the resurrection of the dead and in the participation of the human race in the reign of God in eternity.

22. *The Complete Poetry and Selected Prose of John Donne.* Modern Library Series, edited by Charles M. Coffin.

PART THREE

Universal Redemption

9

Biblical and Patristic[1] Bases

For as all die in Adam, so all will be made alive in Christ.

1 CORINTHIANS 15:22

L ET US PAUSE FOR a moment and review the thread of my discussion to this point. I began by justifying belief in God and in evolution as the means whereby God created the universe as we know it. But did God have a particular purpose in creating the universe by evolutionary means? I affirmed that God did and that the purpose was twofold. First, to produce persons made in God's image, designed with the capacity to truly and freely love as God loves—and thus to form with God an extended[2] eternal community of mutual love (Ephesians 1:4). Now it is contradictory to suppose that the ability to love God truly and freely could have been imposed by fiat. So I suggested that the capacity for free will, love, and rationality is built into the very nature of the evolutionary process from the start. This freedom inevitably leads to distortions, which is why God's ultimate intention from before the foundation of the world is the renewal of all things, including *H. sapiens.*

Second, the process of evolution would also create persons with the capacity to rationally share in the governance of the world and by implication, the universe in its present form (Genesis 2:19–20).[3] Note the phrase "in its present form." This expression is meant to draw our atten-

---

1. Patristic: related to the early church fathers, both Greek and Latin.

2. "Extended," because such a community already exists eternally within the Trinity.

3. The Hebrews and other ancient peoples conceived of angels as sharing in the governance of the universe, or at least of this world. I am personally doubtful of the existence of an angelic realm, but if it exists, I assume it is provisional, pending the full development of *H. sapiens.*

tion to the fact that although the world and wider universe evolved as they did in order to produce human persons made in God's image, the universe in its present form is not God's ultimate intention. Rather, God's ultimate design has always been "the new heaven and the *new* earth" (Revelation 21:1, emphasis added), which will be inhabited by the eternal community of mutual love and which could not be realized apart from perfected human beings. In the age to come, perfected human beings will be coworkers with God in the perfecting of the universe, which has been distorted by the very process of evolution that created it.

In Chapter 2 we also explored the ways in which the Genesis narrative is compatible with evolution and further, how evolution actually illumines some aspects of that foundational narrative, such as the origin of evil, the original sin, and the fall. In Chapter 3 we followed the biblical narrative through the rest of the Old Testament, observing how God dealt with the human disposition to sin—which I defined as pursuing ends not in accord with God's twofold purpose in creation. We took note of God's covenantal relationships with the representative figures of Adam, Noah and Abraham, Moses and David. We traced God's dealings with the tribes and nation of Israel, through whom God intended to bless all nations. We saw how their history incorporated triumph and folly, exile and return, and how God nevertheless maintained relationships with them in spite of their sinfulness, as God did with nations of the world other than Israel. That discussion led us in Chapter 4 to a summary survey of the Axial Age, which coincided with the era of Israel's prophets but also saw the emergence of the major world religions familiar to us today.

All this development was preparatory to the Christ event, described from a bottom-up perspective in Chapter 5. In Chapter 6 we explored from the New Testament record the ways in which the apostles and other notable disciples attempted to discern the meaning of the Christ event as they formulated the gospel they proclaimed to the world. This is the process we term contextualization. We found no definitive formulation of the atonement in the early church, but rather a host of images and metaphors—kernels of what in the centuries ahead would become a veritable harvest of theories or models of the atonement. We surveyed eighteen of these models in Chapters 7 and 8, concluding with a précis of my own atonement model, which incorporates the concept of universal atonement or salvation.

It may be useful to remind the reader of my earlier distinction between salvation and atonement. A drowning woman may be saved by a rescuer apart from any intention of establishing a personal relationship with her. So rescue and communion are two different though potentially related events. Similarly, in my perspective salvation is the larger concept and includes the whole universe. Atonement is limited to the human race and has to do with uniting humankind with God the Father (at-one-ment)[4]—that atonement or reunion being the means of ultimate salvation for *H. sapiens* and eventually the whole creation.

This distinction is a real one, but since the two concepts are nestled one within the other, it will not always be possible in our discussion to maintain a sharp distinction between them. In this current chapter and the next, we will consider the prospect of universal salvation and atonement together. In subsequent chapters we will explore the ethical, socio-political, and missional dimensions of the renewal of all things. Finally, I will present a gospel for the twenty-first century in Chapter 12, entitled "My Gospel," the good news of God's reign insofar as I have been able to understand and appropriate it.

Background of Universal Redemption

We begin by recognizing that in the Genesis narrative God judged his creation to be good, and with the emergence of the human race, *very* good. This goodness does not imply that either nature or humankind is perfect (they are still evolving), only that the creation was well suited to God's intended purpose and met with his approval. By embedding free will into the material nature of the universe, as the evolutionary scenario suggests, God knew that deviation from his purpose was inevitable; but there is no reason to believe that God proposed that if creation strayed from its end God would abandon or destroy it altogether. In fact, the story of the deluge and its aftermath presents this notion as a temptation (Genesis 6:6–7) that God rejected. A significant part of God's creation (that is, *H. sapiens*) was made in God's image, after all.

---

4. In contrast with the model of Eric Stetson, my model of the atonement has to do with reconciliation rather than making amends. Cf. Stetson, *Christian Universalism*, 20. Stetson's understanding of atonement appears to have incorporated certain Gnostic features into his theology. His book is otherwise a lucid exposition of Christian universalism, however.

It is essential to note that God values his creation. God sustains it, providentially provides for it, and most importantly, loves it. God loves most especially the human race, with which he initiated personal fellowship. The Bible read closely reveals that God will not destroy his creation, though it is certain that love will impel him ultimately to destroy the accumulated evil in it as he renews all things. Meanwhile, however, in space and time there are attending "curses" attached to any deviation from God's original purpose by either nature or humankind that require God's judgments (Genesis 3:15, 21). But these judgments ensure salvation, not damnation.

The Christian tradition recognizes that the world—and by extension the universe—has deviated from God's original purpose. The apostle Paul refers to this deviation in Romans 8:18–24. He notes that the creation groans under its subjection to the bondage of decay—think of the second law of thermodynamics. Paul sees this subjection as within the will of God; I described it earlier as inherent in the way God created the universe through evolution.

Paul goes on to affirm that the creation will be renewed only in association with the freedom and glory of the [redeemed] children of God. Paul grounds this redemption in the Christ event, and with this the various major Christian traditions (Orthodox, Roman Catholic, and the various Reformation traditions) agree. Ultimate redemption is presumed to occur at the second coming of Christ (Acts 1:11), followed by the resurrection of the dead (1 Corinthians 15) and the appearance of a new heaven and a new earth (Revelation 21).

The world includes the human race, of course. But when it comes to determining the extent of the redemption afforded *H. sapiens* through the Christ event, there is vast disagreement. As we have seen, some Christians believe in limited atonement. Jesus died only for the elect, they insist, and the elect are relatively few. Other Christians maintain that the atonement is unlimited. Jesus' death atoned for everyone; therefore it is potentially but not inevitably efficacious for all persons. They maintain that an individual as the possessor of free will is free to refuse the proffered atonement. In either case, however, the Christian accepts the reality that the vast majority of all human beings who have ever lived have perished or will perish. Only a minority—those who have heard the gospel and have confessed Jesus as Savior and Lord—will enter the kingdom of heaven.

Naturally, this scenario has some variations. For example, some Christians believe that sincere, humble persons of any religion or no religion who have not had an opportunity to hear about Jesus may yet be saved by God's grace. "To those who by persistence in doing good seek glory, honor and immortality, [God] will give eternal life" (Romans 2:7; cf. 4:11–12). But even with such a proviso, most Christians agree that "small is the gate and narrow the road that leads to life, and only a few find it" (Matthew 7:14).

The model I am proposing sets forth a third alternative: God determined from eternity past not only to redeem the universe but also to save and renew the human race in toto—everyone who has ever lived or ever will live. Why would God assign to the scrap heap most members of a species that was the end product of God's long creative process?[5] Especially a species made in his own image. Rather, God purposed to reconcile every wayward will to himself. In the Christ event God indeed made manifest the reconciliation of the world, including all human beings, to himself (2 Corinthians 5:19).

This is clearly a minority proposal—some will call it heretical—so I will do my best to make the case within the narrow constraints of this chapter and the next along three lines. First, I will explore with the reader the extent to which there is specific biblical support for the notion of universal redemption in both the Old and New Testaments. Second, I will draw attention to the fact that the prospect of universal salvation was well established among the church fathers of the first five centuries. And third, in Chapter 10 I will approach the matter philosophically, as it were, contesting the traditional notions on various grounds. In agreement with some notable evangelical universalists, I will argue that the biblical, patristic, and rational support we find justifies abandoning the traditional positions and embracing the joyful expectation of universal renewal. It goes without saying that if universal salvation is God's intent, then the atonement also is universal in its effect.

---

5. One good friend has suggested that this sentence, particularly the word *majority*, is a bit "over the top," since up to one-third of the world's population today is professedly Christian. But his calculation overlooks the fact that that this fraction applies only to the past two or three generations at best, and many of those professing Christians are only nominally so. There have been hundreds, perhaps thousands, of generations of *H. sapiens* since "Adam." Only a tiny percentage has professed Jesus Christ as Lord and Savior, and these only within the past few thousand years.

The Old Testament

To those with eyes to see, the clear thrust of the Old Testament narrative is universal, meaning it has the entire world with all its peoples as its horizon. The Old Testament narrative begins with the creation of the universe and the human race, followed by a moral fall and the promise of redemption. All this within the first three chapters of Genesis, in which Adam and Eve, the only two human actors in the story, represent all humanity. After the deluge, God renews his covenant with all humanity; this time Noah represents the human race. The table of nations recorded in Gen 10 ensures that God, even in these early chapters, is concerned and involved with the human family as a whole.

The subsequent singling out of one family, Abraham's, alerts us to a change in God's missional strategy but it does not indicate a change in the universal direction of the narrative. On the contrary, Abraham's call and the promise associated with it is specifically directed to "all peoples on earth" (Genesis 12:3). God established a special relationship with Abraham, Isaac, Jacob, and Joseph. Yet although God's covenant was made with Isaac, God did not abandon Abraham's other son, Ishmael. "God was with the boy" and promised to grow him "into a nation" (Genesis 21: 20, 13).[6]

Human nature being what it is, and human societies being what they are, Jacob's sons choose to leave the promised land and reside in Egypt. There they are subsequently enslaved. God rescues them in the exodus and leads them back to the promised land. The exodus is Israel's salvation, but the mission of God remains the same: the blessing of all the nations. Christopher Wright approvingly quotes John Goldingay: "Israel's story (the world's story) is not ultimately about deliverance but about blessing" [to all the nations].[7]

Although the biblical narrative centers on Israel, this focus does not mean that God was uninvolved with other nations. It is hard to overestimate the significance of the questions Amos poses as coming from God:

> "Are not you Israelites the same to me as the Cushites?" declares the Lord. "Did I not bring Israel up from Egypt, the Philistines from Caphtor and the Arameans from Kir?" (Amos 9:7).

6. The Arab nations of today claim descent from Abraham by way of Ishmael.

7. Goldingay, *Old Testament Theology*, Vol. 1, *Israel's Gospel*, 471, cited in C. Wright, *Mission of God*, 226.

Working through the Psalms, Christopher Wright summarizes God's relationship with the heavens, the earth and all the nations as follows:[8]

- The Lord made them (Psalm 33:6–9; Jeremiah 10:10–12).

- The Lord owns them (Psalms 24:1 and 89:11; Deuteronomy 10:14).

- The Lord governs them (Psalm 33:10–11; Isaiah 40:22–24).

- The Lord calls them to account (Psalm 33:13–15).

- The Lord speaks truth to them (Psalms 33:4; 119:160; Isaiah 45:19).

- The Lord loves all that he has made (Psalm 145:9, 13, 17).

- The Lord saves all who turn to him (Psalm 36:6; Isaiah 45:22).

- The Lord guides them (Psalm 67:4).

- The Lord will bring them peace (Psalm 46:8–10).

Apart from the above, numerous other psalms reflect a universalist perspective, e. g., Psalms 22:27;[9] 47:9;[10] 67:4;[11] 72:17;[12] 86:9;[13] and 145:8–12. As noted earlier, King Solomon recognized that the temple he had built for Israel's worship would also attract foreigners from abroad. The prophet Isaiah would subsequently cite as God's word that the temple was meant to be "a house of prayer for all nations" (Isaiah 56:7). I recall that as a young missionary in Cyprus, visiting Egypt for the first time, I was intrigued by such passages as Isaiah 19:24–25; 25:6–8; 45:22–23, and as already noted, 56:7. All these texts clearly reveal God's concern for nations other than Israel and indeed, for all the nations of the world. Even when Israel was in exile in Babylon, the Lord urged them to seek the prosperity of the alien city in which they found themselves, and to pray for it, for "if it prospers, you too will prosper" (Jeremiah 29:7). God is concerned here for the prosperity of Israel, but in the larger context of the prosperity of the Babylonian Empire.

Upon the conclusion of this brief overview the reader is apt to respond: But none of this speaks specifically to the issue of whether or

8. Wright, *Mission of God,* 104.

9. "All the ends of the earth will remember and turn to the Lord."

10. "The nobles of the nations assemble as the people of the God of Abraham."

11. ". . . for You rule the peoples with equity and guide the nations of the earth."

12. "Then all nations will be blessed through him, and they will call him blessed."

13. "All the nations you have made will come and worship before you, Lord . . . ."

not individuals face a life-and-death alternative as regards their eternal destiny. That is true. The reason for that lack of specificity is that the Old Testament as a whole is vague regarding the afterlife. Matters of heaven and hell as eternal destinations do not emerge in full effect until the inter testamental period, the four hundred years between Malachi and Matthew. The Old Testament's concern is this-worldly for the most part, hence its universalism focuses on God's love for all humanity and his intent to bless it by way of a specially chosen people.

One of the texts we used in a course I taught at Palmer Theological Seminary[14] was Lucien Legrand's *Unity and Plurality: Mission in the Bible.* Legrand, a longtime Roman Catholic missionary to India, asserts that the Old Testament texts bear witness to "a universality potentially capable of embracing all that is human."[15] He further affirms that the God of Israel is the God of "cosmic benedictions."[16] What I will be arguing in this chapter and the next is that the universality referred to is not merely potential but actual, and will be fulfilled eschatalogically, that is, in the renewal of all things at the end of this age.

The New Testament

The universalist thrust of the Old Testament continues in the New. John's gospel opens with the declaration that "the true light that gives light to *everyone* was coming into the world" (John 1:9, emphasis added). Not all were prepared to respond to the light, yet Jesus himself predicted that "Many will come from the east and the west, and will take their places at the feast with Abraham, Isaac, and Jacob in the kingdom of heaven" (Matthew 8:11). The feast he referenced is the Messianic banquet of Isaiah 25:6, which is "for all peoples." To his disciples Jesus observed that he had not come to be served but to serve, "and to give his life as a ransom for many" (Mark 10:45). In both the Matthean and Markan texts, and else-where, the words *many* or *the many* are frequently a technical phrase for the Gentile nations. Jesus tells a parable about a shepherd who, losing even a single sheep, perseveres until he finds it (Luke 10:4). And of course, there is Jesus' post-resurrection Great Commission. Repeated in each of

---

14. Formerly Eastern Baptist Seminary.

15. Legrand, *Unity and Plurality*, 14.

16. Ibid.

the gospels and the book of Acts, the commission specifically directs the apostles to proclaim the good news to the ends of the earth.

Up to this point, God's intent is clear from both the Old and New Testaments. God intends to bless his entire creation and most especially the human race by means of the witness of his chosen people. The blessing entails renewal and salvation: "God our Savior, who desires *everyone* to be saved and to come to the knowledge of the truth" (1 Timothy 2:3b–4, emphasis added). This text, however, does not answer the obvious question: Will everyone therefore be saved and come to a knowledge of the truth? Or are some (many? most?) doomed to annihilation,[17] eternal separation from God, or unending torment in hellfire? Eastern Orthodox Christians, for instance, believe that God "forgets forever"[18] those who finally choose not to respond to his love (cf. Matthew 7:23, Luke 13:27).

Texts Suggesting Universal Redemption

In response to this crucial question, Will everyone be saved? We turn now to an admittedly limited but powerful group of New Testament texts. We have already noted one text, John 1:9.[19] Here are some others (emphasis added in each case). My comments follow the text:

- *John 3:17.* "Indeed, God did not send the Son into the world to condemn the world, but in order that the *world*[20] might be saved through him." God's purpose for the world (John has in mind the world of human beings) is not condemnation, but salvation.

- *John 12:32.* "And I, when I am lifted up from the earth, will draw *all* people to myself." This is a text that Abelard drew inspiration from, and rightly so. The Israelites sinned during their journey through the wilderness. Moses erected a serpent on a pole. "And everyone

17. Annihilation: to destroy completely; to extinguish, to blot out, so that nothing remains. The noted evangelical theologian John Stott tentatively holds this idea as the ultimate destiny of unbelievers. Cf. Bacchiocchi, *Immortality or Resurrection.* .

18. Stăniloae, *Revelation and Knowledge*, 208.

19. "... the true light that gives light to *everyone* was coming into the world" (John 1:9, emphasis added)

20. In each of the instances in this text and all the following ones listed, the Greek word translated *world* is *kosmos*, literally meaning "an orderly arrangement," i. e., an ornament or decoration, and by implication the world in a wide or narrow sense, including its inhabitants, literally, figuratively, or morally (Strong's *Greek Dictionary of the New Testament*, 43).

who is bitten shall look at it and live" (Numbers 21:8). So with Jesus. Not only will he save all those who look to him; he will actually "*draw* men" to look.

- *John 12:47.* "For I came not to judge the world, but to save the *world*." This text is a parallel to John 3:17 above.

- *Acts 2:39.* "For the promise is for you, for your children, and for *all* who are far away, everyone whom the Lord our God calls to him."

- *Romans 5:18.* "Therefore just as one man's trespass led to condemnation for all, so one man's act of righteousness leads to justification and life for *all*." The word *all* assumes great significance in Paul's understanding of the gospel. Christians who are repelled by the idea of universal redemption interpret "all" as meaning "some from every population group in the world." There is no indication that Paul intends this limitation, especially when we consider the texts immediately below.

- *Romans 11:26.* "And so *all* Israel will be saved." Paul looked forward to the complete salvation of Israel and the fulfillment of God's promises to the nation.

- *Romans 11:32.* "For God has imprisoned *all* in disobedience so that he may be merciful to *all*." By the same token that we believe that all are captive to sin and fall short of the glory of God, with no exceptions, so we may believe that all, with no exceptions, receive the mercy of God.

- *1 Corinthians 5:22.* "For as all die in Adam, so *all* will be made alive in Christ." Do we believe that all are subject to spiritual death, "dead in your trespasses and sins" (Ephesians 2:1)? Just so, all will be made alive, not by any virtue or volition on their part, but because "in Christ, God was reconciling the world to himself."

- *2 Corinthians 5:14–15.* "We are convinced that one has died for *all*; therefore all have died. And he died for all, so that those who live might live no longer for themselves but for him." Jesus died representing humanity before God. Paul insists all died with him. But Jesus was raised from the dead, so all are raised with him. Those who are aware of this resurrection will no longer live for themselves. For them the "selfish gene" no longer controls; Darwinian rules no longer prevail.

- *2 Corinthians 5:19.* "In Christ, God was reconciling the *world* to himself, not counting their trespasses against them, and entrusting the message of reconciliation to us." God does not count the world's trespasses against it. This affirmation does not mean that God does not take the trespasses seriously. He does, and he judges them thoroughly. But he does not allow judgment to be the last word. "Mercy triumphs over judgment" (James 2:13).

- *Philippians 2:10.* "That at the name of Jesus *every* knee should bow."[21] This text is parallel to John 12:32. Jesus draws all persons to himself: the precise circumstances are unclear. I assume it to take place at the last judgment, when all human beings will experience God's saving love. Every knee will bow, not reluctantly, as having been forced into submission, but gladly. God does not use the cross to compel submission; God has other ways of coercion, should he wish to conquer through force.

- *Colossians 1:20.* "And through him God was pleased to reconcile to himself *all* things, whether on earth or in heaven, by making peace through the blood of his cross." Here we see that "all" includes not only the human race but the entire creation.

- *1 Timothy 2:6.* "Who gave himself as a ransom for *all*." This verse parallels Mark 10:45, on which we have previously commented.

- *1 Timothy 4:10.* "We have our hope set on the living God, who is the Savior of *all* people, especially of those who believe." Here we approach the crux of the matter. Everything depends on the character of God. He is not the God of death, but of life. God is not the Savior of some, but of all. "Especially of those who believe"—these are the fortunate ones who in this life actually experience God's reign.

- *Titus 2:11.* "For the grace of God has appeared, bringing salvation to *all*." John the evangelist agrees: "From his fullness we have *all* received, grace upon grace" (John 1:16).

---

21. Of this listing, Philippians 2:10 might be considered dubious, in that "subjection" per se does not necessarily imply reconciliation. But we will look at the way in which the early church fathers interpreted this text. Cf. Talbott, I:2, in Parry and Partridge, eds., *Universal Salvation?*, 23.

- *Hebrews 2:9.* "But we see Jesus, who for a little while was made lower than the angels . . . so that by the grace of God he might taste death for *everyone.*" Grace again for everyone.

- *1 John 2:2.* "And he is the atoning sacrifice for our sins, and not for ours only but also for the sins of the *whole world.*" Here John the elder specifically extends the atonement beyond a limited group to include the whole of humanity.

Texts Suggesting Eternal Damnation

Over against these positive affirmations, however, there are other texts that seem just as clearly to assert the opposite, namely, that some persons will be eternally separated in hell from the presence of God and tormented there without end. The following list is taken from Neal Punt's *What's Good About the Good News?* [22] I defer my comments on these texts to Chapter 10.

- *Matthew 7:23.* "Then I will declare unto them, 'I never knew you; go away from me, you evildoers.'"

- *Matthew 25:41.* "Then he will say to those at his left hand, 'You that are accursed, depart from me into the eternal fire prepared for the devil and his angels.'"

- *Matthew 25:46.* "And these will go away into eternal punishment, but the righteous into eternal life."

- *John 5:28–29.* "The hour is coming when all who are in their graves will hear his voice and will come out—those who have done good, to the resurrection of life, and those who have done evil, to the resurrection of condemnation."

- *2 Thessalonians 1:9.* "These will suffer the punishment of eternal destruction, separated from the presence of the Lord."

- *2 Thessalonians 2:12.* "So that all who have not believed the truth but took pleasure in unrighteousness will be condemned."

- *Revelation 22:15.* "Outside are the dogs and sorcerers and fornicators and murderers and idolaters, and everyone who loves and practices falsehood."

22. Punt, *What's Good?* 17–18.

We will examine these texts again in Chapter 10. But for now, let us contemplate what we can or should do when faced with two sets of texts that appear to contradict each other. Rather than dispose of the Bible as incoherent, our first instinct is to try to understand each text, specifically or as a group, in the light of Scripture in its totality. But experience shows that this understanding is not really possible, for each of us interprets the Bible as a whole through a particular set of lenses based on our world-views, presuppositions, contexts, life experiences and, if we are serious Bible students, some particular hermeneutic, such as the grammatical-historical method. It is only by means of these lenses, which others may not share, that we might attempt to reconcile incompatible texts.

A missionary friend who has lived many years in the "fuzzy-set"[23] atmosphere of India[24] has suggested that we need not feel obligated to reconcile the opposing texts. We can simply hold them in tension, as we do with a paradox.[25] I admit this possibility but believe it may subvert the missional calling of the Christian. Holding opposing views in tension is another way of saying, "I do not know," or "It may not be possible to know for certain." But, as the apostle Paul pointed out in another context, "If the trumpet does not sound a clear call, who will get ready for battle?" (1 Corinthians 14:8). If I am to obey the Lord's command to make disciples of all nations, I want to be able to communicate the good news with clarity and conviction.

But a third option is available. We can take the bull by the horns and interpret the "all will be saved" texts through the lens of the "most will be lost" texts; or vice versa, we can interpret the "most will be lost" texts through the "all will be saved" lens.[26] In this chapter I will choose the latter because I judge this approach to be more faithful to the metanarrative of Scripture and especially more faithful to the character of the Father as

23. Fuzzy set: a mathematical model of vague qualitative or quantitative data originated by Lotfi A. Zadeh in 1965 and since then generalized to such other fields of study as anthropology. See Hiebert, fn. 24 below.

24. Cf. Hiebert, *Anthropological Reflections on Missiological Issues*, chapter 6, 107–136 for the distinctions between bounded sets, centered sets, and fuzzy sets.

25. John Ridgway, e-mail correspondence, September 2008.

26. Neal Punt attempts to ameliorate the consequences of interpreting Scripture through such a lens as "all will be lost except those whom the Bible expressly declares will be saved" by suggesting that what the Bible actually teaches is that "all will be saved except those [perhaps relatively few] whom the Bible expressly declares will be lost." (Cf. Punt, *What's Good?*, 2.).

revealed in Jesus. For me, this is the decisive criterion. Keeping that in mind, let us meanwhile take note of what a significant number of early church fathers believed about universal salvation.

Patristic Thought

Twenty centuries have elapsed since the Christ event and, as we saw when we surveyed models of the atonement, believers have understood the gospel in varied ways in different contexts. The early Christians read the Old Testament in the Septuagint (Greek-language) version. The whole of the New Testament, with the likely exception of Matthew's gospel, was also written in Greek.[27] The gospel itself was proclaimed in the first-century Mediterranean world in the Greek language. It seems worthwhile therefore to return to those early church fathers who (a) were in closest proximity to the apostolic proclamation; (b) whose native language was Greek; and (c) who read the Old Testament in its Septuagint version and the apostolic Gospels and Epistles in Greek.

Most of my readers have easy access to Bibles, but until recently access to the early church fathers was more difficult to come by.[28] For that reason, and for the reader's interest, I have allotted more space to the following section than might otherwise be expected.

Irenaeus, the second-century bishop of Lyons, wrote a five-volume treatise tirled *Against Heresies*. The heart of Irenaeus' understanding of the gospel is his theory of recapitulation (Greek: *anakephalaiosis*), which he expounds in books III, IV, and V. By recapitulation Irenaeus theorizes that God in Christ rehabilitates the original divine plan for the salvation of the human race that was interrupted by the fall of Adam, and that God gathers up his entire work from the beginning and restores it in his incarnate Son. In this way Christ becomes for us a second Adam. The Son of God had to become human in order to effect the re-creation of humankind in its entirety.

27. Some scholars believe that Matthew's gospel was originally written in Aramaic.

28. The Ante-Nicene as well as the Nicene and Post-Nicene Fathers (series I and series II) are available free of charge online in their entirety in English translation in the Christian Classics Ethereal Library (CCEL) Rebecca Frey, e-mail correspondence May 2009.

> God recapitulated in himself the ancient formation of man, that he might kill sin, deprive death of its power, and vivify man.[29]

Again,

> What then did the Lord bring at his coming? Know that he brought all newness, by bringing himself, who had been foretold . . . that a newness would come, to renew and give life to man.[30]

And again,

> But now the case stands thus: The Word has saved that humanity which had perished . . . . The apostle says, "Now you have been reconciled in the body of his flesh" [Colossians 1:21]. He says this because the righteous flesh has reconciled that flesh which was being kept under bondage in sin, and brought it into *friendship with God.*[31]

Friendship with God is, of course, the very essence of atonement. The reader will recognize that Irenaeus' concept of recapitulation is not quite the same as the renewal that I have presented, since recapitulation is not identical to renewal. But it is a "kissin' cousin," as it were. Irenaeus does not make an explicit case for universal salvation,[32] although universal salvation is compatible with his recapitulation theory. On the other hand, nowhere does he deny it. Even though it was extant in his time and he was writing "against heresies," he does not include it as a heresy.

Theophilus, bishop of Antioch around 180 c.e., wrote to his pagan friend Autolycus, saying, "Just as a vessel, which, after it has been made, has some flaw, is remade or remodeled, that it may become new and right, so it comes to man by death. For, in some way or other he is broken up, that he may come forth in the resurrection whole, I mean spotless, and righteous, and immortal."[33]

Clement of Alexandria was the head of the famed Catechetical School, a seminary for theologians located in that city during the last

---

29. *Against Heresies*, III:18:7.

30. Ibid., IV:34:1.

31. Ibid., V:14:2. Emphasis mine.

32. Although perhaps he comes close with his assertion above in V:14:2 that in Christ God has "saved humanity." Cf. Gregory of Nyssa below.

33. Theophilus, *"To Autolycus,"* II, xxv.

decades of the second century.[34] He assumes the universality of redemption, having learned it from his predecessor Pantaenus, and attempts to explain its relationship to hell, or Hades. From Clement's *Stromata*:[35]

> The Lord is the propitiation, not only for our sins, that is, of the faithful, but also for the whole world (1 John 2:2); therefore he truly saves all, converting some by punishments, and others by gaining their free will, so that he has the high honor that unto him every knee should bow: angels, men and the souls of those who died before his advent.[36]

Clement says that punishment—or more precisely, chastisement—in Hades is remedial and restorative. God does not punish, for strictly speaking, punishment is vengeance: retaliation for evil. The God who through Jesus instructs us to pray for those who despitefully use us (Matthew 5:44) does not practice vengeance. Upon Clement's death, Alexander, bishop of Jerusalem, wrote to Origen, whom we consider below, bemoaning the passing of "my master and profitable to me." This lament would indicate that Clement's views were not considered heretical by either Alexander or Origen.

Origen (185–254), another citizen of Alexandria who succeeded Clement at the Catechetical School, was the early church's greatest theologian since the apostle Paul. His best-known works are *Against Celsus* (a pagan philosopher) and *De Principiis* (On First Principles). It is with the name of Origen that the doctrines of *apokatastasis* (restoration to the original condition) and universal salvation are usually associated. God is indeed a consuming fire (Hebrews 12:29), Origen notes, but what his fire consumes is the evil in humans, not the humans themselves, nor even Satan:

> We hold that in the mind there is no evil so strong that it may not be overcome by the Supreme Word and God. For stronger than all the evils in the soul is the Word, and the healing power that dwells in him; and this healing he applies, according to the will of God, to every man. The consummation of all things is the destruction of evil.[37]

---

34. Except where otherwise noted, in this section I am following Hanson, *Universalism*.

35. Stromata: Greek for "patchwork," or "miscellanies."

36. *Stromata* VII:16.

37. *Against Celsus*, VIII:lxxii.

Not everyone agreed with Origen about Satan, for they assumed Satan to be intrinsically evil. Origen expounds at great length on 1 Corinthians 15:24–28. The translation from Greek to Latin to English is too complex to include here, but the gist is something like this: If the subjection by which the Son is said to be subject to the Father is good and salutary, one may logically infer that the subjection of even the enemies of God—the rulers, powers, and authorities; Satan; and even death—should also be good and salutary. This subjection of all things will be brought about not by force but by the love of God and the word of the gospel, however long that may take.

> We assert that the Word, who is the Wisdom of God, shall bring together all intelligent creatures, and convert them into his own perfection, through the instrumentality of their free will and of their own exertions. The Word is more powerful than all the diseases of the soul ....[38]

Great though he was, Origen was actually excommunicated by Bishop Demetrius of Alexandria—not because of heresy, however, but because of Demetrius' anger toward bishops who (as he saw it) had usurped his authority. His excommunication was therefore disregarded by the bishops of Palestine, Arabia, Greece, and Cappadocia. Among the early church fathers in the East who followed or defended Origen were Pamphilus and Eusebius of Caesarea, Didymus of Alexandria, Athanasius the staunch opponent of Arianism, Basil the Great, Gregory Nazianzen, and Gregory of Nyssa; and of the Latin fathers, Ambrose of Milan, Hilary of Poitiers, and Jerome, translator of the Bible into Latin (the Vulgate version).

Of the six great theological schools of the early Church—Alexandria, Caesarea, Antioch, Nisibis (later Edessa), Carthage/Hippo, and Athens, only one[39] held to the doctrine of unending punishment in hell for unbelievers. Another favored annihilation. Two favored universal salvation on the principles laid out by Origen. The final two also held to universal redemption, but on the somewhat different principles advocated by Theodore of Mopsuestia.

Theodore of Mopsuestia, born around 350, was one of the founders of Nestorianism, the great missionary movement that reached the interior

---

38. *Against Celsus*, Book VIII.

39. Carthage was an ancient city near Tunis in modern Tunisia; Hippo (or Hippo Regius) was the ancient name of the city of Annaba in modern Algeria.

of China in the eighth century. Although Origen and Theodore were both universalists, they reached their conclusions via different routes. Origen emphasized free will. As long as human beings have free will, he maintained, conversion cannot be ruled out, for God's love powerfully heals all diseases of the soul. Theodore, instead of regarding humans as absolutely free, considered them part of a divine plan whereby they would be ultimately guided into holiness:

> The wicked who have committed evil the whole period of their lives shall be punished till they learn that, by continuing in sin, they only continue in misery. And when, by this means, they shall have been brought to fear God . . . they shall obtain the enjoyment of his grace. For he never would have said, "Until thou has paid the uttermost farthing," unless we can be released from suffering after having suffered adequately for sin; nor would he have said, "He shall be beaten with many stripes," and again, "He shall be beaten with few stripes," unless the punishment to be endured for sin will have an end.[40]

Again, commenting on Romans 6:6,

> All have the hope of rising with Christ, so that the body having obtained immorality, then the tendency to evil should be removed. God recapitulated all things in Christ . . . as though making a complete renewal and restoration of the whole creation in him. Now this will take place in a future age, when all mankind, and all powers possessed of reason, look up to him as is right, and obtain mutual concord and firm peace.[41]

Gregory of Nyssa (c. 335–395) was the renowned bishop of Cappadocia in what is now Turkey. He considered Origen his spiritual godfather and was a fervent proponent of *apokatastasis*. His thoughts on the subject have come to us through a treatise written in Greek but with the Latin title given as *Anima et resurrectione* (On the Soul and the Resurrection), and from a lengthy account he wrote to the monk Olympius:

> What is then the scope of St. Paul's argument in this place [1 Corinthians 15:20–28]? That the nature of evil shall one day be wholly exterminated, and divine, immortal goodness embrace

---

40. *Assemani Bibiotheca Orientalis*, Tom. III, cited in Hanson, *Universalism*, 99.

41. Ibid.

within itself all intelligent natures; *so that of all who were made by God, not one shall be exiled from his kingdom*; when all the alloy of evil ... shall be dissolved, and consumed in the furnace of purifying fire, and everything that had its origin from God shall be restored to original pristine state of purity ... when every creature shall have been made one body. *Now the body of Christ, as I have often said, is the whole of humanity*[42] [emphasis added].

The decline of belief in universal redemption from the sixth century[43] onward in Western Christendom is generally attributed to the influence of the great Latin theologian Augustine. Yet, in addition to the Greek-speaking church fathers I have cited, it is worth observing that such noteworthy Latin-speaking fathers and doctors of later centuries as Ambrose of Milan (Augustine's mentor) and Johannes Scotus Eriugena were convinced universalists. Martin Luther was what we might call a "soft" universalist, meaning he was unwilling to flatly deny the possibility of universal reconciliation. But generally speaking, the doctrine remained submerged until sectors of German Pietism revived it in the seventeenth century.[44] In the eighteenth century the Englishman William Law, author of the classic *The Serious Call to a Devout and Holy Life*, was a universalist.

In our day the late Leslie Weatherhead and William Barclay, both widely read Bible commentators among evangelicals, were believers in universal salvation. So is the highly respected Jürgen Moltmann, now in his eighties and still writing. Three important twentieth-century theologians, the Protestants C. H. Dodd and Karl Barth, and the Roman Catholic Hans Urs von Balthasar, were "soft" universalists. The equally renowned Catholic theologian Karl Rahner has said, "In principle, the entire human race is already saved in Jesus Christ; in virtue of this, the whole of humanity already constitutes the 'people of God.'"[45] That the whole of humanity may constitute the people of God is something we discussed in the previous chapter.

---

42. Ibid., 111.

43. The Fifth Ecumenical Council of Constantinople (553) confirmed the previous edict of the emperor Justinian condemning the doctrine of universal salvation particularly as applied to demons and Satan.

44. Moltmann, *Coming of God,* 238, traces a line from Johann Bengel (d. 1752) though Friedrich Oetinger (d. 1782) to the Blumhardts, father and son (the latter d. 1919).

45. Cited in Dupuis, *Toward a Christian Theology,* 352.

Reflection

The language used by these early Christians sounds strange to our modern ears. Nevertheless, the words I have italicized in the paragraph from Gregory of Nyssa above accurately reflect my own conclusions, stated at the end of Chapter 8: All members of the human race have now been reconciled to God; all humanity is "in Christ." Yet there are some major differences, the chief one being the difference we might understand between restoration (or recapitulation) and renewal.

When Irenaeus and other fathers use the word *renewal*, as they often do, they mean that the human race will be restored to the original condition of innocence that preceded the fall. Readers will recall that in Chapter 1 of this monograph I posited that what we term original sin was already present in the Garden of Eden. In other words, the situation in the Garden of Eden was not one of perfection. So what is needed, and what God has provided in the Christ event, is not a restoration to the presumed innocence of the Garden but a complete renewal, a thorough re-creation that places humankind and all creation on a track that will fulfill in eternity God's twofold purpose in creation by evolution: participation in a freely determined community of mutual love and a share in the stewardship of the universe. Hence the title of this book, *The Renewal of All Things*.

10

A Viable Concept?

He who was seated on the throne said, "I am making everything new!"

REVELATION 21:5

THOMAS TALBOTT, PROFESSOR EMERITUS of philosophy at Willamette University in Oregon, lays out three well-established propositions of Western theology:[1]

1. It is within God's *power* to achieve his redemptive purpose for the world (cf. Jeremiah 32:17, 27; Matthew 19:26).

2. It is God's redemptive *purpose* for the world (and therefore his *will*) to reconcile all sinners to himself (cf. Colossians 1:19–20; 1 Timothy 2:3–4).

3. Some sinners will never be reconciled to God, and God will therefore consign them to a place of never-ending punishment from which there will be no hope of escape, or annihilate them altogether (cf. Matthew 25:46; 2 Thessalonians 1:9).

Texts supporting each of the three propositions are present within the New Testament, and yet . . .

- Those who accept proposition 1 (e. g., those who highlight the sovereignty of God) can and usually do accept proposition 3 but not proposition 2, because to do so would violate the doctrine of limited election.

- Those who accept proposition 2 (e. g., those who highlight the free will of human beings) can and usually do accept proposition 3 but not proposition 1, usually on the basis that humans are free to reject God's grace.

1. Talbott, *Inescapable Love of God*, 43.

- Those who accept proposition 3 (e. g., the great majority of Christians of all denominations) can accept either proposition 1 or 2 but not both, because of the perceived tension between free will and limited election.

- Those who accept both propositions 1 and 2 (e. g., Christians who believe in universal reconciliation) are logically and morally obligated to reject proposition 3. This rejection does not require rejecting the idea of chastisement, restorative punishment, or even purgatory,[2] but it does mean rejecting the fate of unending, conscious torment—that is, the typical notion of hell.

Therefore, which propositions one accepts or rejects will be those the interpreter believes conform most closely to the overall narrative of the Bible and to the portrait of God revealed by Jesus in the Christ event. In other words, whether we acknowledge it or not, we all read through pre-established filters. Therefore, as I indicated in the previous chapter, some texts will have to be interpreted through the lenses of other texts, and some texts necessarily will be given priority over others. Historically, for example, Christian scholars have considered both the Old and the New Testament as inspired by God. But they consistently interpret Old Testament texts through the lenses of New Testament texts. Similarly, they give the New Testament priority over the Old Testament.

Proceeding in this manner, the interpreter will have to accommodate the dissonant texts. Those who believe that the sovereignty of God takes precedence over human free will must put a different spin on the awkward texts that support free will, such as Hebrews 6:4–6. Those who emphasize free will must do the same with the texts that speak of limited election. And the believer in universal redemption will have to interpret the election passages, the "all" passages, and the eternal punishment passages, among others, differently from other Christians. Each has a perfect right to do so. Oddly, in our day free-will Arminians and limited atonement Calvinists are not prepared to excommunicate each other but equally oddly, both agree that universalists are heretics! Consequently, when a devout evangelical scholar writes a book titled *The Evangelical Universalist*, he or she, sadly, must do so under a pseudonym.[3]

---

2. Purgatory: a state or place of chastisement or temporary punishment after death.

3. MacDonald, *The Evangelical Universalist.*

Autobiographical Note

Because belief in universal reconciliation and salvation is a minority view among Christians, most Christians who have come to embrace it started out as believers in the idea that virtually all human beings are destined for an eternity of hellfire. Typically, those who now believe in universal reconciliation have been led to this conclusion by virtue of personal experiences that forced them to return to the Scriptures for more in-depth study. It was so in my case.

Without going into great detail, my vocation as a Christian missionary in the Middle East, East Africa, and Asia during the third quarter of the twentieth century led me to certain conclusions about the essential oneness of all the world's peoples with respect to spiritual experience and moral behavior. Einstein couldn't see much difference between Jews and other ethnic groups with respect to moral behavior (see page 195). Similarly, after years of living cross-culturally, I could discern little difference between the aspirations and moral behavior of most professing Christians and the aspirations and moral behavior of most members of other major religions. The typical Muslim, for example, is not a terrorist, and many Muslims live lives of devotion to God that would put not a few Christians to shame. The same can be and should be said of adherents of other world religions. And the typical Christian, though capable of deep devotion, is also capable, as history shows, of inflicting massive pain on noncombatants in time of war (think of the firebombing of Dresden and the atomic bombing of Hiroshima). As a missionary, I recognize that Christianity itself has been "interlaced with the demonic."[4] And I came to feel a deep solidarity with the human race as a whole, regardless of individuals' particular faith or lack of faith. This sense of solidarity has been reinforced during the past quarter-century as my wife Georgia and I have lived and ministered side by side with inner-city families in Paterson, New Jersey.

Further circumstances of a more personal nature during the final quarter of the twentieth century led me into the fathomless reality of the never-failing love of God—something similar, I suspect, to the experience of the author of Lamentations. Even as the latter endured the destruction of his beloved city, Jerusalem, he was compelled to confess, "The steadfast love of the LORD never ceases, his mercies never come to an end" (Lamentations 3:22).

---

4. Cf. McDermott, *God's Rivals*, 13.

Back in 1963 my decade-long missionary exposure to social injustice around the world led me to reread the Bible from Genesis to Revelation through the lens of *tsedeqah wa mishpat* (the Hebrew term for social justice) and eventually to write *Bring Forth Justice,* published by Eerdmans in 1980. At the end of the century my existential experience of the unfailing love of God, coupled with my sense of solidarity with humanity as a whole, led me to reread the Bible again, this time through the lens of God's love, and to the writing of *What about the Cross?* And now this book.

The Eternal Love of God

In the midst of the carnage of World War I, Frederick Lehman penned these words:

> Could we with ink the ocean fill,
>   And were the skies of parchment made;
> Were every stalk on earth a quill,
>   And every man a scribe by trade;
> To write the love of God above,
>   Would drain the ocean dry;
> Nor could the scroll contain the whole,
>   Though stretched from sky to sky.[5]

God is love (1 John 4:8,16). This is an ontological assertion.[6] That is, it bespeaks God's very essence. Love is not a property or attribute or a trait of God; love is, I repeat, God's very essence. And it is through the lens of God's love that I have come to read Scripture. In doing so, I have found that the texts that support universal reconciliation, listed on pages 123–25 above are more consonant with God's love than the opposing texts listed on page 126. When we assert that God is righteous or just, we mean he will never act in an unrighteous or unjust manner toward anyone. Similarly, if God is love, he will never act in unloving fashion toward anyone, not even toward his most adamant enemies. Nor would Jesus, in faithfulness to the

---

5. Lehman, *Songs That Are Different*, vol. 2, Hymn 329. This is the third stanza of the hymn, *The Love of God*. This stanza is based on a Jewish poem, *Haddamut*, said to have been written in Aramaic in the year 1050 c.e. by Meir ben Isaac Nehorai, son of a cantor in Worms, Germany. Lehman wrote a short pamphlet titled "History of the Song, The Love of God," that was published privately in 1948.

6. Ontology is the branch of metaphysics that deals with the nature of being or reality.

loving character of his heavenly Father, have instructed us to bless even those who persecute us.

John the elder also affirms with other biblical writers that God is light; that is, that God is holy (1 John 1:5). Holiness too is God's very essence. Therefore, God's holiness and God's love are of a kind. God's love is expressed in holiness; and God's holiness is expressed in love. Similarly, Jesus notes that God is spirit (John 4:24). Spirit is not mere disembodiment; it is the faculty of relationship, what it means to be a Person. Spirit, holiness, love—these convey the essential nature of God. Back in chapter 2 we noted that *agape* love, a term Christians use to identify God's love, is "the generous, unconditional, self-sacrificing, and thoughtful good will that both desires and works for the welfare of the other." Agape love is consistent with punishment or chastisement only when such chastisement is for the purpose of rehabilitation and restoration, not retribution or retaliation. God's justice is not punitive but restorative.

We will return to the subject of wrath and judgment, punishment and chastisement, further on. For the moment, let us reflect a bit more on the love and goodness of God. Thomas Talbott quotes William Barclay as saying, "The only possible final triumph is a universe loved by God and in love with God."[7] Closely associated with God's love is God's goodness. The Psalmist prays, "Answer me, LORD, out of the goodness of your love" (Psalm 69:16). The apostle Peter praises "him who called us by his own glory and goodness" (2 Peter 1:3). But it is not only the goodness of God's character that intrigues me; it is the fact that God pronounces seven times over that his *creation* is "good" and "very good." And as Christopher Wright correctly observes, "A good creation can only be the work of a good God." He goes on to assert, again rightly, "This affirmation of the goodness of creation is the seal of divine approval on the *whole universe*."[8]

The universe is imperfect, to be sure—not least because of human sin—but it is incredible that God would utterly destroy that which he deems good if it is within his power to perfect the imperfect. Thus the "new heavens and the new earth" foreseen in Revelation 21 will not be another creation *ex nihilo* (out of nothing) but a true renewal of all things

---

7. Talbott, *Inescapable Love,* 133, epigraph.
8. C. Wright, *Mission of God*, 398–399. Emphasis mine.

out of the old (*ex vetere*).[9] The new creation will include God's human creation, *H. sapiens*.

Bishop Pearson's Problem

One evening, Bishop Carlton Pearson tells us,[10] he was watching the nightly news, holding his baby daughter in one hand and eating his supper with the other. The news report showed women and children with bellies swollen, collapsing to the ground; and mothers with withered breasts, flies gathered in the corners of their eyes and mouths, bones protruding through their black, leathery skin. Feeling guilty and angry, he berated God:

"I don't know how you can sit on your throne there in Heaven and let these poor people drop to the ground hungry, heartbroken and lost, and just randomly suck them into hell, thinking nothing of it, and be a 'Sovereign God,' not to mention a 'God of love.'"

He heard a voice respond within him: "Is that what you think we're doing, sucking them all into hell?"

"That's what I've been taught," he responded angrily.

"And what would change that?" the voice replied.

"They need to get saved so they can go to heaven," he answered confidently.

"And how would that happen?" the voice responded.

"Somebody needs to go over there and get them saved by preaching the gospel to them."

"Well, then," the voice resounded, "put down your food and your baby, turn off that big-screen television, and catch the first plane over there!"

Pearson burst into an emotional mix of tears of grief, compassion, shame, guilt, and anger. Then he retorted,

"Don't put that burden on me, Lord. My hands are full. I can't save the whole world!"

"Precisely," the voice responded. "That's what we already did. But these people don't know it and regretfully, most of you who claim to be

---

9. Cf. Moltmann, *Coming of God*, 265.

10. Pearson, *Gospel of Inclusion*, 2. For our purposes I have condensed the story and paraphrased it to read in the third person.

my followers don't believe it. We redeemed and reconciled all of humanity at Calvary. That is what the cross was and is all about."

Hell as Never-ending Torture

On the World Wide Web a California pastor assures us that "The reality of hell is the most horrifying, terror-striking, fearful truth known to man. It encompasses the worst possible fear and the meanest conceivable existence: continual, never-ending torture . . . . It is a literal place where literal people suffer the torment of a literal fire."[11]

Hell is a problem for a lot of Christians these days, not because of some unwarranted delicacy of feeling, but because it seems so hard to square with the goodness and love of God. What loving father would consign his son to never-ending torment, even if his son had blatantly rebelled against him? Fathers (certain Roman emperors, for example) have indeed murdered their offspring, but no one would dare to call them good or loving. To this some would protest, "You can't compare God to earthly fathers!" But in reality, that is exactly what Jesus did:

> Which of you, if your son asks for bread, will give him a stone? Or if he asks for a fish, will give him a snake? If you, then, though you are evil, know how to give good gifts to your children, how much more will your Father in heaven give good gifts to those who ask him!" (Matthew 7:9–11).

The good bishop handled his dilemma by concluding that hell is on earth.[12] Others metaphorize hell. Still others, such as many contemporary evangelicals, redefine it at "separation from God" (cf. 2 Thessalonians 1:9). Before we pursue the matter further, however, we need to consider carefully the biblical terms we translate as "eternal" and "everlasting."

Aiōn - Aiōnios

The Greek word *aiōn*, which the [Greek language] Septuagint translates as the equivalent of the Hebrew *olam*, is usually translated "eternal" or "everlasting" in English-language Bibles. But *aiōn* does *not*, in fact, denote endless, interminable duration. Rather, it signifies "age-long." This inter-

11. Fish, "Hell," Introduction, lines 1–2.

12. Both the Reformer Martin Luther and the noted contemporary theologian Jürgen Moltmann believe that Jesus "descended" into hell by virtue of the agony of being forsaken by God on the Cross. See Moltmann, *Crucified God*, 250.

pretation negates the traditional doctrine of hell as a place of never-ending, inescapable torment. Eastern Orthodox Christians understand this very well in a way that Western Christians do not.

In the nineteenth century Dr. J. W. Hanson, a Universalist minister who served churches in New England and the Middle West, thoroughly investigated the etymology, lexicography, and usage of the word *aiōn* in Greek literature. [13] Of these three, the latter is the most important. His conclusions: (a) there is nothing in the etymology of the word warranting endless duration; (b) the lexicography not only allows but compels the meaning as being of temporal, indefinite but limited duration, related to an age or an era, and Greek writers before and at the time of the Septuagint always gave the word the sense of limited duration; and (c) so too the Old Testament, and Jewish authors writing in Greek at the time of Christ (e. g., Philo, Josephus).

And so too the New Testament. There is no evidence that the meaning of *olam/aiōn* changed between the two Testaments. Hanson surveys more than 200 New Testament texts to demonstrate that *aiōn* and *aiōnios* derive their meaning from their *subject*, and not vice versa. He focuses on numerous passages in which the words cannot possibly denote endless duration.

Hanson pays special attention to the subject of punishment. This English-language noun appears only eleven times in the New Testament (NIV), translating ten different Greek words. Such paucity, he argues, refutes all attempts to foist the meaning of *endless* on the words. Examining Matthew 25:41 and 25:46 in great detail, Hanson notes that "the word may denote both limited and unlimited duration in the same passage, the different meanings to be determined *by the subject treated*" (emphasis added). He cites Habakkuk 3:6[14] as a clear example.

Hanson also focuses on the biblical meaning of the Greek word *kolasin*. It means primarily chastisement, aimed at the correction and improvement of the offender, hence of limited duration. The Greek word *aidios*, on the other hand, does in fact indicate endlessness, and is used with *timoria* to signify unending torment. Jesus apparently never used this phrase (*aidios timoria*), however. The gospel writers record him as using *aiōnion kolasin*, which has the meaning of age-long correction or discipline.

13. Hanson, *The Greek Word Aiōn–Aiōnios*," Cf. Moltmann, *Coming of God*, 242.
14. ". . . The eternal mountains were shattered . . . the everlasting hills sank low."

Finally, Hanson demonstrates that every universalist and every annihilationist among the church fathers of the first six centuries after Christ used aiōn-aiōnios in the sense of indefinite but not unlimited duration. They consistently added qualifying words when they needed to give *aiōnion* the sense of endless duration. Hanson's research seems persuasive to me. I have only summarized it. His actual paper is fifty-six pages long.

Refuting Traditional Notions of Hell

In this section I will comment on biblical references found on the afore-mentioned *atruechurch* (*sic*) web site that purport to prove the traditional notion of hell. The trend among contemporary evangelical churches in the United States is toward defining hell as "separation from God." I will use this web site as an example, however, because it is typical of many one finds on the Web these days, on religious television shows, and in fundamentalist churches. The kind of language it purveys is the kind I grew up with. Furthermore, in certain folk religions around the world (China being a notable example) similar concepts of hell are widespread. The web site's references are in italics; my comments follow. Scripture citations are from the New Revised Standard Version.

- *Hell is a literal place where literal people suffer the torment of a literal fire* (Matthew 5:29–20 and 10:28; Luke 16:19–31).

The Greek word translated *hell* in the two Matthean texts is *Gehenna.* Gehenna refers to a garbage dump outside Jerusalem, always smoldering, hence a traditional *symbol* of hell. It is a stretch to try to read this literally. The word used in Luke 16 is *Hades,* the Greek translation of the Hebrew *Sheol,* the Hebrew abode of the dead. Gehenna and Hades are not synonyms. How Hades became hell, as suggested in Luke 16, is unclear. Most scholars believe this transition was an intertestamental development, possibly influenced by Zoroastrianism, following Israel's exile in Babylon.

The truth is that the Lukan story is not about hell; it is about greed, about social injustice, about how we treat our neighbor. If the story is read literally, as if it were told by Jesus to prove the literal existence of hell, we would have to conclude that Jesus was expounding salvation by good works, not faith—that one person goes to paradise because he is poor and innocent, and another goes to hell because he was insensitive to a beggar.

- *Those in hell are tortured by God* (Matthew 18:34–35).

The Matthean text is a parable, meant to provoke people to think, or rather, to rethink. Jesus is asking: Is God really like this? The implied answer: No, of course not.

- *God is in hell, consuming them with his fire* (Hebrews 12:29).

The text in Hebrews is clearly not a discussion of hell. By now the traditional notion has become incredible, so I will not pursue the idea of a literal hell further but will turn to other texts dealing with eternal punishment. There are three in particular:

MATTHEW 25:31–46, especially verses 41 and 46.

Verse 41: "Depart from me into the eternal fire prepared for the devil and his angels." Verse 46: "And these will go away into eternal punishment, but the righteous into eternal life." It is reasonable enough for the English-speaking reader to understand these texts as saying that there is an equivalency between "punishment" and "life," since both are said to be "eternal." But bearing in mind that "eternal" means "age-long," two different ages are in view: one age that, no matter how long it may last, is nevertheless limited in duration by virtue of God's love and sovereign purpose; and another that involves the new heaven and the new earth, which is of endless duration because God is eternal. Recall that its *subject* always defines *aiōn*.

2 THESSALONIANS 1:5–9, especially verse 9

"These will suffer the punishment of eternal destruction, separated from the presence of the Lord and from the glory of his might." The context here is the persecution of Christians at Thessalonica by Roman authorities or perhaps by local Jewish leaders (see Acts 17:5). When Christ returns, the persecutors will suffer the retribution of (a) eternal destruction, and (b) separation from the presence of the Lord.

Recall that the meaning of the word *eternal* is determined by the subject, that is, the source of the action. It therefore refers to the *quality* of the destruction, i. e., it is from God. Punishment here is better understood as chastisement, for this is the way the early church fathers understood it. Destruction may imply annihilation but more likely refers to the destruction of the evil within the person. Again, the latter is how the church fathers read it. In any event, it does not imply endless torment. The destruction is uninterrupted within the time frame, whatever that may be, but is not endless. It is possible to interpret this passage through the lens of the traditional concept of hell but it is not necessary to do so. One may use a "loving" lens without losing the aspect of judgment. The old nature will be destroyed but not the person.

Jude 7

"Sodom and Gomorrah . . . serve as an example of those who suffer the punishment of eternal fire." This text is best understood along the same lines as the two previously discussed.

Tears in Heaven?

Commenting on Philippians 2:27, Thomas Talbott observes insightfully that the very thing that makes supreme happiness possible—love—also makes us more vulnerable to misery and sorrow.[15] When the apostle Paul's fellow worker, Epaphrus, became seriously ill and nearly died, Paul was deeply distressed because he had no assurance that the beloved Epaphrus would survive his illness—that is, no assurance of a blessed final outcome. Similarly, Onesiphorus could have no peace of mind until he was assured that all was well with Paul (2 Timothy 1:18). These examples raise the question: How can the believer—or even God, for that matter—be supremely happy in heaven knowing that those she or he loves are forever separated from God and suffering never-ending torment?[16]

Some, including Eastern Orthodox Christians, respond to this dilemma by suggesting that God completely removes from his—and our—memory those whom we formerly loved and who are now damned. Others have said that God in some benign way deceives us about the eternal destiny of those we have loved. Others say that in our perfected state we will identify ourselves so strongly with God's will that it will not disturb us to know that our loved ones are suffering; they deserve what they are experiencing as rejecters of God's love. Still others suggest that in

15. Talbott, *Inescapable Love*, 137.

16. This question was first raised in modern times by the German theologian F. D. Schleiermacher. See Bauckham, "Universalism," 49–50.

heaven we will be so consumed with the beatific vision, i. e., our communion with God, that the fate of others will never cross our minds. All of these arguments seem to me to be lamentably weak, even repugnant.

Justice and Judgment

Mishpat is the Hebrew word for judgment or justice. In the Old Testament, *mishpat* is not a passive impartiality that delegates action to someone else, as in today's West. Rather, it is a dynamic right-doing that sees injustice, steps in to rescue the victim, and rectify the situation.[17] The book of Judges illustrates this concept well. Thus God's judgment is salvific in nature. It is not merely negative and destructive but has a creative element, aiming at *shalom*. God's judgments can vindicate his holiness through a combination of mercy and wrath. To most Christians, a combination of mercy and wrath seems contradictory. But they are not; both are expressions of God's covenant faithfulness.[18] The difference is this: God's wrath is for a moment whereas his mercy is everlasting (cf. Psalm 30:5, Isaiah 54:7–8).

Another aspect of God's judgment and justice is worth pondering. Steven Keillor's book, *God's Judgments*,[19] focuses on the Hebrew word *mishpat* and in particular its special meaning of "sifting out."[20] Judgment sifts out. Keillor's interest is in the judgment of nations, but his thesis is equally applicable to individuals. Future-oriented, God's judgment is not merely a return to the status quo ante; rather, it aims at renewal. And this renewal may take time, centuries, even age-long duration. The church fathers understood the slowness of this process perfectly. Over and over again, with reference to "after death, judgment" (Hebrews 9:27) they speak of the purifying effect of God's justice meant to bring about repentance and create a loving response to God's love.

I find the case of the prophet Isaiah, recorded in Isaiah 6, illustrative, though it relates specifically to judgment within the human lifespan. Isaiah finds himself in the presence of the LORD. "Woe is me," he cries. "I am ruined! For I am a man of unclean lips, and I live among a people

17. This concept of judgment conforms closely to the exposition of judging and judgment in my *Bring Forth Justice*, as well as in *What about the Cross?*

18. Cf. Talbott in Parry and Partridge, *Universal Salvation?* chapter 3, for an excellent exposition of this matter, especially 36–37.

19. Keillor, *God's Judgments*.

20. Keillor derives this meaning from Leon Morris's *Biblical Doctrine of Judgment*.

of unclean lips, and my eyes have seen the King, the Lord Almighty."
A seraph flies to Isaiah with a live coal in his hand. He presses the coal
to Isaiah's lips. A painful experience, no doubt; this is not a matter of
cheap grace. The seraph announces, "Your guilt is taken away and your
sin atoned for." I suspect the "grace-filled postmortem experience" that
open theologian[21] Clark Pinnock posits will be something like this. Each
individual will face a just judgment. The individual will see God as God
truly is: the caring, crucified God. Just as importantly, the individual will
see himself or herself as she or he truly is. "Woe is me!" But that very
twofold vision will incite both repentance and the announcement: "Your
guilt is removed; your sin is atoned for." Love will triumph over hardened
hearts; mercy will triumph over judgment.

I cannot usefully speculate about the precise circumstances of this
experience or about how much time is involved. Are we speaking of
purgatory? Of another age? Apparently the church fathers had each or
both of these in mind in their various writings. Are we speaking of an
instant in time or many centuries by human calculation? Will there be a
difference in the chastisement needed to bring a Hitler or a Mao Zedong
to repentance, as compared to the Ethiopian mother of a starving child
who curses God in her anguish? Apparently so, if the parable Jesus told at
Luke 12:48 is apropos.

The point is this: God's chastisements are not punitive and retributive but disciplinary and therefore restorative. Or, as I have been arguing,
they are meant to prepare us for ultimate renewal and participation in the
new heaven and the new earth.

Objections to Universal Redemption

Gregory MacDonald has conveniently listed some common objections to
universal reconciliation.[22] He also provides clear refutations. I will offer
below my own brief response to each objection MacDonald reports.

Objection: It is often asserted that universal salvation devalues the seriousness of sin and personal accountability. The idea of universal
salvation suggests that we do not deserve hell. In any case, it is God's

21. Open theism is the belief that God does not exercise meticulous control of the
universe but leaves it open for humans to make significant choices that impact their
relationships with God and others. See the glossary for further details.

22. MacDonald, "Reasons Why," para. 2*ff.*

"job" to forgive every one. Universal salvation even suggests that we all deserve to be saved.

I agree that the matter of personal accountability is very important. Sin, especially volitional sin, is serious and sinners are indeed accountable, that is, subject to judgment. In fact, all sin and all sinners have been judged and condemned already in Christ (John 3:18). The wages of sin is death (Romans 6:23). However, whether the wages of sin is death, physical or spiritual, is a different question from whether individual sinners deserve hell. The exact nature of hell is scripturally ambiguous. Hell may not exist in the form in which it is traditionally understood. The issue is not so much hell as a destination but hell understood in terms of never-ending torture. God is not obligated to forgive, as if there were some external standard to which God must conform. He forgives out of mercy and grace because love is God's essence, and because Jesus requested it on the cross (Luke 23:34). Even if we do not deserve to be saved, God has purposed to save us irrespective of merit and desert. His justice, the apostle Paul says, is different from human justice.

Objection: Universal reconciliation rests on a woolly and unbiblical understanding of God's love: God is too kind to hurt a fly, it is said. This undermines the truth of God's justice and wrath.

Now it is true that God is both love and light (and spirit as well). It is a hermeneutical mistake, however, to divorce God's love from his wrath or his justice, as if his love were a mere attribute rather than his essence. Both God's wrath and his justice are expressions of his love. God's wrath and justice can only be understood in the context of his love. God's kindness does not inhibit his justice nor prevent his wrath. Conversely, God's wrath or justice does not preclude his mercy (James 2:13). The biblical question is whether God's wrath and punishment is ultimate. And whether God's justice is retributive, requiring never-ending conscious torment rather than salvific, must also be examined biblically. As to the criticism that those who believe in universal salvation think God is too kind to hurt a fly, let me suggest that the God who lets no fallen sparrow go unnoticed or forgotten (Matthew 10:29, Luke 12:6) may indeed be too kind to hurt a fly, though free-willed nature and human beings may do so without compunction.

Objection: The claim that all will be saved undermines Scripture. The Bible clearly teaches that there is a hell, and it will not be empty.

That the Bible teaches that there is a hell with occupants may be so, but that the Bible's hell is not a place of unending and inescapable, conscious torment has been proven, I think, by Hanson's research noted above, to say nothing of serious reflection on God's essence as love, revealed most notably in the Christ event and decisively at the cross.

> *Objection:* Universal salvation is not fair. Why do we put all this effort into living the Christian life if God is going to save us all, including those evil people who enjoy a life of sin? We may as well have fun sinning now and then let God save us at the end.

This is an old objection (cf. Romans 6:1) and is mistakenly based on the notion of merit or just desert, a notion I dismissed a few paragraphs above. Jesus also countered this notion decisively in his parable of the workers in the vineyard (Matthew 20:1–16). The Bible indeed teaches that we will be accountable for our works (cf. Jesus' parable in Matthew 25:14–30). But it also teaches that God's ultimate justice in providing salvation is not based on works; see Romans 3:24 and 6:1.

> *Objection:* Universal reconciliation undermines the doctrine of the Trinity. Are not most universalists Unitarians?

Certainly Unitarianism is one kind of universalism. But there are understandings of universalism that revere the Trinity. Evangelicals by definition are Trinitarian; some are also universalists.[23]

> *Objection:* Universal salvation undermines the necessity of Christ and the cross for salvation. The believer in universal reconciliation thinks that God will save us through whatever route of salvation we choose, whether it be Christ or some other track: all ways lead to God as surely as all roads lead to Rome.[24]

Again, this position is perhaps one kind of universalism in that it assumes the relativity of all religions. In my opinion, this objection misunderstands the basis of salvation. We are saved not on the grounds of our religious choice, not even the Christian choice—most people do not choose their religion—but because God has elected the human race for salvation. Christ and the cross are necessary because therein God's reconciliation with the human race is both effected and revealed. God may have other, perhaps pedagogical, or restraint-of-sin purposes for the

---

23. See MacDonald, "A Trinitarian Universalist Prayer," para. 1–4.

24. See for example Hick, *Metaphor of God Incarnate.*

religions[25]—including Christianity—that relate to other aspects of salvation. We will discuss these possibilities in the following chapter.

> *Objection:* Universal salvation undermines the necessity of faith in Christ alone for salvation. Even if the Christian believer in universal redemption insists that all who are saved are saved through Christ, he or she still believes that God will save everyone through Christ whether or not they have heard of Christ, or whether they have received him or rejected him.

This objection must be considered in two parts: (a) whether people have heard of Christ (Romans 10:14); and (b) whether they have received or rejected him.

As to the hearing, we must acknowledge the stark fact that more than 90 percent of all humans who have ever lived have never heard of Jesus. If salvation depends on hearing in a strict literal sense, then the significance of the human race in God's economy is seriously undermined, making humans no more important than trilobites or dinosaurs, and God's good creation must be judged an utter failure. If only a tiny percentage of all the human beings who have ever lived have heard the Gospel, it surely cannot be said that the universe has an anthropic propensity, and that God created the universe with human beings in mind.

As to rejection, we cannot assume that there is no grace-filled postmortem opportunity for exercising faith. First Peter 3:19 suggests the possibility, as does 1 Corinthians 15:29; and the church fathers believed in it. Further, in my reading of Scripture, judgment necessarily implies salvation. The judge is our Savior,[26] and "if God is for us, who can be against us?" (Romans 8:31). As was true for the early church fathers, it is also my contention that the noncoercive love of God will ultimately win the hardest heart.

> *Objection:* belief in universal reconciliation undermines evangelism and the worldwide missionary effort. Without the threat of judgment, without the threat of God's wrath and hellfire, why should anyone bother to seek forgiveness? If we believe that everyone will be saved

---

25. Some biblical scholars, for example, interpret the statement of 2 Thessalonians 2:6, "And you know what is holding him [the man of lawlessness, the Antichrist] back" as a reference to the role of religion in society.

26. The judge is our Savior: Christians who confess the Apostles' Creed, "whence He shall come to judge the living *and the dead*," (emphasis added) have always allowed for the possibility of the salvation of every person who has ever lived.

whatever they do, then what motivation do we have to proclaim the gospel to them? Who is going to risk their health, safety, families, or their lives to reach the lost if the lost will be saved whether we reach out to them or not?

This is the major objection for many evangelical Christians, but to me it presents no serious problem. There are significant motivations for evangelism and mission within a context of universal salvation. But I will reserve this discussion for the following chapter.

There are two more objections, not mentioned specifically by Gregory MacDonald, but often raised by others. Calvinists believe that God's election is limited to those relatively few chosen before the foundation of the world. And Arminians believe that human free will means that we cannot discount the possibility that some will never submit to God's love.

Against the strict Calvinists, I have argued that God has elected the entire human race, not just a few. I will not repeat the argument here. And against the Arminians, I believe that God, being sovereign, can never be defeated. Sooner or later, all will respond to his unfailing love. This seems to me to be the point of Jesus' parable in Luke 15. God will not be satisfied until the last lost sheep is brought back into the fold. How long this will take is anybody's guess. Perhaps it will be accomplished in an instant at the last judgment. Perhaps it will be the outcome of a lengthy purgatorial process. Even Jesus did not pretend to know all the details of God's coming reign (cf. Matthew 20:23).

The idea of universal redemption and renewal for the cosmos, planet Earth, nations, families, and individuals has far-reaching implications for missiology. Several of the objections I have discussed above are specifically missiological. In chapter 11 we will reflect on a selection of these missiological extensions.

11

Missional Implications

And I, when I am lifted up from the earth, will draw all people to myself.

JOHN 12:32

THIRTY YEARS AGO THE esteemed Dutch missionary to Indonesia, Johann Verkuyl, wrote, "Missiology's task in every age is to investigate scientifically and critically the presuppositions, motives, structures, methods, patterns of cooperation, and leadership which the churches bring to their [missionary] mandate."[1] I shall not attempt that gargantuan task in this chapter, but I do want to reflect on some of the missiological implications of the foregoing chapters.

Our Religiously Plural World

My wife Georgia and I live in Paterson, New Jersey. In this modest city of 150,000 people, nearly forty different languages are spoken in the public schools. These languages reflect ethnic groups from more than ninety different countries. Most of Paterson's ethnic groups are nominally Christian (immigration from Latin America is high), but a good number are Hindu and Muslim—the latter from countries as far-flung as Nigeria, Syria, and Bangladesh. Patersonians also include people who practice folk religion: Chinese, Haitians, Brazilians, and Native Americans. We also have Baha'is in Paterson as well as followers of the Dalai Lama. Others adhere to Zen Buddhism. Both Tibetan and Zen Buddhism are nontheistic religions. And of course we have our share of New Age religious groups as well.

1. Verkuyl, *Contemporary Missiology*, 5.

Thus Paterson is a microcosm of America's religious mosaic and indeed of the world's.[2]

The postmodern world, as Thomas Friedman has famously reminded us, is once again a flat-earth society.[3] Postmodernism, considered not as a philosophy but as a culture embodied in the World Wide Web, is hardly distinguishable from globalization, and it is the rapid progress of globalization that has made religious pluralism inescapable. The noted English historian Arnold Toynbee considered the most important event of the twentieth century to be the first large-scale encounter of Eastern and Western religions.

The situation is even more complex, however, because in the Western world, the impact of the Enlightenment and the rise of science have eroded faith and created agnostics and atheists in many quarters. Some have reacted by reverting to neopagan religions or astrology as ways of connecting to reality. Existentialism is another example of a philosophy that, while currently dormant, still underlies a variety of secular and religious worldviews. And over the past century the spread of communist ideology, not only in the former Soviet Union but also in China and the West, has added hundreds of millions to the rolls of those who consider themselves atheists.

In addition, it is reasonable to ask, "Is Christianity the religion founded by Jesus?" A recent paper published by the World Evangelical Alliance (WEA) indicates it is.[4] The WEA statement may have been a concession to its intended Muslim audience; even so, it reflects a common perception among Christians as well. Yet this perception is hardly warranted. In the whole of the New Testament there is scant evidence that Jesus intended to found, much less did found, a new religion. The prime evidence might be the two isolated passages in which Jesus speaks of "my church" and "the church" (Matthew 16:18 and 18:15–17). But "church" is the English translation of the Greek *ekklesia* and the Hebrew *lahaqah* and *qahal*. Both the Greek and Hebrew terms refer to a gathering or assembly of people, not a formal religion per se. In fact, in early Greek democracy, the *ekklesia* identified a political gathering.

2. Cited by Carman, "My Pilgrimage in Mission," 136.

3. Friedman, *World Is Flat*.

4. World Evangelical Alliance, May 2008. "We Too Want to Live in Love, Peace, Freedom and Justice: A Response to a Common Word between Us and You," para. 1. This paper is a welcome development in evangelical ecumenism.

As I read it, Matthew 16:18 tells us that Jesus Messiah intended to gather a new community of people united with him in spirit who would constitute, in the later words of the apostle Paul, a temple or a dwelling place for God's Spirit (cf. 1 Corinthians 3:16). This community would manifest the reality of the reign of God in life, word, and deed. In my judgment, whatever it was that Jesus had it mind all too quickly *became* a religion, or more precisely, a diversity of religious expressions that we call Christianity. Before the end of the very first century of the common era we hear Ignatius of Antioch declaiming, "Do nothing without the bishop and presbyters."[5] Although the gospel is not a religion, and the kingdom of God is not a religion, the variegated Christianity of our time is certainly a religion comparable to other religions. All religions are in large measure human creations developed in response to God's own initiatives to his world. This is what Marjorie Hewitt Suchocki identifies below as God's call and our response.[6]

So it is permissible to discuss Christianity as one religion amongst the world's religions, philosophies, and ideologies as long as we do not confuse the formal Christianity that has evolved with God's great salvific purpose of renewing all things. And if the word *all* in "all things" is to sustain any coherence, it must include both Christianity and all other world religions and ideologies—a startling idea indeed.

With the advent of globalization, not only the kingdom of God but all the religions of the world are "at hand." That being so, the kinds of questions raised at the end of the previous chapter, and others as well, are unavoidable.

Resources

As might be expected, in this chapter I draw on my more than half-century of missionary experience. In addition, I write with the earlier chapter 4 on the Axial Age in mind. The majority of the world religions and philosophies that emerged during the Axial Age are with us today, along with pre-Axial Age tribal religions that maintain themselves in parts of Africa, Latin America, and elsewhere. I write also with the biblical material that we have previously reviewed firmly in mind and with the commentaries of the early

---

5. Ignatius, *Epistle to the Magnesians*, 7.
6. Suchocki, *Divinity & Diversity*.

church fathers in view. Additionally, I keep in mind the lights and shadows that science and evolution cast on the Christian mission enterprise.

Beyond these, in this chapter I am interacting more specifically with discussions by four contemporary thinkers: an evangelical, a representative of mainstream Protestantism, and two Roman Catholic missiologists. I hope that this selection will keep my own discussion from being too simplistic. Although I will not be discussing his thought in this chapter, readers will recognize that throughout this book I have often referred to the writings of the Eastern Orthodox scholar Dumitru Stăniloae.

God's Rivals

Gerald McDermott, the evangelical author of *God's Rivals*, asks this question: Why has God allowed different religions? Note the word *allowed*. McDermott, a professor at Roanoke College in Virginia, had previously penned *Can Evangelicals Learn from World Religions?* He maintains that:

> [T]he biblical authors and early church theologians saw the religions not simply as human constructions but as spiritual projects as well. The religions are living and breathing beings, if you will, that have inner souls, derived in part from spiritual entities called "gods" by the Old Testament and "powers" by the New Testament.[7]

As I have indicated in earlier chapters, I cannot agree that there are supernatural entities (other than God) that can be said to animate the world religions. The "gods" and "powers" McDermott references are, in my opinion, natural forces inherent in the religions—as well as in other cultural building blocks: family, commerce, government, the military, education, and the like. Nevertheless it is safe to say that McDermott's perspective prevails in evangelical and other Christian circles today.

In addition to surveying the two Testaments on the subject of other religions, McDermott also presents the thinking of four early church theologians: Justin Martyr, Irenaeus, Clement of Alexandria, and Origen.

Justin, known as the Martyr because he was beheaded in 165 C.E. for refusing to sacrifice to the Roman gods, argued that some portions of pagan religions were inspired by Christ. That is, Christ the eternal *Logos* (Word of God) had been present from the advent of *H. sapiens*, enlightening everyone (John 1:9) in different degrees; and that therefore, truth

---

7. McDermott, *God's Rivals*, 11.

may be found in the world's philosophies and religions. Justin went even further: some non-Christian thinkers, such as Socrates and Heraclitus, were actually Christians insofar as they were able to appropriate the seeds sown by the Word. Similarly so were certain "barbarians" of the Old Testament: Abraham, Melchizedek, Job, and Elias, for example.

Irenaeus, whom we met back in chapter 7, saw the other religions from a pedagogical perspective. He taught that God has always been at work in all the religions, using them to prepare the nations to receive the fullness of the gospel. As with the Hebrews, so with the other nations: God planned a gradual course of preparation for all peoples to receive the incarnate Word. He instituted a series of historical stages—the religions as *praeparatio evangelica* (preparation for the gospel)—that eventually culminated in the supreme event of the incarnation. The first stage was creation. The second stage was the history of the Jews. The third stage was the incarnation, reversing the features of the fall on behalf of all the peoples of the world.

The result of this recapitulation was the "readmission of a new redeemed race to the privileged position held by Adam as companion of God before the Fall."[8] Thus Irenaeus believed that the religions of the world are analogous to the religion established by Moses. They were conditioned by God in some measure to ready the nations for the coming of Christ.

Clement of Alexandria, whom we met earlier in chapter 9, believed that God actually gave some religions as covenants to the Gentiles, similar to the covenant of the law given to Jews. "The same God that finished both the [Old and New] Covenants was the giver of Greek philosophy to the Greeks," Clement asserted.[9] Clement saw the best of the Greek philosophers as being equivalent to the Hebrew prophets. Thus he wrote of Homer's "theology" and Orpheus "the theologian."[10] Greek philosophy was for Clement, in McDermott's words, a unilateral gift of God to train a people for further revelation and closer relationship to himself. Still, Clement asserted, the wisdom of the Greeks could not compare with Holy Scripture. They had truth, but it was mixed with error, and thus while

---

8. Ibid.,109.

9. Clement, *Stromata* 6.5, cited in McDermott, *Rivals*, 122.

10. McDermott, 123.

useful, it was not essential for faith. Greek philosophy was a way *toward* salvation, but was not a way *of* salvation.

Origen, whom we also met in chapter 9, had a more negative attitude toward the religions, cautioning that malevolent spirits were behind Christianity's rivals. (The evangelical McDermott is clearly a disciple of Origen in this respect.) Only mature Christians should investigate other religions, Origen opined, for what is profitable to the mature believer can be fatal to babes in Christ. Behind every religion, Origen supposed, are angelic or demonic powers. These invisible agents account for their mixture of good and evil, truth and falsehood. Surprisingly, as we have seen, Origen believed that God is leading every soul to eventual salvation—universal salvation—by means unknown to us. He grounds this notion on the radical freedom of God, which over the long haul overwhelms human freedom.[11]

So why has God permitted the emergence of other religions? Putting the most positive "spin" on the teachings of the early church theologians, McDermott says,

> God permits what is less than the best . . . . Rather than abandon his creatures because of their stubbornness, God works with them where they are. And by a long process of education and discipline . . . humans are called to a higher truth.[12]

The implications for McDermott are these:

1. We should change the way we think about the religions. They are not mere human creations but involve cosmic powers.

2. People of other religions, therefore, are not our opponents; cosmic powers are.

3. The fact that believers of other faiths are not our enemies suggests patient persistence, not hostile argument. Thus we need to share the Gospel with more respect and sensitivity.[13]

4. Christians have much in common with believers of other faiths. "This commonality in knowledge about God and his ways helps re-

---

11. For myself, I differ from Origen in that I believe it is God's love, not his power or his freedom, that conquers all.

12. McDermott, *God's Rivals*, 160.

13. For an excellent contemporary example of this attitude, see the writings of Nabeel Jabbour.

strain sin and evil in us all, so that the world is a happier place than it would be without these religions."[14]

5. The Holy Spirit can also use the other religions to help Christians understand the gospel more clearly, as well as to judge and purify the church.

6. Nevertheless, in spite of all this, McDermott concludes, "[the] other religions do not provide a road of salvation to the triune God. If believers of other religions are saved, it is only by the work of Christ in his perfect life and death. And it is also through their acceptance of the gospel."[15]

Divinity and Diversity

I do not know whether evolution is part of McDermott's worldview. It is evident from his books, however, that it plays no role in his missiology, at least as that relates to other religions, philosophies, and ideologies. Such is not the case with Marjorie Hewitt Suchocki, a process-relational theologian,[16] professor emerita at the Claremont School of Theology in California, and author of *Divinity & Diversity*. Theistic evolution is clearly embedded in her worldview, as is the assumption (her word, not mine) that God—not demonic powers or gods (as per Origen and McDermott)—is involved, salvifically no less, in the making of religions.[17]

Suchocki presents four Christian "ingredients" in her thesis that Christians should celebrate, not oppose or merely tolerate, the reality of many religions. Her four ingredients are rethought theologies of creation, incarnation, image of God, and the reign of God.

First, the diversity of creation is an evolutionary response to call and response. God calls; nature and humans respond. Out of chaos (not *ex nihilo*; see Genesis 1:2) God calls, "Let there be light," and the universe responds. To every response or lack of response, God issues new calls in the form of new possibilities through the millennia. "The cumulative past provides the always new context in which the next stage of call and

---

14. McDermott, *God's Rivals*, 166.

15. Ibid., 168.

16. Process-relational theology: the view in which relationships to others are integral to identity and to existence itself. Cf. Whitehead, *Process and Reality*; Cobb, Jr., *A Christian Theology of Religions*; and Mesle, *Process-Relational Philosophy*.

17. Suchocki, *Divinity & Diversity*, 16 and 27.

response can occur."[18] Creation by call and response takes creatures into covenant, Suchocki avers. From this intentional process irreparable diversity is inevitable. If creaturely response is integral to the Creator's call, then there is simply no way there could ever be a world without great diversity.[19] This variety includes the phenomenon of religion, the diversity of which is presaged in the story of the tower of Babel in Genesis 11.[20]

Second, having called the religions into existence by way of human response to God's "upward call" (Philippians 3:14), it follows that God is present to save in all religions. We know this because of the Christ event, which reveals the true nature of God. That is, radical incarnation is the way God works. God is present in every realm of life. But if this be so, one might reasonably ask how can there be Truth with a capital T? Jesus: "I am *the* Way, *the* Truth, and *the* Life; no man comes to the Father but by me."[21] How does Suchocki understand this declaration? She first notes that truth is always bound up with the way we abstract information from our experience in order to explain and control experience. How truth is perceived varies from place to place and from time to time. Further, she points out that the nature of religious language, plus the nature of incarnation, generates multiple truths.

For Suchocki this multiplicity means that although God is known in one form (or formlessness) in other religions, one cannot know God as *Father*—as infinitely caring, in the way that Christians do—except through Jesus. This reality does not suggest that the other religions have no truth or salvific dimensions themselves, however. Indeed, this possibility is clearly open. Other religions may know God truly in other ways than Father.

Third, the image of God has traditionally been seen in the individual. Suchocki suggests instead that if God's image reflects the trinitarian nature of God, as we believe, we must define it also in terms of community. No individual apart from Jesus reflects the fullness of the image of God. Only in the diversity of community is this fullness to be found. Suchocki suggests that the image of God means that all of humanity in its *togetherness* is a reflection of the divine image. We are called to be a world community of

18. Ibid., 29.

19. Ibid.

20. An observation made by Laurel Van Der Wende, September 2008, e-mail correspondence.

21. John 14:6.

communities. "This communal way of being is our call; it is yet before us; we have not yet achieved it," Suchocki declares.[22] In a beautiful section too long to reproduce here, Suchocki evokes Psalms 145–150, describing how these psalms alternate between prayer and praise expressed directly to God but also expressed to one another within the human community. These psalms portray the kind of God in whose image we are made, and these are the kinds of works in which we should engage, and this is the kind of communities we should build, she insists.

Fourth, justice characterizes the reign of God in the Hebrew Bible. We recognize the reign of God in the community's ability to succor the needs of the widow and orphan, and especially the stranger, in its midst. In today's world that stranger includes the person of another faith. Suchocki notes that

> ... within Christianity, our proclivity for valuing our kind meets its ultimate test in relation to those whose religious ways are not our own .... In our history, we have often demanded conversion as the test of community .... We have often extended well-being to the other in the hope that the other will, in fact, become like us.[23]

Suchocki goes on to suggest that we should accept as permanent the diversity of religions and witness to the reign of God in the world for the sake of friendship, through which we all might turn the world itself into a community of communities and, more importantly, a community of friends.

Naturally such a vision raises questions from such evangelical Christians as McDermott: What is happening on the cross of Jesus Christ? Does religious plurality mean that Jesus does not save everybody? If other religions are valid in and of themselves, what happens to the historic mission of the Christian church? To answer these queries, Suchocki adds two chapters on "Saving Grace" and "Mission in a Pluralistic World."

What happened on the cross, as Suchocki sees it, was not a cosmic conflict such as Irenaeus envisioned, or an Anselmian satisfaction, but an Abelardian revelation of the nature of God. God is a consistent and insistent drive toward love, and lures the world to do the same. This revelation has the power to transform lives.[24] And with this definition as

22. Suchocki, *Divinity & Diversity*, 68.

23. Ibid., 80.

24. Ibid., 102.

background, she eloquently presents her own model of Christian mission as the cultivation of the friendship among the world's religious communities. She quotes Jesus: "You are my friends if you do what I command you .... This I command you, that you love one another" (John 15:14, 17). "My conviction in writing this book," she avers, "is that God is calling religious peoples in particular to model new ways of friendship in today's world."[25] This modeling has to be accomplished locally as well a globally, with respect to systemic injustice as well as one-to-one ministry.[26] Dialogue, then, is the future of Christian mission.

A Theology of Religious Pluralism

While asserting the permanent diversity of other religions, and believing that God (whether known by that name or another) is present in all religions, Suchocki writes from within the Christian tradition. The same is true of Jacques Dupuis, author of *Toward a Christian Theology of Religious Pluralism*.[27] Dupuis was a long-time Jesuit missionary in India and later professor of theology at the Gregorian Institute in Rome. Of the four books I am summarizing in this section, Dupuis' treatise is the most erudite and extensive.

Dupuis reviews the witness of the Old and New Testaments with respect to the Gentile nations and their religions, emphasizing the roles of the Word, Wisdom, and Spirit. He then proceeds to describe in much the same manner as McDermott the thinking of the early church fathers. He concludes his review by quoting appreciatively the Roman Catholic theologian Karl Rahner's observation that the world religions "were an unconscious Yes or No to the Word of God who was to come in human flesh."[28] These words echo Suchocki's theme of call and response.

But Dupuis is writing primarily to a critical Roman Catholic readership and must necessarily trace the long history of that church's thinking about and relationships with other religions. And he must deal in depth with Cyprian's famous dictum, "No salvation outside the Church."[29] He traces in detail the evolution of the [Roman Catholic] church's teaching

25. Ibid., 11.

26. Ibid., 118.

27. Dupuis, *Religious Pluralism*, 7.

28. Ibid., 83.

29. St. Cyprian, bishop of Carthage about 250 C.E.

on the subject through the medieval period and the Counter-Reformation before examining the situation surrounding Vatican II.[30] This project consumes the first half of his book. Dupuis regards Vatican II as a clear watershed in Catholic thinking about the religions of the world.

It seems to me that Dupuis finds a middle position between McDermott and Suchocki. He believes with Suchocki that the plurality of religions in the world today is God-ordained, resting primarily on "the superabundant richness and diversity of God's self manifestations to humankind . . . . Religious pluralism in principle rests on the immensity of a God who is love."[31] But with McDermott, Dupuis regards the goal of Christianity as being something much more than a global community of friends.

In the second half of his book, Dupuis presents his own theological position, set off against both the exclusivism of such evangelicals as McDermott and the radical pluralism of a number of contemporary scholars, of whom Suchocki is an apt example.

Dupuis' thinking moves along two distinct but related paths. One he terms regnocentrism because he sees the kingdom of God as a framework that transcends the church's previous insistence on "no salvation outside the church." He believes it also transcends the typical evangelical insistence on exclusivism: no salvation without a profession of faith in Jesus Christ as the one and only way of salvation. The other is what he calls Trinitarian Christology. Trinitarian Christology is Dupuis' framework for countering the radical pluralism of those who insist on the validity of all religions.

According to Dupuis, God created the universe and the human race as a diversified unity by means of his Word and Spirit. Throughout the long history of humanity God communicated with the human race by his Word and Spirit with a view to its ultimate salvation. It is out of this interaction that the strongly contextualized religions and philosophies of the world, including Christianity, emerged and are sustained. This interaction continues to the present day and will continue into the foreseeable future. This is the Trinitarian aspect of Trinitarian Christology. Dupuis quotes the following paragraph approvingly:

30. Vatican II, the Second Ecumenical Council of the Roman Catholic Church, convened by Pope John XXIII in 1962. It concluded in 1965 under Pope Paul VI. Pope John conceived it as an *aggiornamento*, an 'updating' of the Church.

31. Dupuis, *Religious Pluralism*, 387.

> Its experience of the other religions has led the Church in Asia
> to [a] positive appreciation of their role in the divine economy
> of salvation. This appreciation is based on the fruits of the Spirit
> perceived in the lives of the other religions' believers: a sense of
> the sacred, a commitment to the pursuit of fullness, a thirst for
> self-realization, a taste for prayer and commitment, a desire for
> renunciation, a struggle for justice, an urge to basic human good-
> ness, an involvement in service, a total surrender of the self to God,
> and an attachment to the transcendent in their symbols, rituals
> and life itself, through human weakness and sin are not absent.[32]

Meanwhile God manifested himself to the nation of Israel and at
the appropriate time revealed himself to the world in the saving "particularity" of the incarnation of the Word in Jesus Christ.[33] By his death,
resurrection, and ascension to the right hand of God, Jesus saves—or
more precisely, God saves through Jesus. This is the Christology aspect
of Trinitarian Christology. Christians are free to witness to salvation in
Jesus, therefore, without having to deny that God also works within and
through the world religions to move the human race toward the salvation
that will be fulfilled in the reign of God. As I read him, Dupuis stops short
of affirming salvific efficacy in the world religions. They only move the
nations *toward* salvation in Christ; the reader should recall Clement of
Alexandria.

As regards the mission of the Church, Dupuis, without devaluing the
proclamation of the gospel in any way, insists that all evangelization be
done in the spirit of dialogue. "The spirit of dialogue must inform every
aspect or element of the evangelizing mission."[34] Dialogue is a distinctive
integral element (along with presence, service, liturgical life, proclamation, and persuasion) of that mission in its own right.

I imagine Dupuis would consider this summary of his 400-page
tome to be woefully inadequate but I trust that it serves to show how
contemporary Roman Catholic thinking agrees with and differs from
both mainline and evangelical Protestants.

---

32. Theological Advisory Commission, no. 48, 7.

33. Dupuis, *Religious Pluralism,* 297–300.

34. Ibid., 360.

God's Chosen Peoples

After serving as a missionary in Tanzania, Walbert Bühlmann has been for many years now the general secretary of Capuchin[35] missions worldwide. The book under review here is his *God's Chosen Peoples*. Note that the word *peoples* is in the plural. In some respects Bühlmann is a more radical thinker than Dupuis, with bolder ideas.

Bühlmann's book has four parts. In Part I he describes how "the chosen people" (singular) came to be, first as Jews and then as Christians, and how both groups have understood their election in exclusive terms. In Part II he works out in excoriating detail how this theological exclusivism has generated two millennia of ideological exclusivism, resulting in rejections, divisions, persecutions, inquisitions, and crusades, with heretics, scapegoats, and pagans doomed to hellfire. This divisiveness simply cannot continue, he declares.

In contrast to the way in which the chosen people have viewed the "not-chosen" peoples, in Part III Bühlmann discusses how the not-chosen ones view themselves. In some respects this section is the most interesting and valuable part of his book. He gathers together a great deal of research on the pygmies, shepherds (nomads), and farmers or hunters of Africa and other continents. He shows how each of these groups and their myriad subgroups understands itself to be the chosen people of a supreme deity who is in covenant with them (and in many cases is known to them as "Our Father!") Bühlmann includes some African tribal prayers to God, beautiful to read, and notes, "It would not be difficult for us to take such prayers as these upon our own lips, and pray together with 'pagans' such as these to our common God."[36]

In like manner Bühlmann reviews the putative "higher" religions of the Axial Age, ferreting out similarities and differences in their notions of God, the afterlife, salvation, forgiveness, and the like.[37] He concludes that all peoples are religious, and that therefore religion has something to do with being human as such. He notes that while the origin of the higher religions is a matter of record, the beginnings of primitive religions are

35. The Capuchins are an autonomous branch of the Franciscan Order.

36. Bühlmann, *God's Chosen Peoples*, 145.

37. John Carman, longtime professor at Harvard Divinity School's Center for the Study of World Religions, notes that "Several times in my research I was surprised to find out how striking the similarities are between very different faith traditions in naming the attributes of God." Carman, "My Pilgrimage," 138.

lost in the shadows of prehistory. "Their myths assert that God's relationship with human beings began with their very first creations. Naturally, there is no empirical demonstration that this is the 'way it was' . . . but neither can we prove the contrary."[38]

Sadly, Bühlmann notes that wherever we find an explicit covenant consciousness in primal as well as higher religions, we usually find an unattractive exclusivist side as well—or worse, a spirit of aggressiveness, with rueful effects on the "others," who are not considered equally the peoples of God.

In Part IV Bühlmann deals with most of the questions that have been raised by the other three writers we have been discussing. Is there true revelation in other religions? Are other deities identical with Yahweh and the Father of our Lord Jesus Christ? Have incarnations similar to Jesus' incarnation occurred in other religious settings? What is the actual salvific value in other religions? And finally: why, where, and how should we evangelize?

> Today it can be said that a third phase of salvation history has begun, in which one people is no longer singled out to represent the others, but all peoples are discovering that they are a chosen people all together, that they form, in common, the "Third People of God," comprised of all humanity . . . . They already live all together within sight of the kingdom of God, and it is the proper task of the church to cry this out to them, to make proclamation of this kingdom.[39]

Interfacing with the Religions

"Universal salvation? How wonderful!" This was the response I received recently from the widow of perhaps the most highly regarded missiologist of the late twentieth century when I casually mentioned to her that I am writing on the subject. She continued, "I have come to the 'insight' that our God is so much greater than Christianity, and I believe that God speaks to people where ever they are, and through the faith they grew up in. The Holy Spirit is busy with each of us, whatever our background."[40]

---

38. Bühlmann, *God's Chosen Peoples*, 179.

39. Ibid., 268.

40. Annemie Bosch, e-mail correspondence, August 2008.

In this book I am pressing the thesis that in the Christ event God was reconciling the world to himself. More than that: the world has in fact been reconciled, and that the salvation of everyone who has ever lived or ever will live is assured. This salvation will be fully realized in the context of the second coming of Christ, the last judgment (cf. Romans 2:16) and the resurrection of the dead. Obviously, such a scenario is at variance with the exclusivism of Gerald McDermott and most other evangelicals.[41]

Universal salvation as I have presented it, is not identical, however, with the radical pluralism suggested by Marjorie Suchocki, for she seems to envision a salvation limited to this present world to be hopefully realized in a "community of communities of friends." We live in an unbearably violent world, so I empathize with Suchocki's vision of a peaceable kingdom. But for me the community that God purposes to create is an eternal community of mutual love whose members not only are united to God in Christ but also destined to share in the stewardship of the universe in life eternal.

My thesis is also at some variance with the Roman Catholic theology of religious pluralism as presented by Jacques Dupuis. Catholic doctrine in its present form, like that of evangelicals, accepts the distinction between saved and lost and assumes that not all will be saved[42]—though many more will be saved than we have traditionally thought because there are aspects in every religion through which God moves people toward salvation. What I find compelling in Dupuis' thesis is his emphasis on the kingdom of God (as over against the church as an institution) and his Trinitarian Christology. The former can be understood as a guarantee against exclusivism. The latter seems to preserve both the particularity of the Christ event while affirming God's presence through Word and Spirit with all the world's peoples.

Though Walbert Bühlmann does not take up the topic of universal redemption per se, I agree most with his presentation, perhaps because of his lifelong missionary experience with which I identify, but primarily because he seems to grab the bull by the horns and insist that we take a hard look at our history and make the mental and spiritual changes necessary to relate properly to a globalized world of religious and ideological pluralism.

41. Cf. Netland, *Encountering Religious Pluralism*.

42. Dupuis, *Religious Pluralism*, 311.

Having noted these caveats, I want to reaffirm my conviction that the gospel of universal renewal as I have presented it has special meaning for our times. In East Asia and sub-Saharan Africa, for example, Christian missionaries find that concern for the fate of deceased ancestors keeps many from considering conversion to Christ.[43] Missionaries often are in a quandary trying to respond to this concern in terms of traditional Christian dogma. God's promise of universal salvation in the renewal of all things provides the missionary with a message that enables him or her to relate compassionately and convincingly to worries about ancestors.

Religious pluralism, here intended to include all the variant philosophies and ideologies that create our worldviews and underlie our cultures and civilizations, increasingly impinges on us. We can no longer accept as a given the "clash of civilizations" that Samuel Huntington predicts. Suchocki is right: we are impelled to promote understanding and friendship among the world's peoples.[44] This promotion is impossible if we cling to the notion that our religion as it has evolved is superior to others and that therefore our faith must prevail over others.

Once we realize that all peoples are on equal footing, that "God has bound everyone over to disobedience so that he may have mercy on them all" (Romans 11:32), and that God purposes to save the human race in toto, we are psychologically enabled to pursue conversions—yes, conversions[45]—graciously in the context of Christian presence, service, liturgy, proclamation, dialogue, and persuasion. But such conversions in a postmodern world are better directed, in my judgment, to the person of Christ and his kingdom than to formal Christianity—though I admit that maintaining the clear distinction between these two is not easy for most of us.

Up to this point, I have not said much about service, though it is central to my own practice of holistic ministry. Service (in the form of building and staffing hospitals, schools, orphanages, and the like) has

43. Recall our earlier discussion of "Tears in Heaven?"

44. As Dr. Nabeel Jabbour does in his book *The Crescent through the Eyes of the Cross.*

45. René Girard suggests that "conversion is our discovery that we are persecutors without knowing it. The sacrificial system disguises this reality by insisting that the victim is actually guilty of something. But Satan 'is a liar and the father of lies,' Jesus declared (John 8:44 NIV). The King James Version translates this as "he was a murderer from the beginning." Girard, *Evolution and Conversion*, 198, 223.

always been a part of Christian mission. Within the evangelical community during the early years of my ministry it, like dialogue, and certainly liturgy, was generally downplayed. Evangelism and church planting were the major emphases. But during the second half of the twentieth century evangelical missionaries, beginning with Bob Pierce and the formation of the World Vision organization during the war in Korea, embraced it more and more. Today such megachurch pastors as Rick Warren are major proponents of service. Asked about dialogue with Roman Catholics and Orthodox leaders overseas, Warren says, "I'm not really that interested in interfaith dialogue. I am interested in interfaith *projects*. Let's do something together."[46]

The Insider Movement

The earliest generation of followers of the Way asked: Is it incumbent on Gentile converts to forsake their Hellenistic culture and adopt the Jewish way of life? Today's Christian missionaries are asking a similar question: Is it necessary for Muslims or Hindus or Buddhists to abandon their respective cultures, embedded as these cultures are in the religions of Islam, Hinduism, and Buddhism, in order to become authentic disciples of Jesus Christ? This is precisely the kind of question that the reality of religious pluralism forces upon us. Some of my younger missionary colleagues in The Navigators organization, now middle-aged but not yet retired, are active in what is called "The Insider Movement."[47] To understand this movement, a little background is required.

In 1998 John Travis, a missionary in Central Asia, published an article describing six approaches to evangelization–or more precisely, the outcomes of six different approaches—that he laid out on a contextual spectrum or continuum labeled C1 to C6.[48] Travis developed his spectrum in a Muslim context, but the spectrum can be applied to any religion or ideology. C1 represents very low contextualization; that is, a church that reflects the culture of the foreign missionaries who planted it or a long-

---

46. *Christianity Today*, October 2008, 44. Warren is the pastor of the Saddleback Church in Lake Forest, California. He has launched a global P.E.A.C.E. Plan (Promote reconciliation. Equip servant leaders. Assist the poor. Care for the sick. Educate the next generation) to help meet the United Nations' Millennium Goals. See http://www.the peaceplan.com.

47. Cf. Petersen and Shamy, *The Insider*.

48. Travis, "The C1 to C6 Spectrum," 407–8.

established minority indigenous church, such as the Coptic Church of Egypt. C5 represents an unusually high level of contextuality; for example, Christians who identify themselves not merely as followers of Jesus, but "*Hindu* followers of Jesus," or "*Buddhist* followers of Jesus." C6 represents secret believers and is not really an integral part of the continuum.

The Navigators colleagues I referred to are missionally involved at the C5 level. They point to such passages as 1 Corinthians 7:17–24 and 9:19–23 to argue that just as Paul did not require Gentiles to convert to Judaism, so we should not encourage Hindus or Buddhists to convert to "Christianity."[49] C5 missionaries point out that Jesus commanded us to make disciples, not converts (Matthew 28:29). C5 workers, if anything, desire to convert Muslims or Hindus to Jesus and his kingdom, not to the religion we call Christianity.

Followers of Jesus cannot live in isolation. National insiders at the C5 level are already embedded in an established community of Buddhists, Hindus, or some other faith. Of course they want to be yoked also with others who are followers of Jesus. Rather than withdrawing from their indigenous community and joining a Christian church, however, they share their faith in their natural networks of family, co-workers, fellow students, etc. As these natural network members profess in turn their faith in Jesus, they form a cohesive, expanding body of believers within their home culture. One such insider, a Chinese layperson working in China, described his situation this way:

> Lay people like me appear to the locals to be just like them, professionals with demanding work schedules, limited time for family, etc. We do not seek out strangers as such, but live and function as salt and light in our relational networks, attracting people by our lifestyle—essentially a friendship and process approach. At appropriate times, we share relevant stories and experiences leading to the good news. No hell fire stories are needed: just presence, service, dialogue. Proclamation? From a pulpit, probably not, because most of the intended audience doesn't sit before a pulpit. From a public place? Hardly, for that is not allowed. Witnessing privately in a *jiaoliu*, yes.[50] Persuasion? Hardly necessary: our wit-

---

49. Cf. Joshua Massey, "God's Amazing Diversity," 8.

50. *Jiaoliu*: Mandarin for a mutually agreeable dialogue, as in "iron sharpening iron" (Proverbs 27:17).

ness is perceived as good news and welcomed because it is relevant and meaningful.[51]

Or, as Carl Raschke, the iconoclastic professor of religion at Denver University, puts it,

> Paul did not go around in clear Christian dress. He was something of a covert operator. He wanted to show that the relativity of proliferating spiritual viewpoints could be captured in the net of the gospel itself and turned into the presence of a Christ in whom there was 'no east or west.'[52]

My own interest in the Insider movement stems from what I see as its potential to advance some of the major themes of this book, not only with respect to the world of religious pluralism but also to the secular world. Insiders are perfectly placed for dialogue, for mutual giving and receiving from the home culture. They can participate in whatever God is already doing within that culture as God moves peoples and nations toward the salvation he intends for all. Once convinced that God purposes universal salvation, the insider is free to share his or her good news and allow things to develop as they may. Such flexibility is an acknowledgment of the radical freedom God has to work lovingly in and through all cultures and religions.

Interfacing with the Secular World

Jesus told this parable: The kingdom of heaven is like a man who sowed good seed in his field. But while everyone was sleeping, his enemy came and sowed weeds among the wheat, and went away. When the wheat sprouted and formed heads, then the weeds also appeared. His servants asked him, "Do you want us to go and pull them up?" "No," he answered, "because while you are pulling the weeds, you may uproot the wheat with them. Let both grow together until the harvest."

Jesus' disciples then asked him to explain the parable. He replied: The one who sowed the good seed is the son of Man. The field is the world, and the good seed stands for the people of the kingdom of heaven. The

51. Sik Ming Chong, e-mail correspondence, July 11, 2008.
52. Raschke, *GloboChrist*, 154.

weeds are the people of the evil one, and the enemy who sows them is the devil. The harvest is the End of the Age.[53]

Although not *of* the world in a certain sense, we disciples of Jesus are thoroughly embedded *in* the world. This participation suggests that we have a responsibility to understand and apply the gospel to both local and global problems, some of crisis proportions. In this chapter we are thinking globally. We are not the only ones interacting with these problems, however. Men and women of good will everywhere, as well as men and women with evil intentions are also engaged. By evil intentions I mean intentions that are motivated by what I previously termed Darwinian rules and the selfish gene, and that aim at personal harm and destruction. A few of these global problems are essentially unique to our time; most of them, however, are longstanding.

I mention first the novel phenomenon of globalization, which we have already discussed briefly. It is not a crisis, properly speaking, for there are benefits attached to it. But it constitutes a major problem for large portions of the world that are drawn into the process against their will and who are without the resources to compete successfully in the system. Something akin to globalization was occurring in Jesus' time: the Hellenizing of culture and the Romanizing of the economic-political order throughout the whole of the Mediterranean world. Jesus ministered directly to those who were marginalized in the process.

As followers of Jesus, we must be sensitive to all those who are being marginalized today by the processes of globalization. More than that, love of neighbor will lead us to advocate on their behalf. "Speak up for those who cannot speak for themselves, for the rights of all who are destitute" (Proverbs 31:8). Certain Christian organizations specialize in providing small-scale entrepreneurial opportunities for the poor; these should be supported. We Christians in the West cannot identify ourselves so completely with the consumerist culture and with the agents of globalization that we become unwitting oppressors ourselves.

Another issue relatively unique to our time is the global population explosion. When I was born the world's population numbered two billion. Today it is six billion, and within fifty years it is projected to be ten billion. Again, population expansion is not bad per se. In fact, some believe that it is part of God's plan of salvation—more people to work on the grand

---

53. Matthew 13:24–30, 36–43.

project of the deification of the world.[54] Population increase presents no problem when global resources are distributed equitably, but such is not the case today. Multiplied millions today live in what we routinely describe as abject poverty. They themselves are acutely conscious of living on the underside of history, dispossessed and angry. The world becomes a boiling cauldron that carries the very real potential for global revolution, or a series of regional revolutions, on a scale heretofore unknown.[55] The temptation for Christians in the West is to side passively with the haves against the have-nots. Rather than taking sides, followers of Jesus would better serve as peacemakers and brokers, cooperating with all people of good will in promoting social justice. In our day there are multiple means of doing this.

The third issue, which gets ample attention in the media and is gradually impressing itself on the public mind, has to do with the environment.[56] As Willis Jenkins of Yale Divinity School has pointed out, "Ecosystems, species, skies, and wetlands make up the context of mission, just as do cultures, languages, markets, and health clinics."[57] Global warming is prominent here, but there are other matters of equal importance, such as deforestation of the Amazon and the development of alternative energy sources. If, as I have argued, God purposes that *H. sapiens* act as stewards of the environment, then clearly we have to take the lead or cooperate with those who are, in tackling environmental challenges. We can understand this task as colaboring with God in preparation for the renewal of all things.

The Canadian missiologist Allan Effa documents the emerging consensus among Roman Catholics, conciliar Protestants (including the Orthodox churches), and evangelicals that missional theology requires rethinking in three major areas: creation, salvation, and eschatology. With respect to creation, a shift from an anthropocentric to a theocentric understanding is called for. "Human beings are God's image bearers, but

---

54. E. g., Stăniloae, *Creation and Deification*, 206: "Through the multiplication of human beings as factors of good and evil, always original but endowed with memory of the past, God is leading the world toward ever new phases."

55. Cf. Attali, *Millennium*.

56. The October 2008 issue of the *International Bulletin of Missionary Research* has two helpful articles on this subject: Effa, "The Greening of Mission," 174–76; and Jenkins, "Missiology in Environmental Context," 177–79.

57. Jenkins, "Missiology," 177.

... other elements of the creation declare the glory of God in ways that humans cannot duplicate."[58] What Effa says is true, but I do not fully agree that this conclusion requires a shift from one perspective to another; rather, both perspectives must be held in creative tension.

Some missiologists are calling for a shift from a personal view of salvation to a cosmic one. Again, this is tendentious as a conclusion. But as I hope this book has made clear, I fully support a greater emphasis on the cosmic dimensions of salvation. As to eschatology, in some parts of the global Christian community, there is, as Effa puts it, "in this line of thought people get saved, wait until Jesus raptures them away, and then get to watch the planet burn"—an eschatology of abandonment. Effa concludes that a shift to an eschatology of restoration is under way.[59]

Willis Jenkins presents a set of useful questions for persons engaged in global mission:

- How does mission fit into an ecological context?
- How and how well are Christian mission practices responding to environmental threats to community life?
- How does "place" matter for spiritual experience and geography for interreligious engagement?
- How might environmental mission practices help reimagine or re-shape theologies of salvation, the patterns of Christian friendship, or the character of Christian witness?
- How do mission practices reframe questions about locality and sustainability, place and global community?[60]

I do not want this chapter to become unbearably long, but we must also acknowledge some of the global problems that have been with us from the beginnings of human civilization, and which the gospel of the kingdom is superbly equipped to address. Poverty, famine, and disease top this list. The abuse of state power and oppression follow closely, as do national chauvinism, especially the exercise of war in the pursuit of national agendas and unbridled free-market capitalism. According to Jesus, people of the kingdom of heaven are the "good seed" planted in our

58. Effa, "Greening of Mission," 174.

59. In this book I have suggested that renewal is a more biblical concept than restoration.

60. Jenkins, "Missiology," 182.

world. Of all peoples, we are best positioned to attend to the point of view of the others, working toward global *shalom*. We cannot allow ourselves to revert to the kind of private pietism that has characterized evangelicals and other Christians in the recent past. And by the same token, we must not allow ourselves to be coopted by partisan politics of either left or right.

Role of the Holy Spirit

Jesus promised that when he "went away" he would send the Spirit, whom he called the Advocate, the defense attorney, to be with us. The Advocate would fulfill two roles. On the one hand, he would "prove the world to be in the wrong"; on the other, he would "guide you into all the truth" (John 16:8 and 16:13). Later Jesus would forecast other roles for the Spirit, but for now let us focus on these two. As to the first, during the past two millennia the Spirit has surely been sifting the nations, unmasking the root causes of the violence that besets *H. sapiens*. As to the second, it seems clear to me that the Spirit simultaneously has been directing the world into ever-deepening understandings of truth and reality, not least in the secular world.

I see this deepening, for example, in the emergence of modern science. We have learned that the world revolves around the sun, not vice versa. We are learning how to interact physically with the moon and other planets in our solar system. We are slowly learning how to conserve and protect the world we inhabit. We are gradually discovering the underlying causes of diseases and ways to combat them. As Girard has pointed out, victimizing and scapegoating are routinely condemned today—think of our negative reactions to the Holocaust and to the ethnic cleansings of Cambodia and Rwanda. This rejection of violence has not always been the case and is almost certainly the consequence of gospel-seepage into Western culture and beyond.[61] The theologian Jürgen Moltmann sees this secular activity of the Holy Spirit as a fulfillment of the Spirit's being poured out on "all flesh" (Joel 2:28; Acts 2:16–17). T. David Beck, in his highly regarded *The Holy Spirit and the Renewal of All Things*. strongly

---

61. Of course, we have also managed to create atomic bombs and other weapons of mass destruction. And our scientists are not always ethically prescient. The Spirit oversees this combination of good and evil and ceaselessly works toward the ultimate freedom of the human race. This oversight reflects God's call and human responses, and it seems to have intensified in recent centuries.

disagrees, attributing Moltmann's position to faulty exegesis.[62] But even if Moltmann's exegesis of the specific texts is wrong, I think he has captured the larger picture correctly.

I see this intensification also in relation to the Christian world mission. The Spirit has worked incrementally through time to reveal God's true purpose for humanity. The Spirit has not only empowered God's people to witness to the world but also to witness more effectively. The Spirit has shown the Church the futility of such measures as crusades and inquisitions, witch trials and forced conversions. In our day the Spirit has, in part through theologies of hope and liberation, revealed more clearly the holistic nature of the gospel and God's concern for social justice. In the fall of 2008, we witnessed the nomination of an African-American to be President of the United States. Those of us who attended the funeral of Martin Luther King, Jr. in 1963 had not expected such a nomination to occur in our lifetime. The Spirit has, through the contemporary process of globalization, made us more conscious of the human race as constituting one family, and the ways in which our destinies are tied to one another. Through the current emphasis on environment, the Spirit is reminding us that we are also bound irrevocably to nature.

In earlier centuries few Christian people were able in their narrow exclusivism to envision such a glorious reality as universal redemption. Today the Spirit is empowering us to overcome our natural prejudices toward the "other." The Spirit is enabling us to conquer the Darwinian spirit of exclusiveness—the selfish gene—that for so long has gone hand in hand with the belief that only "we" are God's chosen people, giving way to the realization that God has elected all peoples for redemption and renewal.

Motivation for Mission

A number of Christian leaders today envision the future in apocalyptic terms. Specifically, they interpret the immediate future of Christian mission as an inevitable clash of eschatologies between Islam and Christianity. Some call for a radical, relational type of postmodern mission to counter the lure of Islamic fundamentalism.[63] Such others as Nabeel Jabbour, whom I cited earlier, urge mission along traditional evangelical lines but with much greater sensitivity toward the peoples of *Dar al Islam* (the

---

62. Beck, *Holy Spirit and Renewal*, 152–53.

63. E. g., Raschke, *GloboChrist*, chapter 5, 116–33.

global community of Muslims). Still others believe Islam to be the antichrist and appear to be arousing Christians, especially those in North America, to counter Islamic jihad with one of their own.[64]

For me, working within a Christian paradigm, the primary motivation for making disciples is to share the reality and finality of God's salvation with everyone so that they might "have life and have it more abundantly" (John 10:10). The reality of judgment and the godly sorrow that leads to repentance (2 Corinthians 7:10), in this life or post mortem, also motivates me, for to be created is to be accountable. Some protest that the vision of universal redemption removes the issue of personal accountability and strips the motive of urgency from the missionary's arsenal. Therefore, they ask, why should you bother to reach out to the nations? To this I reply: Why? Simply because I have been blessed by the good news and want to share it with others! There is a sense in which my blessedness has made me their debtor (cf. Romans 1: 14). I want others to know that God loves them, that Jesus laid down his life for them, that they have been liberated from their past, that the Father has forgiven them. I want to share with them the joy of spiritual transformation. I want them to know that an eternal community of mutual love welcomes them. I want to urge them, "Respond now to the Father's love! Be reconciled to God!"

64. E. g., Murk, *Islam Rising*, Book I.

12

My Gospel

I press on to take hold of that for which Christ Jesus took hold of me.

PHILIPPIANS 3:12

As I MENTIONED IN the preface, by "my gospel" I do not mean anything authoritative or dogmatic, in the sense that the apostle Paul, for example, wrote of "my gospel" in his letters (e. g., Romans 16:25, Galatians 1:9). I simply mean the gospel as I am able to understand it and appropriate it at this stage of my life, and which, as a missionally minded Christian, I wish to share with others.

Its essence is clear to me; its nuances I am still trying to absorb and communicate to others. What is that essence? I find it in the first explicit mention of "the gospel" in the Bible: "Peace ... good tidings ... salvation ... Your God reigns!" (Isaiah 52:7).

Your God reigns! That is the heart of it. The good news is all about God: that God is good, and unconditionally loving, and has a gracious purpose for the universe and humankind that he will fulfill. The nuances are found in the phrases "peace," "good news," and "salvation," which become God's specific gospel for human beings.

"Your God reigns" is not a tag line on the order of one mission society's "God has a wonderful plan for your life." In fact, to announce "your God reigns" to an unbeliever in America or China or Patagonia is not likely to provoke much of a response at all. The phrase in itself does not have as much evangelistic import today as the equivalent phrase Jesus used in his day: "The kingdom of God has come near" (Matthew 4:17). Still, it suggests to me and perhaps to others, a new order in the universe to be consummated in eternity but present proleptically even now in the world. The apostle Paul had this precise thought in mind when he declared, "The old has gone; the new is here!" (2 Corinthians 5:17).

"Your God reigns" conveys a worldview and a philosophy of existence. It has as much a this-worldly dimension as an otherworldly one. Its social implications parallel its individual import. To repeat it is to remind oneself of Ezekiel's famous question, "How then can we live?" (Ezekiel 33:10)—a question somewhat mangled in the title of Francis Schaeffer's best-known book.[1] So I am unable to abbreviate "my gospel" to a thirty-second sound bite. Allow me in this chapter to lay out some of the distinctive aspects of my experience of the Gospel.

"Your God," of course, is the God of Abraham, Isaac, and Jacob—and of Noah and Enoch and Adam before them. My ancient forbears were Celts (with a smidgen of Norse and Dutch thrown in), distantly related to the Galatians to whom the apostle Paul wrote. The Celts of central Europe who eventually made their way to Wales, Scotland, and Ireland worshipped Lugh, the sun god, and a host of local gods.[2] Their underworld god was Balor, the leader of the Fomorii, evil beings who lived in that netherworld. Lugh corresponds to the Welsh god Lleu and the Gallic god Lugos. The names of such modern cities as Lyons and Leiden were derived from Lugh's name.

At some point in time my forefathers and mothers were introduced to the God of the Bible in much the same manner, I would think, that the apostle Paul introduced the one true God to the Athenians on Mars Hill (Acts 17). I inherited this knowledge of God from my parents and from the hermetic Christian community in which I was reared. But to grasp personally the full import of "our God reigns," to experience the peace and salvation God provided in the Christ event, and to share it with others has been the preoccupation of my life. No reader should suppose, however, that I might ever think my understanding exhausts the fullness of the good news we proclaim. That would contradict the central thrust of this monograph, which has tried to highlight the variegated tapestry of the gospel.

Multiple Dimensions

The first characteristic of the biblical good news of salvation as I have appropriated it is that it is multidimensional. In Christ God intends to

1. Cf. Schaeffer, *How Should We Then Live.*
2. Proulx, "Lugh," para. 1*ff.*

save—to rescue, reconcile, renew—the entire cosmos, our planet earth and its nations, families, and individuals. Of course, human interest in salvation is usually in reverse order. We wish above all to experience salvation individually and personally, in terms of our emotional and physical well-being and our eternal destiny. Nevertheless, I want to discuss it in the order I have listed, for I experience personal salvation within the larger framework.

The universe. As the title of this book suggests, it is God's intention to renew all things or, in the words of the apostle Paul, "through Christ to reconcile all things, whether things on earth or things in heaven" (Colossians 1:20; cf. Ephesians1:10, "to bring unity to all things in heaven and on earth under Christ"). This renewal is not a restoration of all things, a return to the innocence of the Garden of Eden, as many have imagined. It is a genuine making new (Revelation 21:5). The analogy may be imperfect, but imagine a potter with her clay. She shapes it to a given end. The vessel subsequently becomes marred; perhaps she foresaw that it would. She decides to use the same clay, not to restore the vase to its original condition but to fashion from the original material a new vessel altogether for a greater purpose. Eastern Orthodox Christians refer to this process as the deification of the universe, bringing the universe into perfect communion with God.

Planet Earth. God's salvation includes our still-evolving world; that is, the earth we live in and its inhabitants, its plants, and its animals.[3] Isaiah prophesied that at some future point,

> The wolf will live with the lamb, the leopard will lie down with the goat, the calf and the lion and the yearling together, and a little child will lead them .... Infants will play near the hole of the cobra; young children will put their hands into the viper's nest ... for the earth will be filled with the knowledge of the Lord as the waters cover the sea (Isaiah 11:6–9).

The Eastern Orthodox tradition teaches us that human beings created by God through the evolutionary process are true persons in the sense that we are the only self-conscious beings on the planet (and perhaps the universe) able to find and experience the true meaning of our existence. This meaning—and here the Latin church father Augustine agrees with

---

3. Cf. Moltmann, *Coming of God*, 70.

the Greek fathers—is found in communion with God.[4] This communion is our ultimate destiny. But it is also the ultimate destiny of the universe *and our earth.* "For the earth will be filled with the knowledge of the glory of the LORD" (Habakkuk 2:14), and perfected (glorified) human beings will be God's chief agents in achieving this destiny.[5] Our responsibility to our global environment is self-evident. As mentioned earlier, already we have begun to take tentative steps toward the moon and other planets in our solar system.

Nations. The omega book of the Bible speaks of a future city in which neither sun nor moon are necessary, "for the glory of God gives it light" and "the nations will walk by its light, and the kings of the earth will bring their splendor into it . . . the glory and honor of the nations will be brought into it" (Revelation 21:23–26). God has a wonderful future ahead for the nations—every tribe and language and people. These are the same nations we have known in history, only perfected. Their best will be preserved, renewed, and incorporated into the new age. It is an intriguing intellectual exercise to reflect on the particular contributions that specific nations have made to the human family.

Families[6] and individuals. To be a person is to be in community, the smallest unit of which is the household or family. When Jesus made the statement, "the Son of Man came to seek out and to save the lost" (Luke 19:10), he was speaking directly about a man named Zacchaeus and his household. He would save them from the *angst* and futility of life in the world in its present form. He would offer them this-worldly "life to the full" (John 10:10). This is the peace or *shalom* that Isaiah prophesied.

For many whom Jesus met in his daily walks, salvation meant healing from physical and mental disorders. Everywhere he went Jesus healed people physically and emotionally as a sign of God's reign. He continues to do so today. The gospel also promises salvation to individuals beyond death: salvation as the transition from temporal existence to eternal life. Speaking of the future resurrection, the apostle Paul argued, "If it is only in this life we have hope in Christ, we are to be pitied more than all others" (1 Corinthians 15:19).

---

4. *"Inquietum est cor nostrum donec requiescat in te"* (Our heart is restless until it reposes in you.) Augustine, *Confessions,* I, lines 6–7.

5. Cf. Stăniloae, *Creation and Deification,* 45.

6. The conversion of households is a prominent theme in the Acts of the Apostles; cf. Acts 10:2 and 16:31.

The Bible is reasonably clear with respect to the final resurrection of the dead, but I have not yet found in the New Testament that which really helps me to anticipate life immediately beyond death. Paul says that "to be away from the body" is to be "at home with the Lord" (2 Corinthians 5:8); but he doesn't describe exactly what it means to be absent from the body or to be at home with the Lord. Are we to become disembodied spirits of some sort while we await the resurrection? Many Christians believe so.

My own belief, which I admit is of little consequence, is that when my body dies and disintegrates, I die thoroughly, fertilizing the earth for a future generation. My body, including my soul, which is integral to my body, will be re-created at the Resurrection as a renewed, transformed body and soul. Meanwhile the real me is preserved perfectly in the memory of God, which I take to be the meaning of "at home with the Lord"; and from God's memory I will be resurrected and renewed, along with every other member of *H. sapiens* who has ever lived. As Daniel Harrell reminds us, "It's just as if the time between [death] and the end of time had already transpired . . . the dead themselves experience no passage of time."[7] Life in eternity will be an experience of continual growth toward perfection, toward becoming fully human even as I increasingly "participate in the divine nature" (2 Peter 1:4).

Good Friday

At the heart of the gospel I hear the proclamation that "Christ died for our sins" (1 Corinthians 15:3). I live and minister from within the conservative evangelical community, but by now it will be clear to the reader that the contemporary North American evangelical worldview is not fully identical with my own. The contemporary evangelical community understands "Christ died for our sins" primarily in forensic terms: Christ died to pay the penalty for our sins.[8] For reasons presented previously in chapter 7, and in more detail in my *What about the Cross?*, this forensic theory of atonement is unsatisfactory to me. Instead, as with the Gospel generally, I see what occurred at Calvary in a multidimensional way. Let me share seven dimensions of Good Friday that I find meaningful.

First, I see what occurred on that special Friday as being the inevitable outcome of a life lived in perfect obedience to the Father and in total

---

7. Harrell, *Nature's Witness*, 125.

8. E.g., Bridges, *Gospel for Real Life*, 29.

solidarity with the human race. Human life ends in death. Human life lived in obedience to the Father and in solidarity with those who are poor, powerless, and oppressed often ends in *violent* death. "Indeed, all who want to live a godly life in Christ Jesus will be persecuted" (2 Timothy 3:12), and many will be martyred. It is happening in our own day.[9] As the son of God and son of man, Jesus was executed on the twin charges of religious blasphemy (Matthew 26:65) and political insurrection (Luke 23:2). No other explanation, theological or otherwise, is needed to account for the fact of Jesus' crucifixion. As a human being I am deeply implicated, if often unwittingly and passively, in a world system that "kill[s] the prophets and stones those sent to you" (Luke 13:34). I need to be forgiven and reconciled to God.

Second, I am concerned not only for the *fact* of Jesus' death (after all, 6,000 followers of Spartacus were crucified as part of a victory celebration along the Appian Way in 71 B.C.E.)[10] but for the *meaning* of it, so the cross is revelatory. By dying this death Jesus limned God's true nature and God's true relationship to the human race. God is one who suffers with human persons in their *angst* and despair. With Abelard, I believe that the revelation of love has the power to reconcile human beings to God and to each other. In my long and turbulent life I have experienced this reconciliation in full measure.

> God is love. Whoever lives in love lives in God, and God in them. This is how love is made complete among us so that we will have confidence on the day of judgment: In this world we are like Jesus. There is no fear in love. But perfect love drives out fear, because fear has to do with punishment (1 John 4:16b–18).

Third, I believe that Jesus' death was truly sacrificial, but in a way that unmasked and nullified the worldwide religious institution of bloody sacrifice which entails the execution of an innocent victim, a scapegoat. The institution of sacrifice was never unique to Israel; it was a feature of many, perhaps most, religions. But it was an institution based on the primal murder of an innocent victim, as Girard's classical research demonstrates. As such it mocks the kind of godly sacrifice whereby, as Jesus himself pointed out, a person lovingly lays down his life for a friend (John 15:13). And we cannot forget that on the cross Jesus forgave those who made him a scapegoat.

9. Cf. the twenty contemporary accounts in Bergman, ed., *Martyrs*.

10. Appian, *Bella Civilia*, 1.120, cited in Zias, "Crucifixion in Antiquity," para. 2.

As the institution of sacrifice evolved among the nations, including Israel, two motives came to predominate; both are evident in the book of Leviticus. One motive is that of gratitude; a person offers something precious to God as a token of gratitude, adoration, and loyalty. It is in this sense that Jesus offered up his life as a sacrifice. The other motive is that of appeasement. One offers something precious to God in hope of warding off his wrath; this is atonement in the sense of making amends. It involves the death of an innocent victim, human or beast, and it is this false understanding of sacrifice that God unmasked through Jesus' death on the cross. The Psalmist foresaw this falsity when he wrote, "Burnt offerings and sin offerings you did not require" (Psalm 40:6).

It is my contention that bloody sacrifice (that is, the sacrifice of an innocent victim, a scapegoat) is a misunderstanding of the true covenant that exists between God and human beings. It is true that God accommodated the sacrificial system in Israel and used it pedagogically, but only until the fullness of time would come—the time when the son of God would unveil the inherent violence in this kind of sacrifice and nullify the institution altogether as contrary to the nature of God the Father who is love. By eliminating violence as an active, atoning feature at the very heart of religion, including Christianity as it developed as a religion, God's Spirit creates in us a different mindset. The new mindset allows us, for example, to approach people of other faiths or no faith in a spirit of friendship rather than contention and mimetic rivalry. I suspect that it was insight into this perverse dimension of religion, exemplified in Christianity's inability to prevent the horror of the Holocaust, which led the martyr Dietrich Bonhoeffer to project a "religionless Christianity."[11]

Fourth, at Golgotha Jews and Gentiles alike were complicit in Jesus' execution. When Jesus asked the Father on the cross to forgive his torturers on the basis that they were acting according to their nature—"they know not what they do"—God did so, no questions asked. In truth God, like any good parent, had forgiven the human race long before we had come to our senses and requested it. But God made it public at Calvary. As I accept God's forgiveness I discover within myself the ability to forgive others for wrongs done to me and to ask forgiveness for the wrongs I have done to others. The apostle Paul recognized this aspect of forgiveness and declared that in shedding his blood on the cross Jesus reconciled

---

11. Bonhoeffer, *Letters and Papers,* 280, 285.

all divisions of humanity, putting to death their mutual hostility through his own death (Ephesians 2:16). In the modern world where religions can and do incite bloody regional clashes, and even clashes of civilizations, this meaning of the cross has unmatched import.

Fifth, the cosmic conflict understanding of the cross expounded by the early church fathers also has great relevance to me today with respect to both individual psychology and social morality. Evolution has bequeathed to us humans a set of malevolent powers over which we have virtually no control. These powers, which I regard as natural forces, not personified spiritual entities, are violent and oppressive. At the personal level they occur as sickness and sinfulness, and during his earthly minis-try Jesus demonstrated his authority to deal with both. At the level of entire societies they occur as oppression and persecution. Jesus dealt with both on the cross, not in the way we might anticipate, but in the weakness of God that absorbed evil like a sponge and negated its powers (1 Corinthians 2:25). In my fellowship with the Lord I have learned, as the apostle Peter learned, to "not repay evil with evil" (1 Peter 3:9).

Sixth, by his death on Calvary God renewed his eternal covenant with humankind. We have seen in our Old Testament survey that God had renewed the covenant more than once, and it is God's faithfulness to his own covenant that is our salvation. Jesus himself made this faithful-ness explicit in his comments at the Last Supper, and in such as way as to dispose of the idea of bloody sacrifice when he took bread and wine rather than the Passover lamb and wine. The New Testament book of Hebrews provides the clearest exposition of this theme. With this fresh and final covenantal commitment I am personally assured that in spite of my failings God in Christ loves me, embraces me with unfailing love, and intercedes for me through his Spirit (Romans 8:27).

Seventh, I want to draw the reader's attention to the connection I see between the cross and universal salvation. With Jürgen Moltmann, the theologian of hope who also wrote *The Crucified God*, I believe that "the true Christian foundation for the hope of universal salvation is the theol-ogy of the cross."[12] And he associates this theology, as did the apostle Peter, with Jesus' descent into hell. Moltmann understands hell not as a specific place but as an existential reality and suggests that Jesus experienced hell

---

12. Moltmann, *Coming of God*, 251. Moltmann derives this concept from Martin Luther.

while he was on the cross. There he vicariously suffered God-forsakenness on behalf of all sinful human beings. Moltmann goes on to assert:

> Only if disaster (forsakenness by God, absolute death, the infinite curse of damnation and sinking into nothingness) is gathered into God himself, does community with this God become eternal salvation, infinite joy, indestructible election and divine life.[13]

Eternal salvation, infinite joy, and divine life indeed describe the eternal community of love we envision in the new heaven and new earth. But so does indestructible election. And indestructible election assures universal salvation only because at Calvary the son of God gathered up into himself, as I believe, all the evil of the universe and bore it on our behalf.

Beyond Calvary

Jesus' atoning (reconciling) death is usually regarded as the climax of the Christ event. That may well be so, although there are a variety of ways of perceiving the import of the crucifixion, as we have seen, including the idea of penal substitution, which I believe to be mistaken. But the Christ event is more than Calvary. After his execution Jesus' body, we are told, was placed in a tomb, whence his spirit descended to the realm of the dead and proclaimed liberty to those held captive there by Satan. On the third day he was raised from the dead with a recognizable yet transformed body. His resurrection pointed directly to the renewal of all things, when we together with all creation will be resurrected to eternal life.

After forty days with his disciples, instructing them further about God's reign, Jesus ascended to the right hand of God and poured out his Spirit to "all people" (Acts 2: 17, quoting Joel 2:28). I put "all people" in quotation marks because on that specific occasion he poured out his Spirit on a limited number of people, followers of the Way. Yet the apostles recognized the universal significance of this outpouring. "The promise [of the Spirit] is for you and your children *and for all who are far off*" (Acts 2:39, emphasis added). They recognized that the whole human race is the intended recipient. At the right hand of God Jesus today directs the affairs of God's dominion, moving the creation through his Spirit toward its renewal. Of more immediate consequence, Jesus ministers to each of us individually from the right hand of God, sustaining us in our imperfec-

---

13. Ibid., 246. I have modified Margaret Kohl's translation slightly to enhance clarity.

tions in an imperfect world—recall Kierkegaard. We too are destined for total renewal; this is our promised salvation.

Just how will God the Father almighty, maker of heaven and earth, effect this total renewal? Were we to rely on Christian tradition, we would likely envisage some wild apocalyptic event. Such popular English-language novels as *The Late Great Planet Earth* predispose us to picture a catastrophic apocalypse. The imagery of the book of Revelation (*apokalypsis* in Greek) also influences us in this direction, as does some of Jesus' own imagery in Matthew 24, paralleled in Mark 13, and oftentimes called the "Little Apocalypse." From this perspective an appropriate analogy might be that of a potter breaking to pieces a finished product and starting over.

But as I have maintained, the cosmos and earthly nature, including humankind, is not a finished product. Rather, all is in a state of God-ordained evolution. And it may well be that the more appropriate analogy is the one I have previously suggested: that of a potter who uses the still-malleable material in an unfinished piece of work to fashion something better suited to a larger purpose. In this scenario it is not necessary to assume a cosmic cataclysm. This scenario, in fact, accommodates an evolutionary process ongoing from the past to the present and into the indeterminate future. This prospect approximates that which the Eastern Orthodox churches have always envisioned, long before the emergence of the modern scientific theory of evolution.

First Corinthians 15:24–28 seems to suggest that God through Christ is even now in the process of renewing all things. When Christ has destroyed "every ruler and authority and power," including death itself, then comes the end [of this age] and he hands over the kingdom to the Father. Here as elsewhere in the New Testament, the language is metaphorical and coded, so we cannot be certain of the mechanics, as it were; but we know they involve the Spirit, the Word, and the witness—including the martyrdom—of the saints (Revelation 7:9–17).

The New Testament presents the end times in the context of the second coming of Christ and the Last Judgment. It is my belief that these events are apocalyptic in the most precise sense (that is, revelatory or unveiling), as I discussed earlier in my remarks on judgment. At the same time they are part of the total renewal God purposes; and as such, they can be envisioned within a larger evolutionary framework.

Evolution and the Gospel

I consider evolution as important background for appropriating the good news in the twenty-first century because it alleviates if not eliminates the tension that many late modern and postmodern people have experienced between religion and science during the past four centuries. This tension has been felt predominantly in the West, but with the onset of globalization it is being integrated within much of the non-Western world as well. Recently I received a newsletter from a home missionary who specializes in discipling international students. He tells of one Chinese couple to whom he has been witnessing for eight years, yet neither the man nor his wife is prepared to embrace the Christian faith. One reason for their reluctance is that for the missionary of whom I speak, an anti-evolution polemic is part of his presentation of the Gospel. The Chinese couple, both now university professors, were reared in a communist environment that took evolution for granted. How much more effective would it have been for this missionary to say when discussing the first two chapters of Genesis, "Evolution does not have to be an issue; one can understand it simply as God's method of creation." This recasting is a modest example of one kind of intellectual peacemaking that is implicit in the gospel.

A theistic evolutionary framework also illumines other aspects that pose problems for traditional Christian ways of explaining reality. For instance, we claim the Christian gospel transforms people, yet to the naked eye it does not appear to have made a decisive impact on human nature during the past two thousand years—a fact that disturbs many observers.[14] Wars and oppression continue apace; Christian people daily commit sin. This reality appears to undermine the "already" aspects of the eschatological salvation that Christians proclaim. Yet one can also point to significant changes in morality and ethical behavior around the globe under the influence of the gospel that have occurred incrementally through the centuries. Marjorie Hewitt Suchocki makes a particularly cogent observation with which I agree:

> The slow nature of the evolutionary process is because the cumulative past makes a difference to what the present can become. In a world such as ours, weighted with enduring structures that impose their own influence on each present moment, evolution is a slow, incremental affair.[15]

14. Cf. Beck, *Holy Spirit and Renewal*, 153.
15. Suchocki, *Divinity & Diversity*, 27.

Here in the United States we still execute criminals—but not for taking a coat off the rack, as occurred in England not all that long ago. We are more sensitive to human rights violations than we once were. Apartheid is everywhere denounced, as is the kind of ethnic cleansing we witnessed in the Holocaust, and in Cambodia and Rwanda. We are becoming aware of our ecological crimes. Everything we know about evolution suggests that it is a very slow process. But Christians have been united to Jesus in a way that makes possible victory over the selfish gene. We are free to develop "the mind of Christ" (Philippians 2:1–5). But the total renewing of human character under the influence of the spirit of Jesus will span millennia, not mere decades, as the earliest Christians anticipated.

Evolution also illumines the mystery that confounded that same first generation of Christians, namely: Why had the Messiah not returned? Why the hiatus that has now extended for two millennia and counting? Evolutionary theory suggests that God is renewing all things, preparing a new order of existence, but incrementally. Two thousand years have passed; it is not inconceivable that perhaps two or many more millennia have yet to pass before this age ends and the new one begins. I do not mean to suggest that the kingdom of God will emerge in ordinary future time by natural evolutionary processes alone. Rather, I mean that evolutionary processes under the specific influences of the Word and Spirit are contributing to the moment when God will deem the time is ripe for the dissolving of the old age and the total renewing of the new.

Let me say at this point that the fact that I privilege theistic evolution over creationism and intelligent design as embraced by many Christians today does not mean that science is the only source of true knowledge. It is not, as the famed polymath Michael Polanyi has shown us.[16] Nor does it mean that God does not intervene in human affairs or relate personally to human beings; the Christ event demonstrates otherwise, as do God's responses to our daily prayers.

The Enigma of Natural Evil

I like many others have been sometimes frustrated by the apparently meaninglessness of life, by the devaluation of human worth implied by what we call natural evil, or euphemistically, "acts of God." It is clear that some level of corruption exists in the universe that God created, some

---

16. See Polanyi, *Personal Knowledge*.

level at which God's original purpose for the universe has been at least partially perverted. If the gospel is to be true good news, it must speak to the problem of evil, particularly natural evil.

I began this book with a chapter on evolution because I believe that theistic evolution explains this corruption or alienation, as I am calling it, more helpfully than traditional readings of Scripture do, and this alternative reading becomes part of the good news for me. Rather than understanding nature's corruption or perversion as being caused by the putative revolt of an angelic Lucifer or by the act of a single individual such as Eve, I see it as the inevitable and God-foreseen result of the Creator's embedding into nature the freedom to make itself and be itself by way of the evolutionary process.

I wrote of God's original purpose as having been partially perverted. I believe the anthropic principle indicates that the universe was meant ultimately to produce the human race made in the image of God by evolutionary means. That was the original purpose. By image of God I mean primarily the capacity to radically love as God loves, but also having the capacities for free will, self-reflection, and the rationality necessary to share in the governance and perfection of the universe. From this perspective we can say that the universe indeed fulfilled God's purpose, for here we are, you and I, with these specific potentials—marred or incomplete but in place.

The hard truth, however, is that the declaration "our God reigns" is always pronounced in the face of its apparent opposite. There are other powers perceived to be at work in the universe. Scientists expect that the universe will ultimately burn out or freeze itself into oblivion; they cannot as yet predict which. It is against this possibility of utter despoilment that Genesis asserts that God created the universe, that the universe is good, that God is fully and beneficently responsible for it, and that he will ultimately renew it—while yet, surprisingly perhaps, sharing his governance of the cosmos with human beings.

What I have come to believe is that in the renewal of all things the entire cosmos will be remade in the image of God.[17] Once the extended eternal community of mutual love has come into existence, there will be no need for the universe to be free to make itself, and therefore no need for the possibility of sin. In other words, God will change his fundamental

17. Cf. Stăniloae, *Creation and Deification*, 18–20; also Moltmann, *Coming of God*, 273.

relationship to the universe and refashion creation's present elemental laws. Randomness and free will, like tears and death, will be things of the past. The universe will continue to evolve in perfect harmony with God.

As for planet Earth, contemporary jeremiads predict the dissolution of our world by global warming or nuclear holocaust or another ice age or asteroids from outer space. There is much in the recorded history of humankind that seems inexplicable, even unjustifiable, from our perspective: deformed children, mysterious diseases, tsunamis, volcanic eruptions, wars, diseases, famines, social injustices, and the death of innocents amid immense suffering. During the time I have been writing this chapter, eighty thousand lives were lost in a vicious cyclone that wasted lower Myanmar (formerly Burma), and seventy thousand more in an earthquake in western China. At the end of 2004 nearly two hundred thousand lives were lost in the wake of the tsunami that devastated Sumatra and the surrounding region.

The early seventeenth-century philosopher Gottfried Leibniz rationalized that we live in the best of all possible worlds. But in the aftermath of the horrendous earthquake of 1755 in Lisbon, Portugal, in which at least sixty thousand people were killed, the French philosopher and novelist Voltaire ridiculed Leibniz (in the person of Pangloss) for his naiveté.[18] Since then, the attempts of theologians to explain these natural evils as acts of the sovereign will of God or conversely as acts of Satan have proved equally unsatisfying, raising more questions about God's goodness and power than they answer. Dismissing these evils as simply the actions of "nature" is no explanation at all, at least in terms of moral meaning.

At this point it seems to me that the theory of theistic evolution again is eminently useful. Evolution continues by the will of God, whose will gives it a moral dimension. And pervasive natural evils can be justified only by the biblical revelation that in due time God will renew all things. The all-too-real suffering that animals and humans experience will be more than made up in the eternity of God's blessing. This approach can be thought of as the "greater good" defense,[19] and this is what the apostle Paul believed:

> The creation [Paul seems to have only planet Earth in mind here] was subjected to frustration, not by its own choice, but by the will

18. Voltaire (François-Marie Arouet), *Candide,* 4.
19. For a contrary view, see Middleton, "Why the 'Greater Good' Isn't a Defense."

of the one who subjected it in hope that that the creation itself will be liberated from its bondage to decay and brought into the freedom and glory of the children of God (Romans 8:20–21).

This liberation is also what John the Seer envisioned when he saw in his mind "a new heaven and a new earth, for the first heaven and the first earth had passed away" (Revelation 21:1). The first heaven and the first earth are not annihilated; they are transformed. What is evil is annihilated, but all that is good in the first heaven and earth are taken up into the new heaven and new earth. The parallel with individuals can be seen in the apostle Paul's description in 1 Corinthians 3:12–15:

> If anyone builds on this foundation [Jesus Christ] using gold, silver, costly stones, wood, hay or straw, their work will be shown for what it is, because the Day will bring it to light. It will be revealed with fire, and the fire will test the quality of each person's work. If what has been built survives, the builder will receive a reward. If it is burned up, the builder will suffer loss but yet will be saved—even though only as one escaping through the flames.

With respect to nations, we must consider not only the judgment Jesus rendered on the Galilean cities of Chorazin and Bethsaida (Luke 10:13), but especially the well-known account Jesus gave in Matthew 25 of the judgment of the nations. "Nations" in this passage are peoples, i. e., ethnic groups, which may or may not be organized as political entities though no doubt most have been and are. We have previously examined some of the theological problems in this passage; at this point I note only that this judgment of the nations is a prelude to the glorious future described in Revelation 21. There is a sifting going on in the universe, in the world, and among nations[20]—a purifying process that is preserving the good and restraining the evil. It has been occurring ever since the first human societies were organized (cf. Genesis 4:17). And this sifting allows for the special honor and glory of each nation to be incorporated into the new City that God is preparing. It is all part of God's salvation, his renewal of all things.

As the apostle Paul foresaw, the nation of Israel is the paradigm. "All Israel will be saved" (Romans 11:26). The sifting of Israel is evident throughout Scripture and has continued to the present day. Meanwhile this small nation has continued to contribute to the wealth of the global

---

20. Keillor, *God's Judgments.*

family of nations in the areas of science, music, psychology, commerce, philosophy, and religion. Three of the seminal figures of the nineteenth and twentieth centuries were Jews: Marx, Einstein, and Freud. Similarly, in ways we cannot always discern, God's sifting goes on in every nation of the world until the last judgment as he prepares all peoples—including those nations who have long since disappeared from history's stage—for their glorious future.

In prescientific ages people had no way of identifying the powers that seemed to them to control the fate of nations except as supernatural entities on the order of angels and demons. Each nation was thought to have a guardian angel to protect it against the demonic powers that would destroy the nation's life. This belief is evident in the imagery of Daniel 10, for instance, and also lies behind much of the imagery in the apostle Paul's letters as he images principalities and powers, authorities and dominions. In my view, such imagery is not as useful today as it once was. Instead, we need to perceive these powers as being naturally inherent in the institutions of government, commerce, education, the family, and every other major organization that shapes the life of nations. Part of the story of salvation is that Jesus unmasked these powers and made possible their ultimate defeat at the cross. The reader should recall the discussion of René Girard's theory in chapter 7 above.

Salvation in the Old Testament was this-worldly when applied to families and individuals. As we saw in chapter 3, before the onset of the Axial Age—that is, before the era of Israel's prophets, families and individuals looked to the gods primarily to ensure the growth of crops, the well-being of herds, and the maintenance of human life with a minimum of trouble. Concepts of an afterlife were hazy at best. Ancient Israel shared this worldview. The Hebrew idea of *Sheol* was that of a shadowy, ghostly abode; only gradually did firm ideas of an afterlife emerge.[21] By the time of the Christ event the Jewish people had developed relatively clear ideas of Hades (though not ideas identical with modern concepts of hell) and paradise. More importantly, the majority had come to believe with the Pharisees in the future resurrection of the dead. Christians recognized in the bodily resurrection of the Messiah that the reality of salvation included the bodily resurrection of all the dead in a renewed form.

---

21. Jewish concepts of the afterlife appear to have been influenced by Zoroastrian ideas during the period of the Babylonian captivity.

> So will it be with the resurrection of the dead. The body that is
> sown is perishable; it is raised imperishable. It is sown in dishonor;
> it is raised in glory. It is sown in weakness; it is raised in power. It
> is sown a natural body; it is raised a spiritual body (1 Corinthians
> 15:42–44).

Yet the good news of the New Testament is also this-worldly. The reign of God that guarantees eternal life has begun now, though it is experienced by relatively few and even by them only minimally. Yet knowing I am reconciled to God frees me from a guilty conscience, frees me from the culture of shame, and frees me to love God and my neighbor with ardor. By the spirit of Jesus I experience victory in varying degrees over my old nature with its selfish genes.

> His divine power has given us everything needed for life and god-
> liness, through the knowledge of him who called us by his own
> glory and goodness. Thus he has given us, through these things,
> his precious and very great promises, so that through them you
> may escape from the corruption that is in the world because of
> lust, and may become *participants in the divine nature*" (2 Peter 1:
> 3-4, emphasis added).

At the same time, we also deal with personal evil in this world. If Adam and Eve are collective names representative of the earliest humans, and if those earliest humans were endowed with both free will and an ambiguous genetic heritage produced by a long evolutionary history, then not only the cultural goods that we experience in music, art, science, and technology, but also the evils we experience at the hands of other humans and our own hands, are explainable in a way that is more satisfying than by assuming that the story of Adam and Eve in the Garden of Eden is to be understood literally and that all evil is derived whether in humanity or in nature from a single bad decision on their part.

As noted in chapter 2, within a theistic evolutionary framework it is possible to conceive of the human race as experiencing an elevation of consciousness (God-awareness and self-awareness) simultaneously with a moral fall. The evolutionary process best explains that proclivity to sinfulness that human beings have always been aware of and that theologians call original sin.

Justification by Faith

A good friend, evangelical to be sure, having reviewed my earlier section on salvation, wonders where the apostle Paul's understanding of justification by faith fits in. This query is answered in part in the following section, but at this point it might be helpful to note that while faith is essential to my understanding of how we appropriate God's good news, justification is less so because it is only one way to understand the Gospel. In Paul's environment, shaped as it was by Jewish and Roman law, it was necessary to explain the Gospel in forensic terms. In the early world of Byzantine orthodoxy, however, it was less so. From the perspective of people in the emerging culture of the European Middle Ages, a forensic perspective became necessary again. I am not sure it is as relevant in the twenty-first century.

To be justified is to be made right, to be placed in right relationship with God, ourselves, our neighbors, and planet Earth. But this is just another way, as Abelard clearly saw, of speaking about reconciliation, about atonement. And it is both possible and preferable in our time to reflect on our atonement from angles other than forensic. Rather than focusing on legal definitions, it might be more helpful to focus on personal relationship. Reconciliation with God is a matter of personal relationship. God's justice is not identical with human justice. God's justice consists of his being faithful to his covenant of grace, which is a covenant of relationship. Objectively I know I have been reconciled to God; subjectively I can now appropriate that marvelous fact by exercising faith; that is, by trusting my loving heavenly Father without reservation.

The Gospel and Election

Since I have lived most of my life in circles influenced by Reformed theology, I have had to clarify my own thinking about the relationship between the gospel and the doctrine of election. If the traditional dates can be relied on, the call of Abraham occurred approximately four thousand years ago. This call is a crucial part of my gospel because it revealed the way out of the human dilemma. It was the call to exercise faith, to trust in the unfailing goodness of God (cf. I John 4:16). Israel had a difficult time appropriating saving faith, yet the awareness of faith in God's faithfulness was preserved through the vicissitudes of Israel's history until the Christ event, when the apostle Paul found in it the basis for the inclusion of the entire world in God's plan of salvation.

The great scientist Albert Einstein, himself a Jew, found it impossible to believe that the Jews are a chosen people. As he wrote to a friend, "As far as my experience goes, [we] are also no better than other human groups, although [we] are protected from the worst cancers by a lack of power. Otherwise, I cannot see anything 'chosen' about [us]."[22] One cannot fault Einstein for his conclusion. Although there was a strong religious dimension in his personality, which he later directed toward reverence of the universe, he had lost personal religious faith as a twelve-year-old. He was not a student of the Torah and never really comprehended the divine reason for Israel's election.

Many Christians today believe that the church has replaced Israel as an exclusive body or God's chosen people. That is not what the apostle Paul proclaimed, however. Rather, Paul believed that Israel as the elect of God has been expanded through the Christ event to include all those chosen by grace from among the Gentile nations (Romans 11:5).

What I am asserting is that the gospel reveals that in Christ the human race in its entirety has been chosen by God for salvation. I think Paul intuited this truth, as we saw when we looked closely at a set of Pauline texts. What I believe is that just as the blessing of all nations was implicit in the election of Israel, so the blessing of the human race is implicit in and is a natural extension of the gospel that centers on the inclusion of the Gentiles. This insight is a kind of theological evolution inherent in the gospel but only gradually realized.

A seminal passage for me is Ephesians 1:3–14, in which the "we" and the "us" include even more than the apostle Paul may have envisioned. In addition, there is that enigmatic assertion of Paul's that the early Christians baptized on behalf of the dead (1 Corinthians 15:29). We cannot know exactly what Paul meant by that statement, and it is doubtful that he was a theistic evolutionist, as some of the church fathers were and as I describe myself. Yet baptism on behalf of the dead suggests to me a way of incorporating *H. sapiens* in its entirety into the body of Christ.[23]

22. Overbye, "$404,000 Wins Letter," *New York Times*, May 17, 2008, A11.

23. A friend suggests that 1 Corinthians 15:29 is better understood as speaking of "people who identify with others who have given up their lives because of their confidence in the resurrection. They are taking the same road." Jim Petersen, email correspondence, October 2008.

Social Justice[24]

For me the call of Abraham reveals another dimension of the gospel, namely, its social dimension. In view of the fact that Abraham was destined by God to "become a great and mighty nation, and all the nations of the earth shall be blessed in him" (Genesis 18:18), God asked, "Shall I hide from Abraham what I am about to do?" And God answered, "No, for I have chosen him, that he may charge his children and his household after him to keep the way of the Lord by doing righteousness and justice; so that the Lord may bring about for Abraham what he has promised him" (Genesis 18:19).

The phrase "righteousness and justice," italicized in the quotation above, is a hendiadys; that is, a figure of speech used throughout the Old Testament as a technical phrase for social justice. Thus the blessing that God intends for the world is not merely individual and private but social. This is what we would expect if whole nations are included in God's salvific plan. The gospel reveals how people are to live together in community. I was reared in a religious environment that was excruciatingly hermetic; separation from the world was emphasized and political involvement of any kind was forbidden. So the social dimensions of Abraham's call came as a revelation to me, culminating in my writing *Bring Forth Justice* in 1980. A key passage in the evolution of my understanding of the gospel was God's declaration through the prophet Isaiah. I cited this passage earlier, but it is worth quoting again:

> Here is my servant, whom I uphold,
>   my chosen one in whom I delight;
> I will put my Spirit on him,
>   and he will *bring justice* to the nations.
> He will not shout or cry out,
>   or raise his voice in the streets.
> A bruised reed he will not break,
>   and a smoldering wick he will not snuff out.
> In faithfulness he will *bring forth justice*;
>   he will not falter or be discouraged
> till he *establishes justice* on earth.
>   In his teaching the islands will put their hope.
>   (Isaiah 42:1–4, emphasis added)

24. This brief extract is taken from Scott, *What about the Cross?*, 93–95.

This is obviously a messianic text. How did the earliest followers of Jesus understand it? The clearest demonstration is in Matthew 12. The chapter opens with Jesus encouraging his hungry disciples to ignore certain Sabbath legislation regarding the plucking of grain (Matthew 12:1–8). The next paragraph (verses 9–14) finds Jesus breaching Sabbath regulations again in order to meet human need. In both instances he pits himself against the religious leadership of the day. The two-paragraph section ends with the Pharisees going out to plot Jesus' assassination (verse 14).

On the surface one might think these incidents were mere examples of rabbinic nitpicking and that Jesus was simply protesting legalistic attitudes. There is much more to them than that, however. One must keep in mind the socio-politico-economic structure of Palestine in Jesus' day and the extent to which religion underlay and interpenetrated the social system. Rich men can afford the luxury of Sabbath regulations prohibiting labor; hungry men cannot. Jesus took the side of the hungry. In so doing he placed himself squarely against the leaders of the Jewish people. Similarly rich men, owners of sheep, usually manage to get an exemption to protect their property. For them mutilated men are less important than damaged property, but not to Jesus. Again he sides with the poor, and immediately a plot is set in motion to destroy him. It is this aspect of the gospel to which liberation theologians of the 1960s and 1970s drew attention. Like Jesus, they too drew down upon themselves the ire of the religious establishment of their day.

That the evangelist Matthew recognized the social justice implications of Jesus' mission is evident from the fact that in verses 15–21 of this same passage, after recounting the two incidents cited above, he says, "This was to fulfill what was spoken through the prophet Isaiah" (verse 17), and goes on to quote the passage from Isaiah 42 I reproduced above. Professor John Yoder is insightful when he says,

> Jesus was not just a moralist whose teachings had some political implications; he was not primarily a teacher of spirituality whose public ministry unfortunately was seen in a political light ....Jesus was, in his divinely mandated (i. e., promised, anointed, messianic) prophethood, priesthood, and kingship, the bearer of a new possibility of human, social, and therefore political relationships.[25]

25. Yoder, *Politics of Jesus*, 62–63.

In short, social justice is an integral part of the good news I proclaim and therefore work for. Our Lord consciously purposed his mission of justice in the spirit of Isaiah's suffering servant. In Isaiah 42:1–4 Jesus is presented as self-effacing, non-triumphalistic, sensitive, supportive, nonviolent, and utterly tenacious. As God's servant Jesus knew he must "suffer many things, and be rejected . . . and be killed [i. e., executed as a common criminal], and after three days rise again (Mark 8:31). As I wrote in *Bring Forth Justice,* "The pervasiveness of sin in our world, the extent to which the whole international order is corrupted by injustice, can be measured only by the depth of the passion of the son of man at Calvary."[26]

I was raised amidst millenarian Christians, that is, believers who anticipate a literal thousand-year reign of Christ on earth—their interpretation of Revelation 20:4. Millenarian Christians have been part of the Christian community since its beginning; for example, Irenaeus was a millennialist. The doctrine itself has been generally rejected, however, making the position a minority position in our time. I do not believe in a literal thousand-year reign but I understand the deeper motives that underlie that belief; it is the felt need that at some point in time the injustice that pervades the world must be visibly overcome, if only for a limited time.[27] I agree that Jesus came to bring forth justice, but his justice, when it is finally achieved, will be everlasting, a feature of the new heavens and the new earth renewed.

Personal Growth and Outreach

We have come to the end of this book. Let me slip again into an autobiographical mode in these final paragraphs. How does all this theologizing impact my daily life? In this matter my understanding of the gospel does not vary significantly from mainstream Christian tradition, except perhaps for my aversion to the exclusivism that has characterized Christianity. I believe that I am being spiritually transformed (2 Corinthians 3:18)—slowly, to be sure, but truly. I rely on the Holy Spirit for this renovation, believing that the Spirit uses my quiet times with God as I read the Bible and pray to prepare me for life in this world and the next.

---

26. Scott, *Bring Forth Justice,* 95–6.

27. See Moltmann's detailed discussion of millenarianism in *The Coming of God,* 146–93.

Scripture memory has played a significant role in my personal growth and ministry. I believe the Spirit also uses the church to keep me Christ-centered. By church I mean first of all my companions on the journey, and second, the great treasury of writing that those who have preceded me on this journey, beginning with the apostles and church fathers, have bequeathed me. I appreciate being in the company of fellow believers week by week, but perhaps because of my Plymouth Brethren upbringing, churchly rituals and sacraments and contemporary charismatic forms of worship have contributed little to my spiritual growth, as nearly as I can tell. Others may suspect that these absences have impoverished my spiritual life, but if so, not in a way I can discern. Importantly, if I had my life to live over, I would make certain that I was a committed member of a small accountability-focused group.

As far as personal ministry is concerned, my self-identity has been centered on my missionary calling. Like the apostle Paul (Romans 1:14), I believe I am obligated to all people everywhere by virtue of being someone to whom God has revealed his love in such depth. I am indebted not only to those who have been reared in other world faiths but also to those who have been raised in other Christian traditions. As I mentioned in the preface, the label "ecumenical evangelical" or "evangelical ecumenist," which I carried back in the late 1970s, fits my gospel identity.

Paul was a preacher. Timothy and Titus appear to have been pastors, at least in their later years. I on the other hand have invested my life in one-to-one disciple making along the lines suggested by 2 Timothy 2:2 and have never regretted doing so. Jesus' lengthy prayer is John 17 has been a steady source of inspiration to me. Even in my eighties I continue this intentional disciple making with younger men. Of course, I am convinced, as I wrote earlier, that disciple making in the kind of world we live in must be holistic, as much concerned with social justice in this world as with salvation in the next. Pursuing both assures me that I am a co-worker with the Creator, who is also my Redeemer, in the renewal of all things.

Appendix

The Standard Theory of Evolution
A Bare-Bones Summary

IN THE BEGINNING

THE BIG BANG HYPOTHESIS proposes that the universe began 13.73 billion years ago (give or take 120 million years) as an infinitely small, infinitely dense, infinitely hot singularity. As the U. S. National Aeronautics and Space Administration (NASA) describes it,

> This immense primordial energy was the cauldron whence all matter and life arose. Elementary particles were created and destroyed by the 'ultimate particle accelerator' in the first moments of the universe. There was matter and there was antimatter. When they met, they annihilated each other and created light ... a tremendous amount of light. Today there is more than a billion times more light than matter.[1]

Shortly after its origin, this singularity exploded from its dense hot state by a process termed cosmic inflation into the immensely vast and much cooler cosmos we are a part of, creating time and three-dimensional space in the process. The Big Bang model is supported by a number of scientific observations, including:

- The astronomer Edwin Hubble's 1929 observation that galaxies are generally receding from us with speeds proportional to their distance; this finding suggests that the universe was once compacted;

---

1. NASA, "Universe," para. 2. Cf. Genesis 1: 3, "Then God said, 'Let there be light'; and there was light."

- The abundance of the light elements hydrogen, helium, and lithium, which according to the theory should have been fused from protons and neutrons in the first few minutes after the Big Bang; and

- The presence of cosmic microwave background radiation, the remnant heat left over from the Big Bang and discovered in 1964 by the radio astronomers Arno Penzias and Robert Wilson.

NASA launched the Wilkinson Microwave Anisotropy Probe (WMAP) in June 2001 aboard a Delta II rocket from Cape Canaveral Air Force Base in Florida. WMAP completed its first two years of mission operations in September 2003. Meanwhile, it had been granted mission extensions that were to end in September 2009. Subsequently, the WMAP team released three-year data in March 2006 collected on the cosmic microwave background radiation, including full polarization data, as well as papers describing the data processing, error analyses, calibration, and other critical aspects of the experiment. All these data appear to confirm the Big Bang theory.[2]

Questioning the Big Bang Hypothesis

Nevertheless, there are problems with the Big Bang model. It does not explain how structures like stars and galaxies came to exist. The temperature of the cosmic microwave background varies slightly across the sky. Why are there such fluctuations, and how do they relate to stars and galaxies? Supporters of the Big Bang hypothesize a very short but especially rapid burst of growth—the cosmic inflation referred to above—in the very early universe; they believe this provides an elegant, though impossible to test, explanation of these puzzles. In May 2004, however, a large international group of scientists, engineers and independent researchers signed and published an open letter to the scientific community in the journal *New Scientist*. In the opening paragraph they say,

> The big bang today relies on a growing number of hypothetical entities, things that we have never observed—inflation, dark matter and dark energy are the most prominent examples. Without them, there would be a fatal contradiction between the observations made by astronomers and the predictions of the Big Bang theory. In no other field of physics would this continual recourse to new hypothetical objects be accepted as a way of bridging the

2. NASA, "Wilkinson Microwave Anisotropy Probe," para. 1*ff.*

gap between theory and observation. It would, at the least, raise serious questions about the validity of the underlying theory.[3]

It is difficult to relate *any* variation of the steady-state or oscillating theories to a creator God.[4] On the other hand, by definition the word *singularity* used to describe the Big Bang implies something that transcends our current understanding of physics. And this implication in turn suggests to many, including myself, a creator God.

Yet even among believers in a creator God there is opposition to the Big Bang theory. For instance, R. V. Gentry, a physicist and young-earth creationist,[5] offers what he calls "irrefutable evidence" against it.[6] The astrophysicist Ryan Scranton, however, forcefully rebuts Gentry's thesis.[7]

Gravity and Galaxies

We will use Sisson's timeline[8] to follow what happened after the Big Bang. As the primal ball of fire expanded, matter in the forms of hydrogen and helium atoms emerged. Of the four fundamental forces in the universe—electromagnetism, the strong and weak nuclear forces, and gravity—gravity is the weakest. Yet under the force of gravity, the scattering atoms of the universe gathered into billions of great clouds. These clouds eventually coalesced into galaxies of stars, our Milky Way being one such galaxy. Astronomers tell us that there are at least a hundred billion galaxies, each with billions of stars separated by millions of light years. A light year is roughly five trillion miles—a barely imaginable distance. At the human horizon, the universe appears infinite.

A half-billion years after the Big Bang, stars began to appear. Stars originate within a galaxy as gravity again compresses clouds of gas and

3. Halton Arp et al., "Open Letter," para.1.

4. Adherents would say it is unnecessary.

5. Young-earth creationist: scientists and laypersons who hold that the Genesis creation account is to be read literally and that the earth was therefore created by God within the past ten thousand years in a sequence of seven 24-hour real-time days. "Flaws in the Big Bang Point to Genesis: A New Millennium Model of the Cosmos," para. 1ff.

6. Gentry, "Flaws in the Big Bang Point to Genesis: A New Millennium Model of the Cosmos," para. 1ff.

7. Scranton, "Debunking Robert Gentry's 'New Red-shift Interpretation Cosmology," para. 1ff.

8. Sissons, *Big Bang*, 218–19. Cf. Cook, *Brief History*; Oppenheimer, *Out of Eden*; also Klein, *Dawn of Human Culture*.

dust. A star may burn for hundreds of millions of years but eventually runs out of fuel and collapses, then explodes, generating intense heat as it does so. Dying stars throw out clouds of cosmic debris. Some of this debris becomes such individual elements as carbon, nitrogen, and oxygen. Each human being is quite literally made of this stardust, created billions of years ago. Our particular solar system began approximately 4.5 billion years ago when one of the spiral arms of the Milky Way collapsed. Our sun was born, followed by its planets, including our Earth, part of the cosmic debris mentioned above.

Once we begin to speak about Earth, we are leaving the larger cosmology and the Big Bang theory for the most part in order to focus on this tiny speck in the universe we call our home. Indeed, when most people speak of evolution today, it is not cosmological evolution they have in mind, but geological (earth-related) and biological (life-related) evolution—biological evolution being the process that we associate with the names of Charles Darwin and Gregor Mendel.

Earth is just the right distance from the sun, which in turn is just the right size to support life on Earth. The Milky Way is unusually dense with matter, making this part of the universe rich with the molecules we need for life. Earth has a radioactive core that warms and protects us. Such observations illuminate the anthropic principle, which posits that the universe is finely attuned to the production and maintenance of carbon-based human life.[9]

Earth has its own long history, and here the more familiar features of evolution come into play. During its first hundred million years the earth was an unstable, violent mixture of molten liquid and ice. For another four hundred million years, as land and sea were formed, Earth was bombarded with space-borne rubbish (e.g., asteroids) from the formation of the solar system. Then somewhere on the planet, quietly, life began.

Life Emerges

Life on earth in its most primitive form—single-celled organisms—mysteriously appeared[10] roughly 3.5 billion years ago during the Proterozoic

9. Polkinghorne, *One World*, 94–96.

10. It is a mystery now; whether it will remain a mystery is moot. Possibly God intervened directly at this point, as adherents of intelligent design suppose, and again at the moment when human persons emerged as creatures in the image of God. But it is not necessary to assume this intervention; see my argument in chapter 2.

era, and multicellular life followed about nine hundred million years ago.[11] What distinguishes living from nonliving matter? Deoxyribonucleic acid (DNA)[12] is considered the identifying mark of a living system; we judge something to be alive if it contains DNA. More eras and periods followed, one after the other, each enduring for millions of years.

Beginning at a point some sixty-five million years ago, scientists begin to divide these eras and periods into epochs measured in mere hundreds of thousands of years rather than millions. In the Middle Pleistocene Epoch, about 780,000 years ago, *Homo sapiens* evolved in Africa. Today we live in the Holocene Epoch, an interglacial period that began only thirteen thousand years ago, after the last Ice Age.

Biologists maintain that DNA analyses show that all forms of life evolved from the first living entities—descent from common ancestry.[13] Within the past billion years, multicellular forms of plants and primitive animals appeared; then sea creatures, insects, flowering plants and trees, reptiles, birds, and mammals, including primates. To the observer, diversity in creation seems to be an end in itself. As the geneticist J. B. S. Haldane once joked, God seems to have had "an inordinate fondness for beetles."[14]

All this variety occurred by way of random mutations and natural selection. For this reason, Richard Colling, a microbiologist who is a confessing Christian, calls God the Random Designer.[15] Mutations are changes in the genetic code resulting from exposure to radiation, chemicals, and other agents. "Random," in the language of science, does not mean without purpose or meaning, which is a philosophical concept, but simply unpredictable. "Natural selection" means that certain life forms adapt more efficiently to their environments and, by passing on their genes to their offspring, ensure the survival of their species. Because mutations are random with respect to natural adaptation, we can say that natural selection is "the nonrandom reproduction of random variants."[16]

11. Biologists now suspect that the first life forms on earth emerged in deep-sea hydrothermal habitats. Cf. Glover, "Worms Who Eat Whales," 11.

12. DNA (deoxyribonucleic acid): a nucleic acid that contains the genetic instructions used in the development and functioning of all known living organisms.

13. Haarsma and Haarsma, *Origins,* 152.

14. Haldane, *Possible Worlds,* 286.

15. Colling, *Random Designer.* Despite the title, the book is not about intelligent design. Colling writes from within the perspective of mainstream science.

16. Domning and Wimmer, "Evolution and Original Sin," 9.

Primates and Us

Primates[17] evolved a mere sixty million years ago, the first apes forty-five million years ago, and the hominoid superfamily (chimpanzees, gorillas, orangutans, gibbons and hominins[18]) less than 25 million years ago. More than 98% of the DNA of chimpanzees is shared with humans. *Homo habilis*, *Homo ergaster*, *Homo erectus*, and perhaps other *Homo* species preceded our species, *Homo sapiens* (hereafter *H. sapiens*).

H. sapiens appeared first in south and east Africa three quarters of a million years ago. Eighty thousand years ago they began migrating from there into other parts of the world. By the year 10,000 B.C.E., not long after the conclusion of the last ice age, human beings had established themselves on every continent.[19]

Strictly speaking, an individual human develops but does not evolve. Our genetic constitution is fixed throughout our lifetime, preserved in the germ cells our bodies use solely for reproduction. Only through generational turnover (births, deaths, and migrations) does the human gene pool change and evolution occur over long periods of time.

Where does it all end? According to scientists, the momentum of expansion, the pull or push of gravity, and the life cycle of the stars, is what determines the evolution of the universe. Some astronomers estimate that about 7.6 billion years from now Earth will be dragged from its orbit by an engorged red Sun and spiral to a rapid vaporous death.[20] Science currently lacks the data to know whether the universe will collapse back into itself (the "Big Crunch") or whether it will expand forever, or whether it will end, if it ever ends, in a ball of fire or a gigantic ice crystal.

17. Primates: mammals characterized notably by advanced development of binocular vision, specialization of the appendages for grasping, and enlargement of the cerebral hemispheres.

18. Hominins: the ancestors of modern humans.

19. Cf. Dorak, "Human Evolution," para. 1*ff.*

20. Moskowitz, "Earth's Final Sunset Predicted," para. 2.

Glossary

Anthropic principle: posits that the universe is finely attuned to the production and maintenance of carbon-based human life.

Apocalyptic: descriptive of the final cataclysm destroying the powers of evil and ushering in the kingdom of God.

Apocrypha (see also Deuterocanonical books below): books included in the Septuagint and Vulgate versions of the Bible but not in the Jewish and Protestant canons.

Arminian: a follower of Arminius, a sixteenth-century Dutch theologian. Against Calvin, they believe in conditional election, universal atonement, and resistible grace.

Astrophysicist: a scientist who deals principally with the physics of the universe, including luminosity, density, temperature, and the chemical composition of stars, galaxies, and interstellar media.

Axial Age: A term invented by the philosopher Karl Jaspers to describe the six-hundred-year period from 800 to 200 B.C.E. During this time unique religious developments occurred in Greece, the Middle East, South Asia, and East Asia.

B.C.E: Before the common era, equivalent to B.C.; also note C.E. (common era), equivalent to a.d.

Centurion: Originally, the commander of a century (company of a hundred soldiers) in the Roman army; by the time of Jesus, however, the number of soldiers in a century was set at eighty.

Contextualize: To place an idea or practice in a particular context.

Cosmologist: An astronomer who studies the evolution and space-time relations of the universe.

Covenant: A binding agreement between two or more parties. It is a concept used in the Bible as a metaphor to describe the relationship between God and humankind. Some covenants are based on the ancient "royal grant" model. They oblige only the superior party, and are called promissory or unconditional covenants.

Dead Sea scrolls: Documents discovered around the Wadi Qumran near the Dead Sea. They contain Old Testament texts that predate 100 B.C.E. and texts related to Essene rituals.

Decapolis: a group of ten cities, centers of Greek and Roman culture at the eastern edge of the Roman Empire. All but one of the cities were located in the present-day state of Jordan.

Deuterocanonical books: see *Apocrypha* above. They include Tobit; Judith; Wisdom of Solomon; Sirach (Ecclesiasticus); Baruch, the Letter of Jeremiah; the Prayer of Azariah and the Song of the Three Jews; Susanna; Bel and the Dragon; 1 and 2 Maccabees; 3 and 4 Maccabees; 1 and 2 Esdras; the Prayer of Manasseh; and Psalm 151.

Diaspora: the scattered colonies of Jews living outside Palestine after the Babylonian exile; today, those Jews living outside Israel.

DNA (deoxyribonucleic acid): a nucleic acid that contains the genetic instructions used in the development and functioning of all known living organisms.

Enoch: A noncanonical scripture written between 150 and 200 B.C.E.; it was well known in Jesus' day.

Eschatology: Theological beliefs related to the final events in the history of the world and humankind.

Essenes: A Jewish religious group that flourished from the second century B.C.E. to the first century C.E. (the Second Temple period).

Gnosticism: The collective name for a number of pantheistic-idealistic sects that flourished from some time before the common era down to the fifth century C.E. Gnostics held matter to be a deterioration of or prison for spirit, and the whole universe a creation of a depraved deity. Valentinus was a leader among early Christian Gnostics.

Godfearer: in Second Temple-period Judaism and early Christianity, a term used to describe the Gentile who believed in the one true God of Israel and denied the idols and foreign gods of the Gentile world.

Ground Zero: The location of the September 11, 2001 disaster in New York City. Two planes manned by Islamic jihadists crashed into the Twin Towers, Manhattan's tallest buildings, and brought them down with the loss of nearly 2,750 lives.

Hellenistic culture: The culture that emerged after the conquests of the Near East by Alexander the Great around 330 B.C.E. It was pervasive in Palestine during the time of Jesus.

Hermeneutics: The art or science of interpreting texts.

Hominins: The ancestors of modern humans.

Indo-Aryans: A group of peoples who originated in the area north of present-day Afghanistan and Pakistan, some of whom later spread eastward to India where they developed Hinduism.

Infinite regression: Circular reasoning. Applied linearly, it signifies an extended causal relationship or relationships for which there can be no beginning, as in "God created the universe." "But who or what created God?" And so on ad infinitum.

Karma: The Sanskrit word for "action" or "deed." The law of karma is action and reaction. One reaps what one sows; what goes around comes around.

Maccabees: A priestly family that led a Jewish national liberation movement in the second century B.C.E. and founded the Hasmonean dynasty. The contemporary Jewish feast of Hanukah celebrates the victory of Judah Maccabee over the Seleucids, one of the dynasties that succeeded Alexander the Great. The story of the movement is recorded in the deuterocanonical books of 1 and 2 Maccabees.

Metanarrative: A comprehensive story meant to explain historical experience or knowledge.

Metaphysics: That part of physics concerned with the ultimate causes and the underlying nature of things.

Missiology: The formal study and practice of mission, especially Christian mission.

Paleontologist: A scientist who studies prehistoric forms of life preserved in fossils.

Patristic: Related to the early church fathers, Greek and Latin.

Perichoresis: A Greek term used to describe the relationships among the Persons of the Trinity. It can be defined as co-indwelling, co-inhering, or mutual interpenetration.

Pharisee: A member of a Jewish religious party that flourished in Palestine during the latter part of the Second Temple period.

Pharisees insisted on the binding force of oral tradition, or the unwritten Torah.

Plasma cosmologist: Plasma is the fourth state of matter, differing from solids, liquids, and gases. Plasma cosmologists theorize about the electrodynamic nature of the universe; gravity and inertia are not the only forces as work.

Postmodernism: A wide-ranging term applied to literature, art, philosophy, architecture, fiction, and cultural or literary criticism. Postmodernism is "post" because it denies the existence of any ultimate principles; it lacks the optimism of a scientific, philosophical, or religious truth that will explain everything for everybody—a characteristic of the so-called modern mind.

Predestination: The (a) actual divine decree foreordaining each individual to salvation or damnation; or (b) the doctrine that expounds the decree.

Primates: Mammals characterized notably by advanced development of binocular vision, specialization of appendages for grasping, and enlargement of the cerebral hemispheres.

Quantum physicist: One who studies the nature and behavior of matter and energy on the atomic and subatomic levels. The German physicist Max Planck first proposed quantum theory in 1900.

Rabbi: The Hebrew term of address for "my master" or "my teacher." In Jesus' day, it was the title of a spiritual leader well versed in interpreting the Torah.

Recapitulation: The teaching of Irenaeus that Jesus Christ as the Second Adam sums up the entirety of human experience in his own life of perfect obedience, thereby setting right on behalf of the human race what Adam got wrong.

Sadducee: A member of the aristocratic Jewish priestly sect that flourished in the Second Temple period. They rejected the Pharisees' reliance on oral tradition.

Samaritans: An ethnically mixed group living in the area between Galilee in the north and Judea in the south. They were held in contempt by the Jews of Jesus' time.

Samizdat: The Russian term for self-published. During the Cold War years (1946–1989) it designated the secret hand-copying and distribution of literature in order to evade official censorship.

Sanhedrin: The Jewish court system in the Second Temple period. The Great Sanhedrin in Jerusalem consisted of seventy-one ruling elders.

Second Temple period: The period in Jewish history roughly between 515 B.C.E. and 70 C.E. After returning from exile, the Jews built a second temple, the first having been destroyed by the Babylonian invaders. This second temple was itself completely renovated and rebuilt by King Herod around 20 B.C.E. Herod's temple was the one Jesus knew; the Romans destroyed it in 70 C.E.

Septuagint: The Tanakh as translated into the Greek language by Alexandrian Jews between the third and first centuries B.C.E. It is commonly designated LXX.

Sirach: A highly regarded second-century B.C.E. deutero-canonical book, also known as Wisdom of Jesus son of Sirach, or Ecclesiasticus.

Tanakh: The Hebrew Bible; the Christians' Old Testament.

Teleological: Having to do with direction toward a final end (meaning and purpose are assumed).

Theistic evolution: The concept that some form of evolution (not necessarily the "standard theory" held by the scientific community) is God's method of creation.

Theodicy: The attempt to justify God's goodness and power in the face of the reality of evil. "Greater good" theodicy, in brief, argues that the greater good that will ultimately ensue from the conflict between good and evil justifies the suffering that is entailed.

Torah: The first five books of Moses (Genesis through Deuteronomy) in the Jewish Bible, the Tanakh.

Vatican II: An ecumenical council called by Pope John XXIII in 1962 and concluded under Pope Paul VI in 1965. It was meant to be an updating or *aggiornamento* of the Roman Catholic Church.

Way: A term used by early Christians, as in "followers of the Way."

Wisdom of Solomon: A deutero-canonical book authored in Septuagint-style Greek sometime in the first or second century B.C.E.

Worldview (German *Weltanschauung*): The overall perspective from which one sees and interprets the world; a collection of beliefs about life and the universe held by an individual or group.

Young-earth creationist: one who holds that the account of creation in Genesis is to be read literally and that therefore the earth was created by God within the past ten thousand years in a sequence of seven 24-hour days.

Bibliography

Abelard, Pierre. "Exposition of the Epistle to the Romans" (excerpt) In *A Scholastic Miscellany: Anselm to Ockham,* 276–287. Edited and translated by Eugene R. Fairweather, Philadelphia, PA: The Westminster Press, 1956.

Alfvén, Hannes C. "The Big Bang." No pages. Online: http://www.plasmacosmology.net/bb.html.

Anselm of Canterbury. *Cur Deus Homo.* Christian Classics Ethereal Library. No pages. Online: http://www.ccel.org/ccel/anselm/basic_works.toc.html.

Aquinas, Thomas. *Summa theologica.* Christian Classics Ethereal Library. No pages. Online: http://www.ccel.org/ccel/aquinas/summa.toc.html.

Arp, Halton, et al. "An Open Letter to the Scientific Community." No pages. Online: http://www.cosmologystatement.org.

Attali, Jacques. *Millennium: Winners and Losers in the Coming World Order.* New York: Times Books/Random House, 1991.

Augustine, St. *The Confessions of St. Augustine.* No pages. Online: http://www.ccel.org/ccel/Augustine/confess.toc.html.

Aulén, Gustav. *Christus Victor: A Historical Study of the Three Main Types of the Idea of Atonement.* Translated by A. G. Hebert. 1970. Reprinted, Eugene, OR: Wipf and Stock Publishers, 2003.

Bacchiocci, Samuel. *Immortality or Resurrection?* Berrien Springs, MI: Biblical Perspectives, 1997.

Baker-Fletcher, Garth Kasimu. *Xodus: An African American Male Journey.* Minneapolis, MN: Fortress Press, 1996.

Baker-Fletcher, Karen, and Garth Kasimu Baker-Fletcher. *My Sister, My Brother: Womanist and Xodus God-Talk.* Maryknoll, NY: Orbis Books, 1997.

Barrett, Justin L. *Why Would Anyone Believe in God?* Lanham, MD: Altamira Press, 2004.

Bauckham, Richard. *Jesus and the Eyewitnesses: The Gospels as Eyewitness Testimony.* Grand Rapids, MI: William Eerdmans Publishers, 2006.

———. "Universalism: A Historical Survey." *Them* 4 (1978) 48–54.

Beck, T. David. *The Holy Spirit and the Renewal of All Things: Pneumatology in Paul and Jürgen Moltmann.* Princeton Theological Monograph Series, 67. Eugene, OR: Pickwick Publications, 2007.

Becker, Jürgen. *Paul: Apostle to the Gentiles.* Translated by O.C. Dean, Jr. Louisville, KY: Westminster/John Knox Press, 1993.

Beckett, Lucy. "Not a Theory, But a Life." *TimesLitSupp,* August 3, 2007, 23–24.

Bergman, Susan, ed. *Martyrs: Contemporary Writers on Modern Lives of Faith.* Maryknoll, NY: Orbis Books, 1996.

Biology Online. "Tutorials >Genetics and Evolution >Theory of Natural Selection." No pages. Online: http://www.biology-online.org/2/10_natural_selection.htm.

Bloesch, Donald G. *Holy Scripture: Revelation, Inspiration & Interpretation.* Downers Grove, IL: InterVarsity Press, 1994.

Bond, H. Lawrence. "Another Look at Abelard's Commentary on Romans 3:26." No pages. Online: http://www.vanderbilt.edu/AnS/religious_studies/SBL2004/larrybond.pdf.

Bonhoeffer, Dietrich. *Letters and Papers from Prison.* Translated by Reginald H. Fuller. 1967. Reprinted, New York, NY: Touchstone/ Simon & Schuster, 1997.

Boyd, Gregory. *Satan and the Problem of Evil: Constructing a Trinitarian Theodicy.* Downers Grove, IL: InterVarsity Press, 2001.

Britt, Robert Roy. "Understanding Dark Matter and Light Energy." No pages. Online: http://www.space.com/scienceastronomy/dark_matter_animated_0304215-1.html.

Bruce, A. B. *The Training of the Twelve.* Grand Rapids, MI: Kregel Classics, 2000.

Bühlmann, Walbert. *God's Chosen Peoples.* Translated by Robert R. Barr. Maryknoll, NY: Orbis Books, 1982.

Calvin, John. *Institutio Christianae religionis.* Berlin: Gustav Eichler, 1834. Christian Classics Ethereal Library. Online: http://www.ccel.org/ccel/calvin/institutio1/Page _Index.html. [Latin edition can be accessed online page by page.]

Carman, John B. "My Pilgrimage in Mission." *International Bulletin of Missionary Research* 32 (2008) 136–140.

Catholic Encyclopedia. No pages. Online: http://www.newadvent.org/cathen/g.htm.

Chaikin, Andrew. "Are There Other Universes?" No pages. Online: http://www.space.com/scienceastronomy/generalscience/5mysteries_universes_020205-1.html.

Chandler, Paul-Gordon. *Pilgrims of Christ on the Muslim Road: Exploring a New Path between Two Faiths.* Lanham, MD: Cowley Publications/Rowan & Littlefield, 2007.

Clancy, M. T. *Abelard: A Medieval Life.* Oxford, UK: Blackwell Publishers, 1997.

Clement of Alexandria, *Stromata (Miscellanies)* in The Ante-Nicene Fathers, ed. A. Roberts and J. Donaldson, vol. 2. Peabody, MA: Hendrickson, 1994.

Cobb, Jr., John B. *A Christian Theology of Religions: A Rainbow of Faiths.* Louisville, KY: Westminster/John Knox Press, 1995.

Coe, Shoki, et al. *Ministry in Context: The Third Mandate Programme of the Theological Education Fund* (1970–77). Bromley, UK: Theological Education Fund, 1972.

Coleman, Robert. *The Master Plan of Evangelism.* Grand Rapids, MI: Fleming H. Revell/ Baker Book House, 2006.

Colling, Richard G. *Random Designer.* Bourbonnais, IL: Browning Press, 2004.

Collins, Robin. "A New and Orthodox Theory." Version 1. No pages. Online: http://home.messiah.edu~rcollins/Incarnational%20Theory%20of%20Atonement.doc.

Cone, James H. *God of the Oppressed,* revised edition. Maryknoll, NY: Orbis Books, 1997.

Cook, Michael. *A Brief History of the Human Race.* New York: Norton Publishing, 2003.

Dalman, Gustaf. *Die Worte Jesu,* 1898. Reprinted, Darmstadt: Wissenschaftliche Buchgesellschaft, 1965. (ET: *The Words of Jesus,* 1909. Reprinted, Eugene, OR: Wipf and Stock, 1997).

Dawkins, Richard. *The Selfish Gene.* New York: Oxford University Press, 2006.

Dawson, David. "The Magic Word and the Logical Machine: Myth and History in Levi-Strauss, Derrida and Girard." Unpublished paper, 2008.

Depoortere, Frederiek. *Christ in Postmodern Philosophy.* London, UK: Continuum/T&T Clark, 2008.

Dhammika, Ven. S. "What Does the Buddha Say About the Origin of the Universe?" No pages. Online: http://www.buddanet.net/ans75.htm.

Domning, Daryl P., and Joseph F. Wimmer. "Evolution and Original Sin: Accounting for Evil in the World." No pages. Online: http://www.congregationalresources.org /About.asp.

Donne, John. *Complete Poetry and Selected Prose of John Donne*. Modern Library Series, edited by Charles M. Coffin. New York: Random House, 1994.

Dorak, M. Tevfik. "Human Evolution." No pages. Online: http://www.dorak.info/evolution /human.html.

Dunn, James D.G. *The Theology of Paul the Apostle*. Grand Rapids, MI: Wm. B. Eerdmans Publishing Co., 2006.

Dupuis, Jacques. *Toward a Christian Theology of Religious Pluralism*. Maryknoll, NY: Orbis Books, 2002.

Edwards, Jonathan. "A Careful and Strict Inquiry into the Modern Prevailing Notions of that Freedom of Will Which Is Supposed to Be Essential to Moral Agency, etc." No pages. Online: http://www.ccel.org/print/Edwards/works1/iii.html.

———. "Dissertation Concerning The End for Which God Made the World." No pages. Online: http://www.ccel.org/ccel/Edwards/works1.iv.html.

———. "Sinners in the Hands of an Angry God." No pages. Online: http://www.ccel.org /e/edwards/sermons/sinner.html.

Effa, Allan. "The Greening of Mission." *International Bulletin of Missionary Research* 32 (2008) 171–75.

Eldridge, Niles, and Stephen Jay Gould. "Punctuated equilibria: an alternative to phyletic gradualism." In *Models in Paleobiology*, edited by T.J.M. Schopf, 82–115. San Francisco: Freeman Cooper. 1972.

Finger, Thomas A. "Anabaptist Theology of Atonement." No pages. Online: http://www .gameo.org/encyclopedia/contents/A86/html.

Fish, Darwin. "Hell." No pages. Online: http://www.atruechurch.info/hell.html.

Friedman, Thomas L. *The World Is Flat*. New York: Farrar, Straus, and Giroux, 2006.

Fristad, Kalen. *Destined for Salvation: God's Promise to Save Everyone*. Kearney, NE: Morris Publishing, 2003.

Gentry, David. "Flaws in the Big Bang Point to Genesis: A New Millennium Model of the Cosmos." No pages. Online: http://www.orionfdn.org.

Gibbs, W. Wayt. "Profile: George F. R. Ellis." *Scientific American* 273 (1995) 4, 55.

Giberson, Karl W. "No Science, Please." *Books & Culture*, September/October 2008. No pages. Online: http://www.christianitytoday.com/bc/2008/sepoct/7.16.html.

Girard, René. *Deceit, Desire, and the Novel: Self and Other in Literary Structure*. Translated by Yvonne Treccero. Baltimore, MD: Johns Hopkins University Press, 1965.

———. *Evolution and Conversion: Dialogues on the Origin of Culture*, with Pierpaolo Antonello and João Cezar de Castro Rocha. New York: Continuum International Publishing Group, 2007.

———. *I See Satan Fall Like Lightning*. Maryknoll, NY: Orbis Books, 2001.

———. *The Scapegoat*. Translated by Yvonne Treccero. Baltimore, MD: Johns Hopkins University Press, 1986.

———. *Things Hidden Since the Foundation of the World*. New York, NY: Continuum International Publishing Group, 2003.

———. *Violence and the Sacred*. Translated by Patrick Gregory. London, UK: The Athlone Press, 1995.

Glover, Adrian. "The Wonders of the Deep, Deep Sea.." *TimesLitSupp,* March 19, 2008. No pages. Online: http://entertainment.timesonline.co.uk/arats_and_entertainment /the_tls/article3584766.ece.

Glover, Jonathan. *Humanity: A Moral History of the Twentieth Century.* New Haven, CT: Yale University Press, 2004.

Goldingay, John. *Old Testament Theology.* Vol. 1: *Israel's Gospel.* Downers Grove, IL: InterVarsity Press, 2003.

Goldstein, Jeffrey. "Emergence as a Construct: History and Issues." *Emergence: Complexity and Organization* 1 (1991) 49.

Greek Orthodox Archdiocese of America. No pages. Online: http://www.goarch.org/en /multimedia/live/isos/supplementary/irenaios_summary.htm.

Green, Joel, and Mark Baker. *Recovering the Scandal of the Cross: Atonement in New Testament and Contemporary Contexts.* Downers Grove, IL: InterVarsity Press, 2000.

Haarsma, Deborah B., and Loren D. Haarsma. *Origins: A Reformed Look at Creation, Design, and Evolution.* Grand Rapids: Faith Alive, 2007.

Haldane, J. B. S. *Possible Worlds and Other Papers.* London: Chatto & Windus, 1927.

Hanson, John Wesley. "The Greek Word Aiōnios, translated as Everlasting—Eternal in the Holy Bible, Shown to Denote Limited Duration." Chicago, IL: Northwestern Universalist Publishing House, 1875. Made accessible online at Tentmaker Ministry. No pages. Online: http://www.tentmaker.org/books/Aion_lim.shtml.

————. *Universalism.* 1899. Reprinted, San Diego, CA: St. Alban Press, 2007.

Harrell, Daniel M. *Nature's Witness: How Evolution Can Inspire Faith.* Nashville, TN: Abingdon Press, 2008.

Heppner, Caleb F. "A Covenantal View of Atonement." No pages. Online: http://www .thepaulpage.com.

Heschel, Abraham J. *The Prophets.* New York: HarperCollins Publishers, 2001.

Hick, John. *The Metaphor of God Incarnate: Christology in a Pluralistic Age.* Louisville, KY: Westminster/John Knox Press, 2006.

Hiebert, Paul G. *Anthropological Reflections on Missiological Issues.* Grand Rapids, MI: Baker Books, 1994.

————. "The Flaw of the Excluded Middle." *Missiology* 10:1 (1982) 35–47.

Holland, John. *Emergence from Chaos to Order.* Jackson, TN: Perseus Books, 1999.

Hsia, R. Po-Chia, editor. *Cambridge History of Christianity.* Vol. 6: *Reform and Expansion 1500–1600.* Cambridge, UK: Cambridge University Press, 2007.

Ignatius, *Epistle to the Magnesians.* No pages. Online: http://www.newadvent.org /fathers/0105.htm.

Irenaeus. *Against Heresies.* Whitefish, MT: Kessinger Publishing, 2004. Also accessible at Augustine Club, Columbia University. No pages. Online: http://www.columbia.edu/ cu/augustine/arch/Irenaeus/advhaer3.txt.

Jabbour, Nabeel. *The Crescent through the Eyes of the Cross.* Colorado Springs, CO: NavPress, 2008.

Jacobs, Joseph, and Moses Buttenwieser. "Messiah." No pages. Online: http://www .jewishencyclopedia.com/viewfriendly.jsp?artid=510&letter=M.

Jaspers, Karl. *The Origin and Goal of History.* Trans. Michael Bullock. New Haven, CT: Yale University Press, 1977.

Jenkins, Willis. "Missiology in Environmental Context: Tasks for an Ecology of Mission." *International Bulletin of Missionary Research* 32 (2008) 176–184.

Jewish Encyclopedia. No pages. Online: http://www.jewishencyclopedia.com/view.jsp?arti
d=121&letterA&search=fatherhood%of%20God.

KaKohain,Reb Yakov Leib. *To Die for the People: A Kabbalistic Reinterpretation of the Crucifixion of Jesus.* No pages. Online: http://www.donmeh-west.com/ToDie.shtml Originally published in *The Priest: A Journal of Catholic Theology,* April 1996.

Keillor, Steven J. *God's Judgments: Interpreting History and the Christian Faith.* Downers Grove, IL: IVP Academic, 2007.

Khan, Omar. "The Ancient Indus Civilization." No pages. Online: http://www.harappa.com/har/har0.html.

Kierkegaard, Søren. *Sickness Unto Death: A Christian Psychological Exposition of Edification & Awakening by Anti-Climacus.* Translated by Alistair Hannay. New York: Penguin Classics, 1989.

Kilmer, Joyce. "Trees." In *Modern American Poetry,* edited by Louis Untermeyer, 119. New York, NY: Harcourt, Brace, and Howe, 1919.

Klein, Richard G., with Blake Edgar. *The Dawn of Human Culture.* New York: Wiley, 2002.

Knapp, Sandra. "In a Green Light." *TimesLitSupp,* March 21, 2008, 12.

Kugel, James L. *How to Read the Bible: A Guide to Scripture, Then and Now.* New York: Free Press, 2007.

Legrand, Lucien. *Unity and Plurality: Mission in the Bible.* Maryknoll, NY: Orbis Books, 1990.

Lehman, Frederick. *Songs That Are Different,* vol 2. Pasadena, CA: n.p., 1919.

Lewontin, Richard. "The Triumph of Stephen Jay Gould." *New York Review of Books* 55:2 (2008) No pages. Online: http://www.nybooks.com/articles/article-preview?article _id=21003.

Ligon, Greg, *Bonhoeffer's Cost of Discipleship.* Shepherd's Notes: Christian Classics. Nashville, TN: B&H Publishing, 1999.

Livingstone, David N. *Adam's Ancestors: Race, Religion and the Politics of Human Origins.* Baltimore, MD: Johns Hopkins University Press, 2008.

Ludemann, Gerd. *Paul: The Founder of Christianity.* Amherst, NY: Prometheus Books, 2002.

MacDonald, Gregory. *The Evangelical Universalist.* Eugene, OR: Cascade Books, 2006.

———."Reasons Why People Think Evangelicals Cannot Be Universalists." No pages. Online: http://evangelicaluniversalist.blogspot.com/2008/04/can-evangelical-be-univers alist.html.

———. "A Trinitarian Universalist Prayer." No pages. Online: http://evangelicaluniversalist. blogspot.com/2008/07/trinitarian-universalist-prayer.html.

MacEvoy, Bruce. "GeoEvolution." No pages. Online: http://www.handprint.com/PS/GEO /geoevol.html.

Marion, Jim. *The Death of the Mythic God: the Rise of Evolutionary Spirituality.* Charlottesville, VA: Hampton Roads Publishing Co., 2004.

Marshall, Christopher D. *Beyond Retribution: A New Testament Vision for Justice, Crime, and Punishment.* Grand Rapids, MI: William B. Eerdmans, 2001.

Massey, Joshua. "God's Amazing Diversity in Drawing Muslims to Christ." *International Journal of Frontier Missions,* 17 (2000), 5–9.

Mathetes. *Letter to Diognetus.* No pages. Online: http://www.ccel.org/ccel/schaff/ant01 .iii.ii.x.html.

Maximus the Confessor. *On the Cosmic Mystery of Jesus Christ*. Selected Writings. Translated by Paul M. Blowers and Robert Louis Wilken. Crestwood, NY: St. Vladimir's Seminary Press, 2003.

McDermott, Gerald R. *God's Rivals*. Downers Grove, IL: IVP Academic, 2007.

McDonald, William. "Kierkegaard." *Stanford Encyclopedia of Philosophy*. No pages. Online: http://plato.Stanford.edu/entries/kierkegaard.

McKnight, Scot. "The Ironic Faith of Emergents." *Christianity Today* 52 (September 2008) 62–63. Online: http://www.christianitytoday.com/ct/2008/september/39.62.html.

McLaren, Brian D. *Everything Must Change: Jesus, Global Crises, and a Revolution of Hope*. Nashville, TN: Thomas Nelson Publishers, 2007.

Mesle, C. Robert. *Process-Relational Philosophy*, West Conshohocken, PA: Templeton Foundation Press, 2008.

Messadié, Gerald. *A History of the Devil*. New York: Kodansha International, 1997.

Middleton, J. Richard. "Why the 'Greater Good' Isn't a Defense: Classical Theodicy in Light of the Biblical Genre of Lament." *Koinonia* 9/1&2 (Fall 1997): 81–113.

Mills, John E., Jr. *Mountain of Fame*. Princeton, NJ: Princeton University Press, 1994.

Moberly, R. Campbell. *Atonement and Personality*. 1901. Reprinted, Whitefish, MT: Kessinger Publishing, 2006,

Moberly, Walter. *The Ethics of Punishment*. London, UK: Faber and Faber, 1968.

Moltmann, Jürgen. *The Coming of God: Christian Eschatology*. Translated by Margaret Kohl. Minneapolis, MN: Fortress Press, 2004.

———. *The Crucified God*. Translated by R. A. Wilson and J. Bowden. 2nd ed. London: SCM Press, 1973.

Morris, Leon. *The Biblical Doctrine of Judgment*. Grand Rapids, MI: William B. Eerdmans, 1960.

Moskowitz, Clara. "Earth's Final Sunset Predicted." No pages. Online: http://www.space.com/Scienceastronomy/080226-vaporizedearth.html.

Muchee, Julius M. "Did the New Testament Contextualize the Old?" Journal of Asia Adventist Seminary (JAAS) 6 (2003). Also Online: http://adra.ph/jaas/vol6-2003/Muchee_testament.html.

Muesse, Mark. *Religions of the Axial Age*. Course guidebook, parts 1 and 2. Chantilly, VA: The Teaching Company, 2007.

Murk, James M. *Islam Rising: The Never-Ending Jihad against Christianity*. Book I. Springfield, MO: Twenty-First Century Press, 2006.

National Aeronautics and Space Administration. "The Big Bang." No pages. Online: http://map.gsfc.nasa.gov/m_uni/uni_101bb test.html.

———. "Life." No pages. Online: http://map.gsfc.nasa.gov/m_uni/uni_101life.html.

———. "Universe." No pages. Online: http://map.gsfc.nasa.gov/universe/uni_life.html.

———. "Wilkinson Microwave Anisotropy Probe." No pages. Online: http://map.gsfc.nasa.gov/m_mm.html.

Netland, Harold A. *Encountering Religious Pluralism: The Challenge to Christian Faith and Mission*. Downers Grove, IL: InterVarsity Press, 2001.

Nicholls, B. J. "Contextualization." In *New Dictionary of Theology*, edited by S. B. Ferguson and D. F. Wright. Downers Grove, IL: InterVarsity Press, 1988.

Öpik, E. J. *The Oscillating Universe*. Colchester, UK: Signet Publishing, 1960.

Oppenheimer, Stephen. *Out of Eden: The Peopling of the World*. London: Constable & Robinson, 2003.

Orthodox Page in America. No pages. Online: http://www.ocf.org/OrthodoxPage /reading /reading.html.

Overbye, Dennis. "$404,000 Wins Letter by Einstein on Religion." *New York Times,* May 17, 2008, A11.

Pagels, Elaine. *The Origin of Satan.* New York: Random House, 1995.

Parry, Robin, and Christopher Partridge, eds. *Universal Salvation? The Current Debate.* Grand Rapids, MI: Eerdmans Publishing Co., 2003.

Paulos, John Allen. *Irreligion: A Mathematician Explains Why the Arguments for God Just Don't Add Up.* New York: Hill & Wang, 2007.

Peat, F. David, "Interview with David Bohm." No pages. Online: http://www.fdavidpeat. com/interviews/text/bohmint.txt.

Petersen, Jim, and Mike Shamy. *The Insider: Bringing the Kingdom of God into Your Everyday World.* Colorado Springs, CO: NavPress, 2003.

Pexa, Stacey. "Ur." No pages. Online: http://www.mnsu.edu/emuseum/archaeology/sites /middle_east/ur.html.

Pinnock, Clark H. *A Wideness in God's Mercy: the Finality of Jesus Christ in a World of Religions.* Grand Rapids, MI: Zondervan Publishing, 1992.

Polkinghorne, John. *One World: The Interaction of Science and Theology.* West Conshohocken, PA: Templeton Foundation Press, 2007.

———. *Science and Providence: God's Interaction with the World.* West Conshohocken, PA: Templeton Foundation Press, 2005.

Prestige, G. L. *God in Patristic Thought.* 2nd ed. London: S.P.C.K., 1952.

Proulx, Nate. "Lugh." No pages. Online: http://www.windows.ucar.edu/tour/link=/my theology/lugh.html.

Punt, Neal. *What's Good About the Good News?* Chicago: Northland Press, 1988.

Rae, Greg. "Chaos Theory: A Brief Introduction." No pages. Online: http://www.imho. com/grae/chaos/chaos.html.

Raschke, Carl. *GloboChrist: The Great Commission Takes a Postmodern Turn.* Grand Rapids, MI: Baker Academic, 2008.

Religion Newswriters Foundation. No pages. Online: http://www.religionlink.org/tip _050808.php.

Rich, Tracy. "Moshiach: The Messiah." No pages. Online: http://www.jewfaq.org/moshiach .htm.

Roberts, J. J. M. "Covenant." No pages. Online: http://www.mb-soft.com/believe/text /covenant.htm.

Ruether, Rosemary Radford. *Feminist Theologies: Legacies and Prospects.* Minneapolis, MN: Fortress Press, 2007.

———. *Women and Redemption: A Theological History,* Minneapolis, MN: Fortress Press, 1998.

Schaeffer, Francis A. *How Should We Then Live: The Rise and Decline of Western Thought and Culture.* Wheaton, IL: Crossway Books/Good News Publishers, 1983.

Schörnborn, Christoph. *Chance or Purpose? Creation, Evolution and a Rational Faith.* Translated by Henry Taylor. San Francisco, CA: Ignatius Press, 2007.

Schwager, Raymund. *Banished from Eden: Original Sin and Evolutionary Theory in the Drama of Salvation.* Translated by James Williams. Leominster, UK: Gracewing, 2006.

Schwarz, Patricia. "The Official Superstring Theory Web Site." No pages. Online: http: //www.superstringtheory.com.

Scott, Waldron. *Bring Forth Justice*. Grand Rapids, MI: Eerdmans Publishing, 1980; Carlisle, UK: Paternoster Publishing, 1997.

——. *Karl Barth's Theology of Mission*. Downers Grove, IL: InterVarsity Press, 1978.

——. *What About the Cross?* Bloomington, IN: iUniverse, 2007.

Scranton, Ryan. "Debunking Robert Gentry's 'New Red-shift Interpretation Cosmology.'" No pages. Online: http://www.talkorigins.org/faqs/nri.html.

Shelton, R. Larry. "A Covenant Concept of Atonement." No pages. Online: http://www.wesley.nnu.edu/Wesleyan_theology/theojrnl/16-20/19-9.htm.

Sissons, Terry Herman. *The Big Bang to Now: A Time Line*. North Charleston, SC: BookSurge. 2006.

Smart, Ninian. *Worldviews: Cross-Cultural Explorations of Human Belief*. 3d ed. Upper Saddle River, NJ: Prentice-Hall, 1999.

Snyder, T. Richard. *The Protestant Ethic and the Spirit of Punishment*. Grand Rapids, MI: William B. Eerdmans, 2000.

Stăniloae, Dumitru. *Orthodox Dogmatic Theology, The Experience of God*. Vol. 1: *Revelation and Knowledge of the Triune God*. Translated and edited by Ioan Ionita and Robert Barringer. Brookline, MA: Holy Cross Orthodox Press, 1994, 1998.

——. *Orthodox Dogmatic Theology, The Experience of God*. Vol. 2: *The World: Creation and Deification*. Translated and edited by Ioan Ionita and Robert Barringer, Brookline, MA: Holy Cross Orthodox Press, 2000, 2005.

Stephenson, James. *The Language of the Land: Living among Stone-Age People in Africa*. New York: St. Martin's Press, 2001.

Stetson, Eric. *Christian Universalism: God's Good News for All People*. Semmes, AL: Sparkling Bay Books, 2008.

Strong, James. *Exhaustive Concordance of the Bible*. Peabody, MA: Hendrickson Publishers, 2007.

Suchocki, Marjorie Hewitt. *Divinity & Diversity: A Christian Affirmation of Religious Pluralism*. Nashville, TN: Abingdon Press, 2003.

Talbott, Thomas. *The Inescapable Love of God*. Boca Raton, FL: Universal Publishers, 2003.

——. Part 1 Chapters 1–3, "A Case for Christian Universalism," 3–53; Chapter 12, "Reply to My Critics," 247–273, in *Universal Salvation? The Current Debate*, edited by Robin Parry and Christopher Partridge, Grand Rapids, MI: William. B. Eerdmans, 2003.

Team C004367. "The Evolution of Language." No pages. Online: http://library.think quest.org/C004367/la1.shtml.

Teilhard de Chardin, Pierre. *The Phenomenon of Man*. Translated by Bernard Wall. London: Collins & Sons, 1963.

Telushkin, Joseph. *Jewish Literacy*. New York: William Morrow and Co., 1991, cited in "The Messiah," Jewish Virtual Library. No pages. Online: http://www.jewishvirtual library.org/jsource/Judaism/messiah.html.

Terrill, JoAnne Marie. *Power in the Blood? The Cross in African American Experience*. Maryknoll, NY: Orbis Books, 1998.

Theological Advisory Commission (Federation of Asian Bishops Conferences) 48, (1987). "Theses on Interreligious Dialogue.". Hong Kong: FABC, 1987.

Theophilus of Antioch. "To Autolycus." No pages. Online: http://www.earlychristianwritings.com/text/Theophilus-book2.html.

Travis, John. "The C1 to C6 Spectrum: A Practical Tool for Defining Six Types of 'Christ-Centered Communities Found in the Muslim Context." *Evangelical Missions Quarterly* 34:4. (1998) 407–8.

Veylanswami, Satguru Bodhinatha. "Karma Management." No pages. Online: www .hinduismtoday.com/archives/2002/10-12/40-50_karma_management.shtml.

Voltaire [François-Marie Arouet]. *Candide.* Translated by Roger Pearson. Oxford, UK: Oxford University Press, 2006.

Weaver, J. Denny. *The Non-Violent Atonement.* Grand Rapids, MI: William B. Eerdmans 2001.

Wenham, David. *Paul: Follower of Jesus or Founder of Christianity?* Grand Rapids, MI: William B. Eerdmans, 1995.

Whitehead, Alfred North. *Process and Reality.* 2d revised edition. New York: Free Press, 1979.

Wilber, Ken. *Integral Spirituality.* Boston, MA: Integral Books, 2006.

Williams, Delores S. *Sisters in the Wilderness: The Challenge of Womanist God-Talk.* Maryknoll, NY: Orbis Books, 1993.

Wink, Walter. *The Powers That Be: Theology for a New Millennium,* New York: Doubleday, 1998.

Winter, Michael M. *The Atonement.* Collegeville, MN: Liturgical Press, 1995.

World Evangelical Alliance. "We Too Want to Live in Love, Peace, Freedom and Justice: A Response to A Common Word Between Us and You." No pages. Online: http://www .worldevangelicals.org.

Wright, Christopher J. H. *The Mission of God.* Downers Grove, IL: InterVarsity Press, 2006.

Wright, N. T. *Evil and the Justice of God.* Downers Grove, IL: InterVarsity Press, 2006.

———. *Jesus and the Victory of God.* Minneapolis, MN: Augsburg Fortress, 1997.

———. *The New Testament and the People of God.* Minneapolis, MN: Augsburg Fortress, 1992.

———. *Paul: In Fresh Perspective.* Minneapolis, MN: Fortress Press, 2006.

———. *The Resurrection of the Son of God,* Minneapolis, MN: Augsburg Fortress, 2003.

Zias, Joe. "Crucifixion in Antiquity: The Evidence." No pages. Online: http://www.century one.org/Crucifixion2.html.